# Portfoolio 11

### • THE YEAR'S BEST CANADIAN EDITORIAL CARTOONS •

EDITED BY **GUY BADEAUX**   TEXT BY **KEN MacQUEEN**

MACMILLAN CANADA
TORONTO, ONTARIO CANADA

© **The Association of Canadian Editorial Cartoonists 1995**

All rights reserved. The use of any part of this publication reproduced, transmitted in any form or by any means, electronic, mechanical, recording or otherwise, or stored in a retrieval system, without the prior consent of the publisher is an infringement of the copyright law. In the case of photocopying or other reprographic copying of the material, a licence must be obtained from the Canadian Reprography Collective before proceeding.

**Canadian Cataloguing in Publication Data**
The National Library of Canada has catalogued this publication as follows:
Main entry under title:
Portfoolio : the year in Canadian caricature

Annual.
ISSN 0839-6485
ISBN 0-7715-7360-X (1995)
1. Canada - Politics and government - 1984 - Caricatures and cartoons.*
2. World politics - Caricatures and cartoons. 3. Canadian wit and humor, Pictorial
NC1300.P67      971.064'7'0267     C89-030416-5

Macmillan Canada wishes to thank the Canada Council, the Ontario Ministry of Culture and Communications, and the Ontario Arts Council for supporting its publishing program.

**Macmillan Canada**
A Division of Canada Publishing Corporation
Toronto, Ontario, Canada
Printed in Canada

Edited by: **Guy Badeaux**
Text by: **Ken MacQueen**
Guy Badeaux is editorial cartoonist for *Le Droit* in Ottawa.
Ken MacQueen is national affairs columnist for the *Ottawa Citizen* and Southam News.

Design: **Mathilde Hébert**
Assistant: **Stéphanie St.-Pierre**
Front Cover Cartoon: **Serge Chapleau**
Back Cover Cartoon: **Susan Dewar**

# NATIONAL NEWSPAPER AWARD 1994

PETERSON, *The Vancouver Sun,* August 12, 1994

# NNA 1994 FINALISTS

RODEWALT, *The Calgary Herald,* December 15, 1994

CORRIGAN, *The Toronto Star,* September 14, 1994

# GRAND PRIX: WORLD CARTOON GALLERY
## (SKOPJE, MACEDONIA)

DUŠAN, *The Toronto Star*

# THE DUNCAN MACPHERSON AWARD

Sponsored by the Southam, Thomson and Sun news organisations and by the Association of Canadian Editorial Cartoonists, the Duncan Macpherson Award is an annual award that honours a budding Canadian editorial cartoonist. A $500 prize, an engraved statuette and an expenses-paid trip to the presentation at the ACEC convention goes to the winner.

### QUALIFICATIONS
Talent (including drawing), ability to caricature, good ideas—preferably political subjects, but some general subjects allowed. No experience necessary; can be published, but full-time cartoonists are not eligible.

### SUBMISSIONS
Send **photocopies** (no originals, entries not returned) of a maximum of four cartoons no larger than 8 1/2 x 11, plus some biographical information about yourself (including name, address and phone number) to: Art Blaine, Award and Jury Chairman, The Duncan Macpherson Award, Box 766, P.O. Station A, Hamilton, Ontario, Canada L8N 3M8
Deadline: April 30th, 1996

Winner: Rick Cepella (Nelson, B.C.)
Finalists:
David Bluestein (Thornhill, Ontario)
James Grasdal (Edmonton, Alberta)

**EXCLUSIVE!! O.J.'s courtroom notes...**

**Portfoolio 11**

# The Newting of America

This was the year that everything in the United States went overboard. Lunatic "patriots" with fertiliser for brains vaporised an Oklahoma office tower and daycare to protest, apparently, the terrible threat of government to the security of the American people.

The O.J. Simpson trial ground on, becoming the longest running joke in America and proving to network television that you do not need a laugh track to tell the American people when to snicker. It gave new meaning to the term "trial and error." It proved American justice was not only blind, but in desperate need of a saliva test.

The White House became a target for homicidal pilots, gun-wielding nutbars and, scariest of all, the U.S. Congress.

Then there was Newt, a reptilian fellow who took all this anger in middle America and peddled it for personal and political profit. Here was a prophet of "traditional American values" who had belly-crawled out of service in Vietnam, and whose personal morals ("Too bad about the cancer, honey. Would this be a good time to ask for a divorce?") were as cold-blooded as his namesake. The president, whose name escapes us, and her husband, wisely kept their heads down and hoped the anger would subside by the 1996 election.

The jury is still out on that. All in all, it was a very bad year for jurors.

ZAHARUK, Union Art Services

ROSEN, *Hour*, Montreal

# AMERICAN GOTHIC...

SEBASTIAN

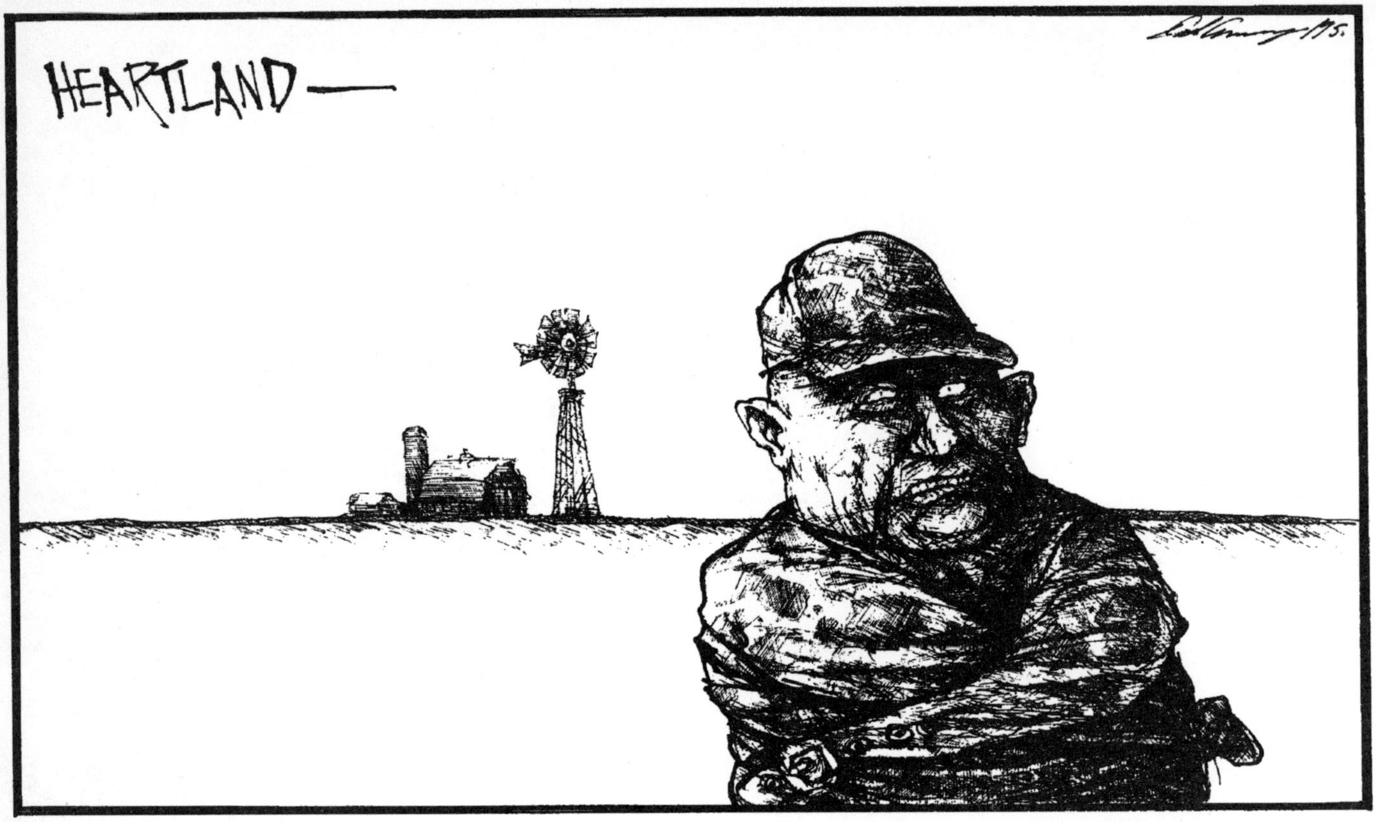
HEARTLAND—

CUMMINGS, *The Winnipeg Free Press*

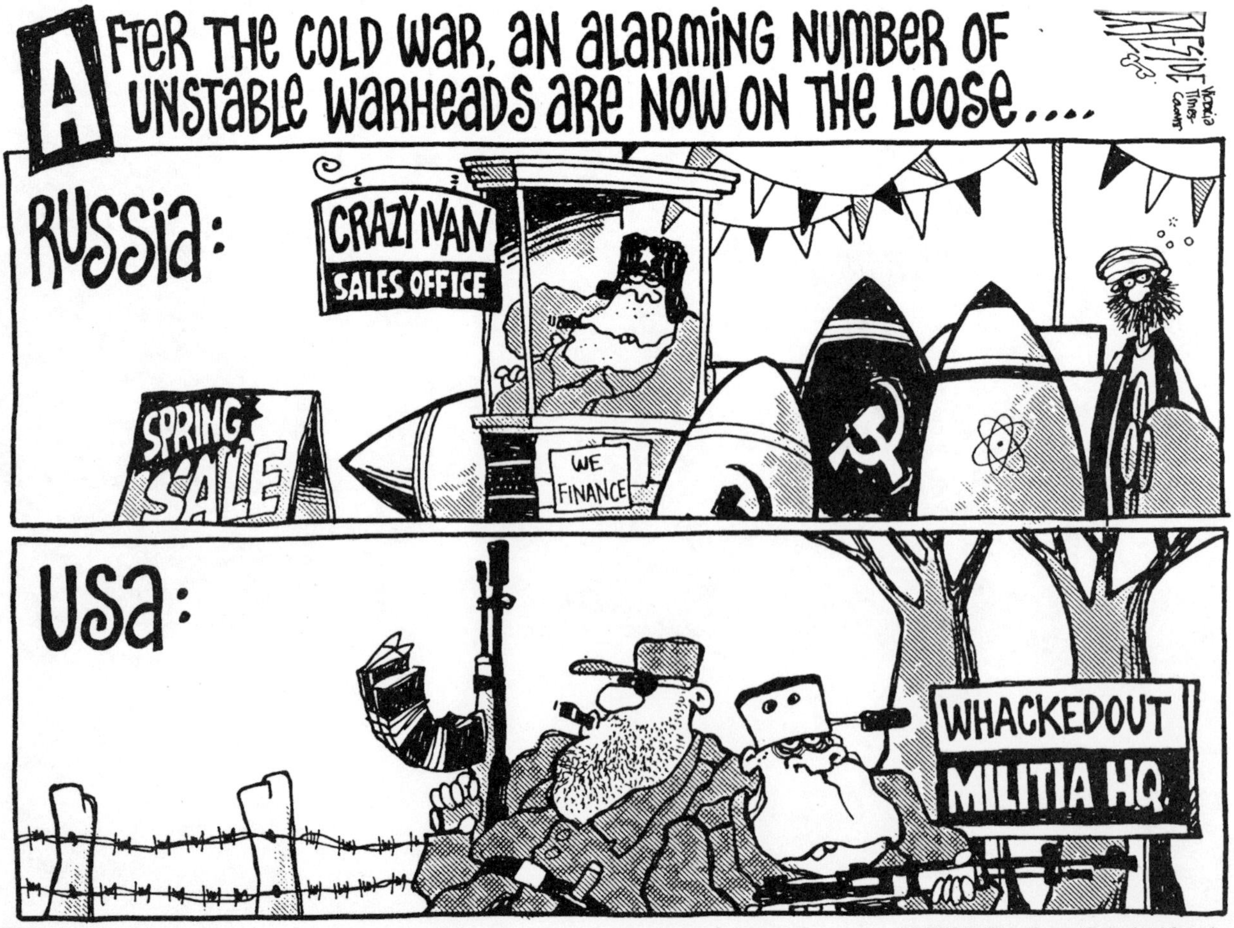
AFTER THE COLD WAR, AN ALARMING NUMBER OF UNSTABLE WARHEADS ARE NOW ON THE LOOSE....
RUSSIA:
CRAZY IVAN
SALES OFFICE
SPRING SALE
WE FINANCE
USA:
WHACKEDOUT
MILITIA HQ.

RAESIDE, *The Times-Colonist*, Victoria

WOULD YOU PLEASE PASS THIS LEGISLATION?
NO!
CLINTON
COULD WE TALK ABOUT WELFARE REFORM?
NO!
COULD SOMEONE TAKE OUT THE GARBAGE?
NO!
HERE KITTY! KITTY!...
NO!
WHAT'S THE GRAVEST THREAT TO AMERICA TODAY?!
MILITIA
BILL CLINTON DICTATORSHIP!!
GABLE

GABLE, *The Globe & Mail*

CUMMINGS, *The Winnipeg Free Press*

OLSON, *The Vancouver Courier*

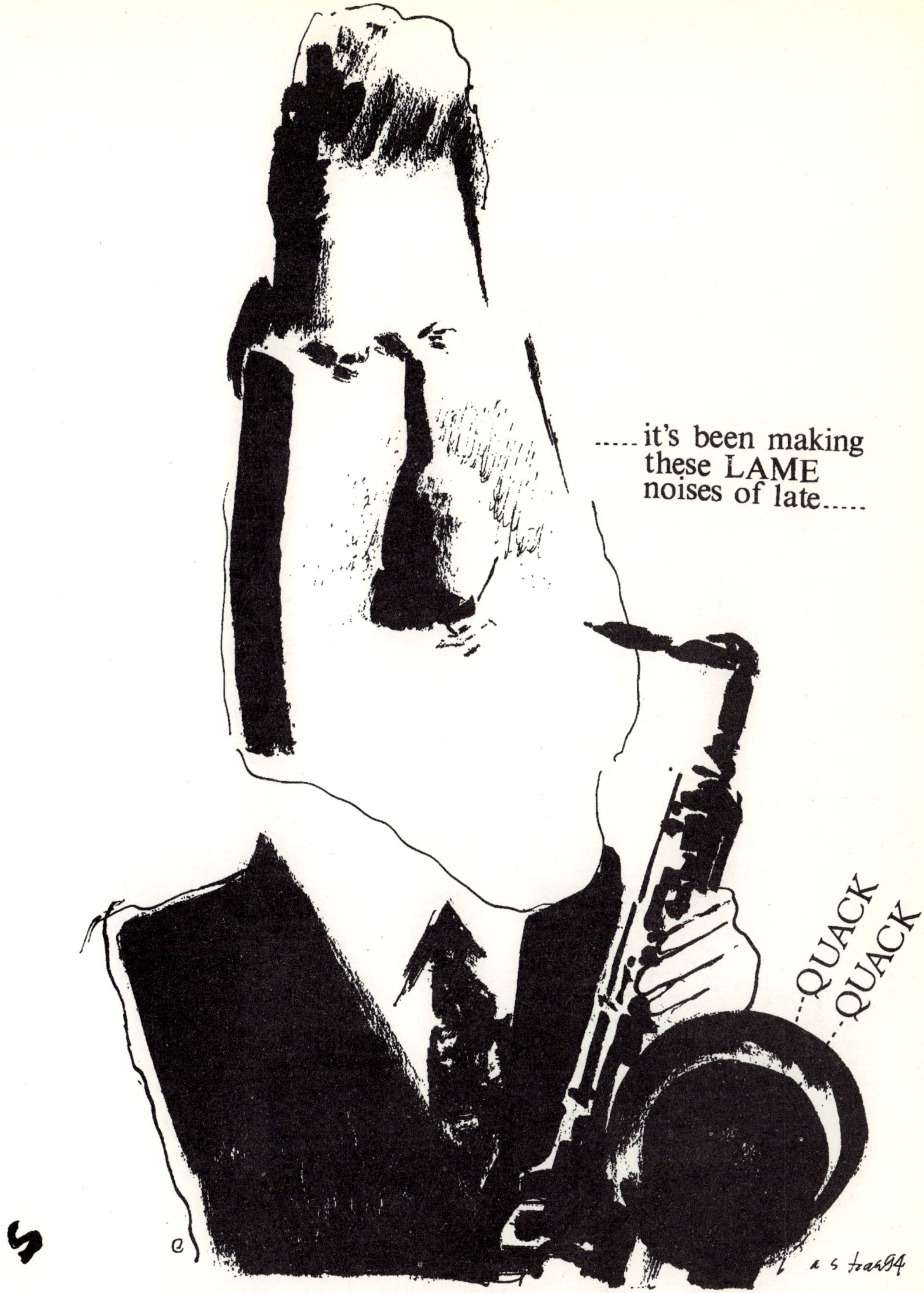
.....it's been making these LAME noises of late.....
QUACK
QUACK

SEBASTIAN

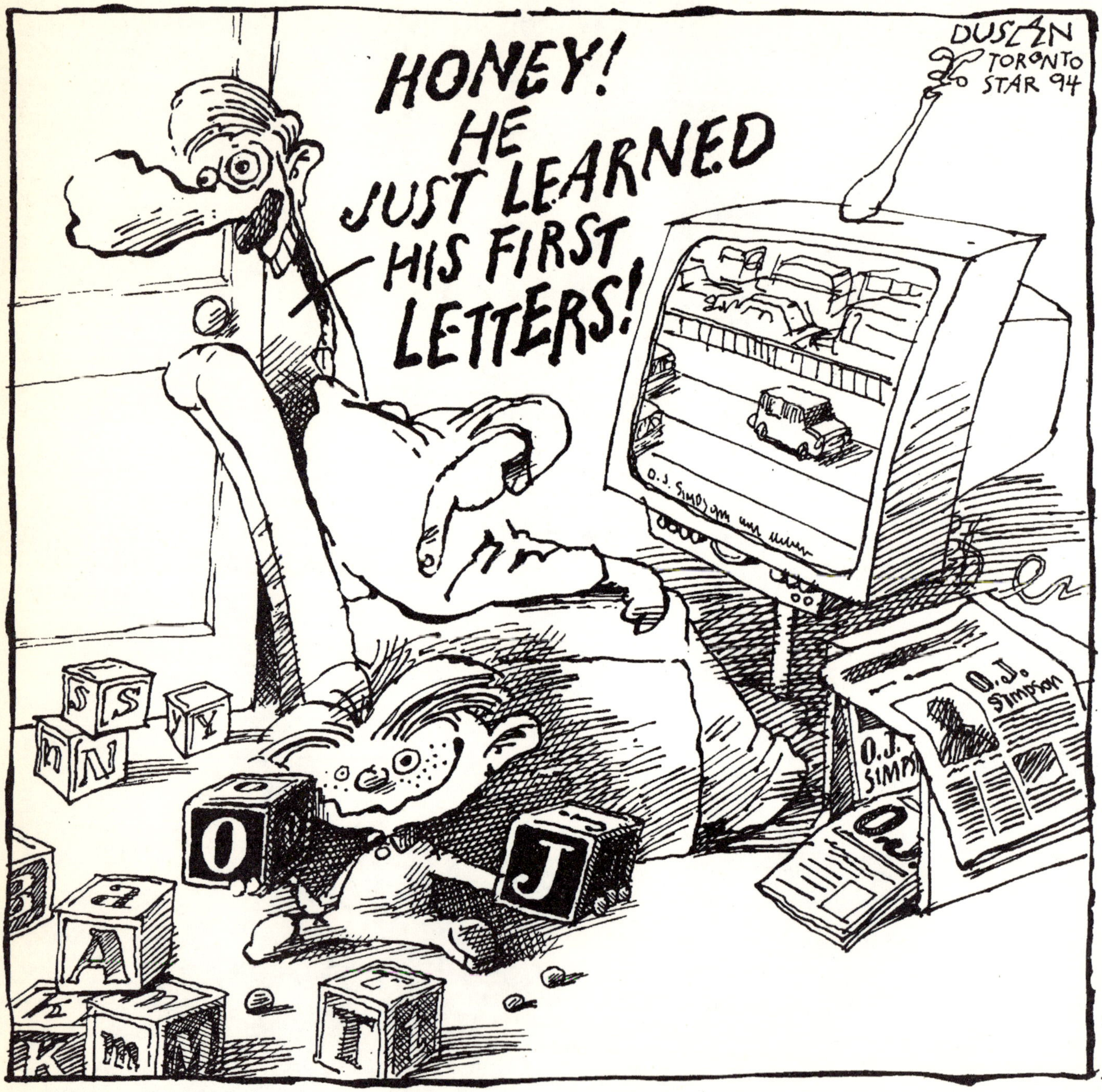
HONEY! HE JUST LEARNED HIS FIRST LETTERS!
DUSAN TORONTO STAR 94
O.J. Simpson
O.J. Simpson
O.J. SIMPS
O
DUSAN, *The Toronto Star*

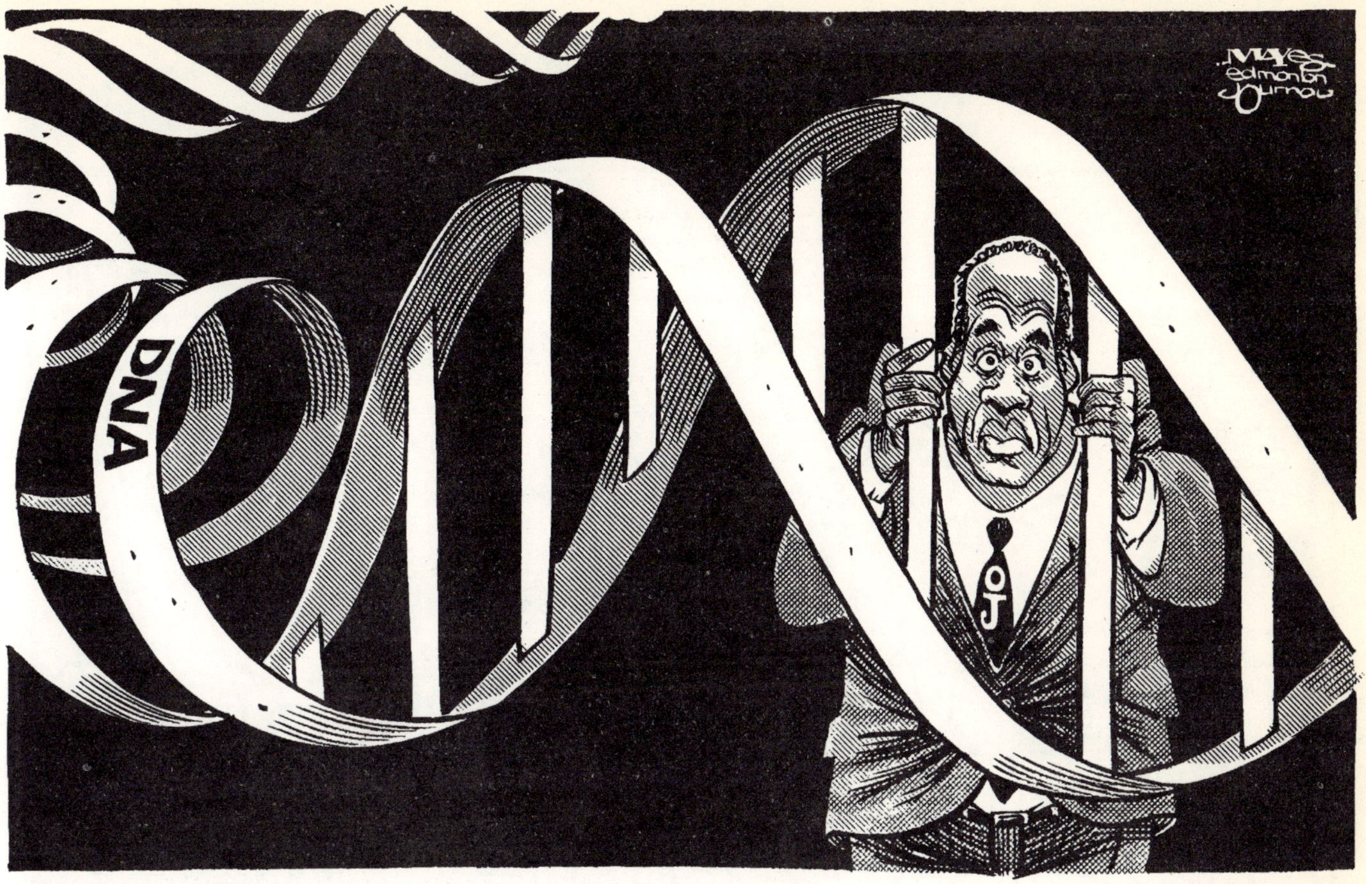
MAYES
edmonton
journal
DNA
OJ

MAYES, *The Edmonton Journal*

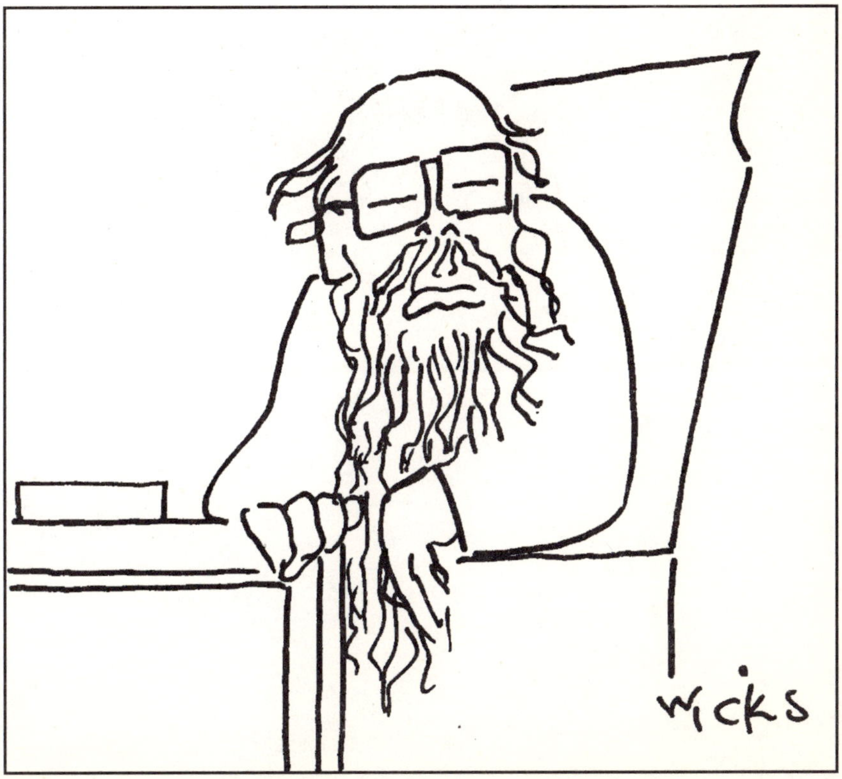
wicks

Members of O.J. jury, have you reached a verdict?

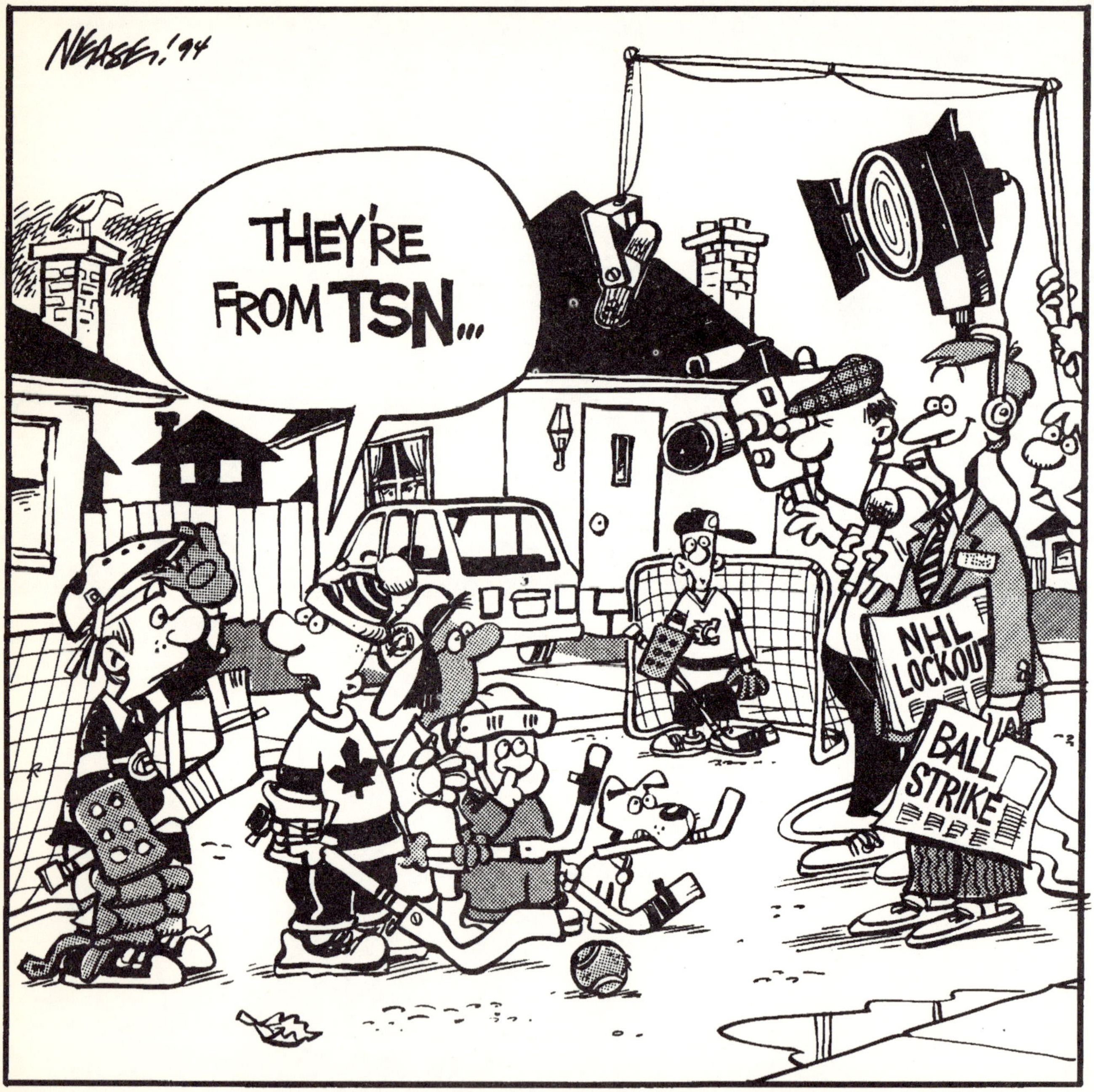
NEASE!'94
THEY'RE FROM TSN...
NHL LOCKOUT
BALL STRIKE

**Portfoolio 11**

# He shoots! He scores!
## Sure sex is fun, 'til somebody loses an eye

By the time you read these words, there will be 35 million Canadians. Six million of them will be in diapers. In years to come, they will be known as the Slap Shot generation. Or maybe the Baby Bat generation. Or maybe just the Strike Babies. They are the direct result of the professional sports strikes that laid the dedicated sports fan low, so to speak.

Odds are, if you are holding an infant even as you read this, you know exactly how it happened.... It was Saturday night, the Sports Network was showing (for the third time) highlights from the Australian Open Dwarf Bowling Semi-Finals. Two blow-dried commentators on CTV were listlessly arguing about the likelihood of darts becoming an Olympic demonstration sport in time for Atlanta. In desperation, you opened the *TV Guide* to the 8 p.m. listing for CBC. It read: "Hockey? Not in Canada." One thing led to another: an offside. A slide into second base. Some stick handling. Ahhh! Safe at home. But not safe enough.

The reason that post-strike attendance has been so slow to recover has nothing to do with fan cynicism. They simply don't see the logic in spending $50 to watch an exhibition of incomprehensible babbling and tantrum-throwing. This they can see at home for the price of a few Pampers.

Besides, there is an inexplicable shortage of babysitters.

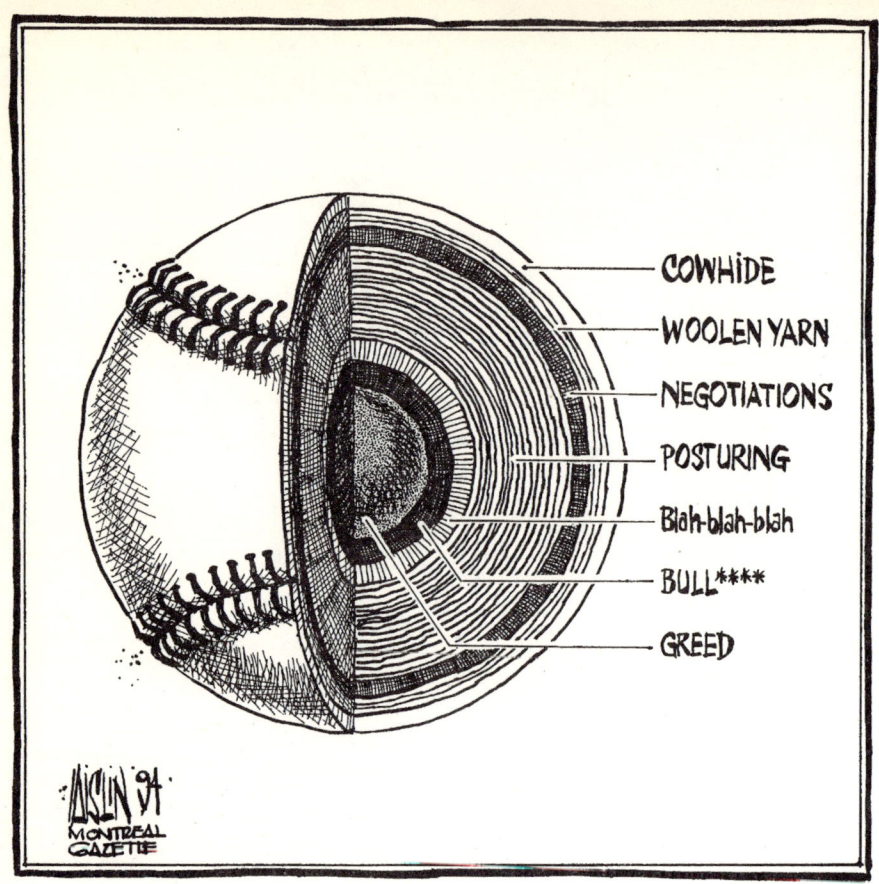

AISLIN, *The Gazette*, Montreal

HOGAN, *The Moncton Times-Transcript*

LACHINE, *The Chatham Daily News*

GABLE, *The Globe & Mail*

PETERSON, *The Vancouver Sun*

PRITCHARD

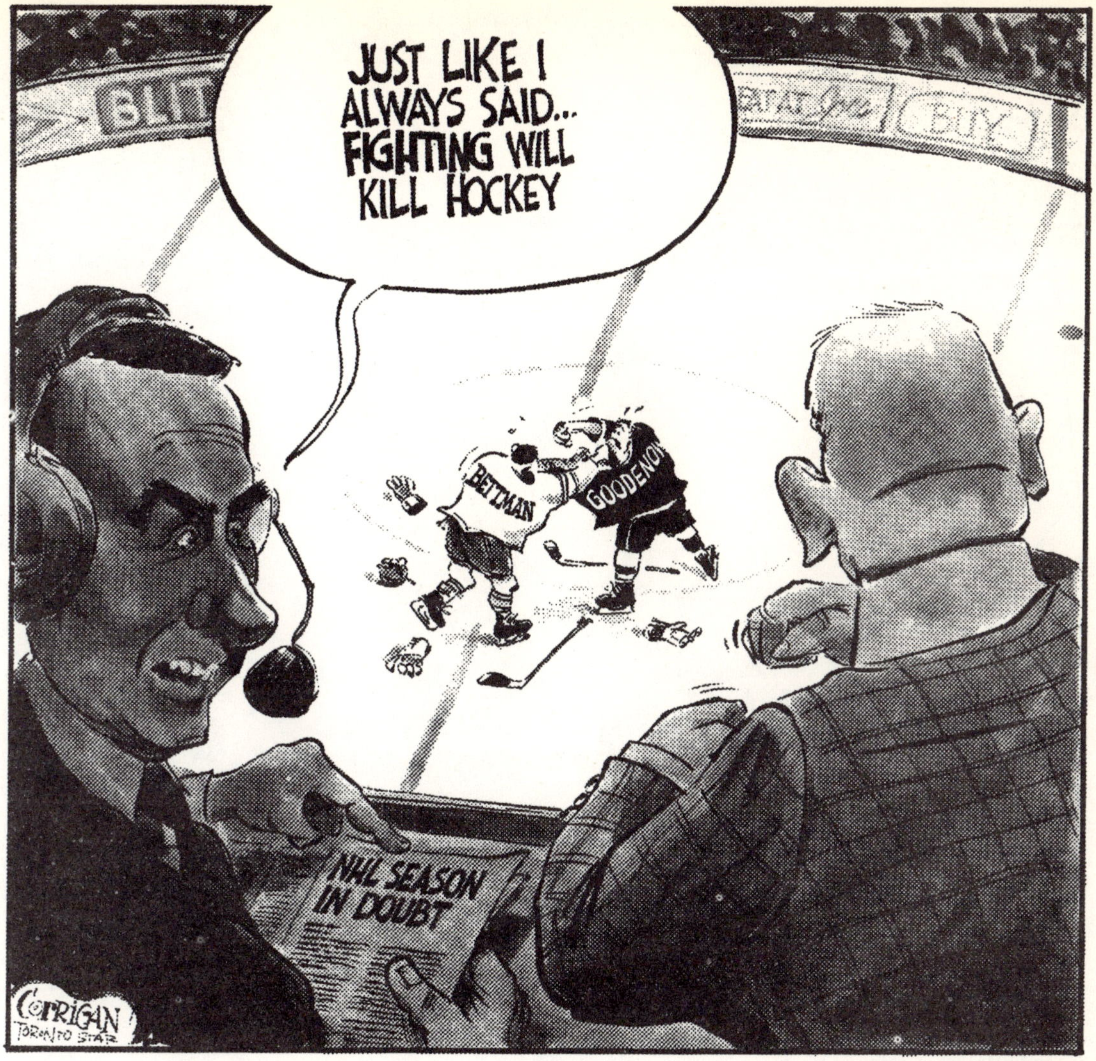
JUST LIKE I ALWAYS SAID... FIGHTING WILL KILL HOCKEY
BETTMAN
GOODENOW
NHL SEASON IN DOUBT
BUY
CORRIGAN
TORONTO STAR

CORRIGAN, *The Toronto Star*

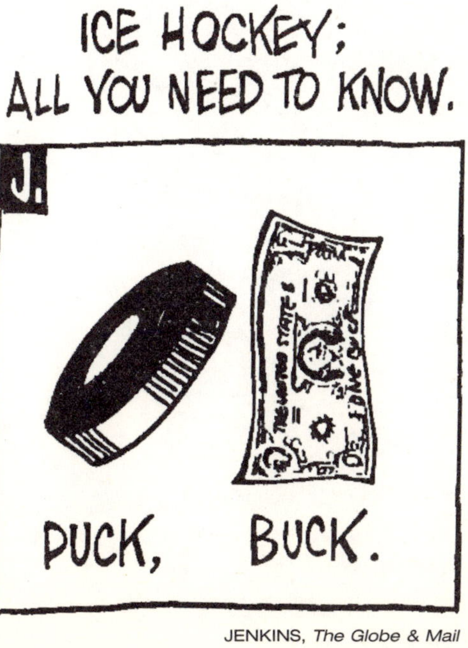
ICE HOCKEY;
ALL YOU NEED TO KNOW.
J.
PUCK, BUCK.

JENKINS, *The Globe & Mail*

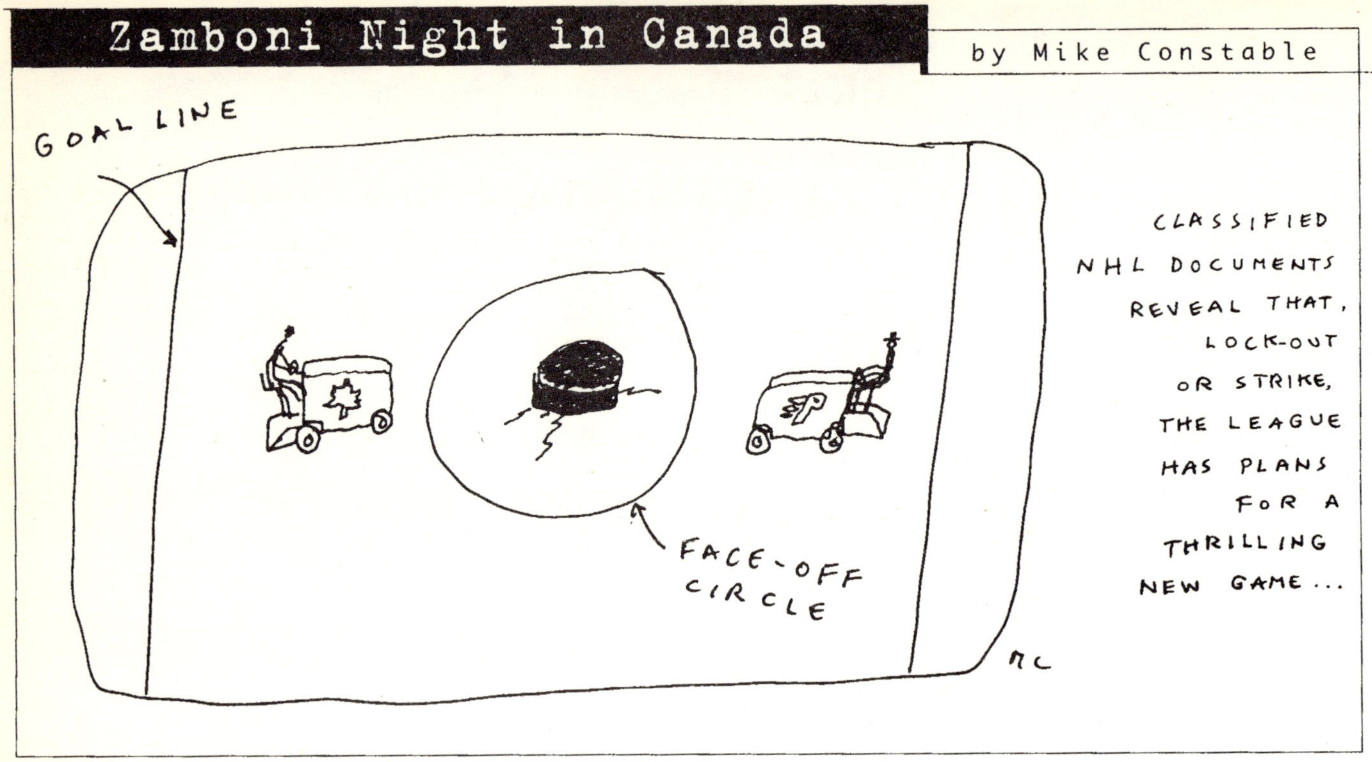
Zamboni Night in Canada
by Mike Constable
GOAL LINE
FACE-OFF CIRCLE
CLASSIFIED NHL DOCUMENTS REVEAL THAT, LOCK-OUT OR STRIKE, THE LEAGUE HAS PLANS FOR A THRILLING NEW GAME...
MC

CONSTABLE, *Saturday Night*

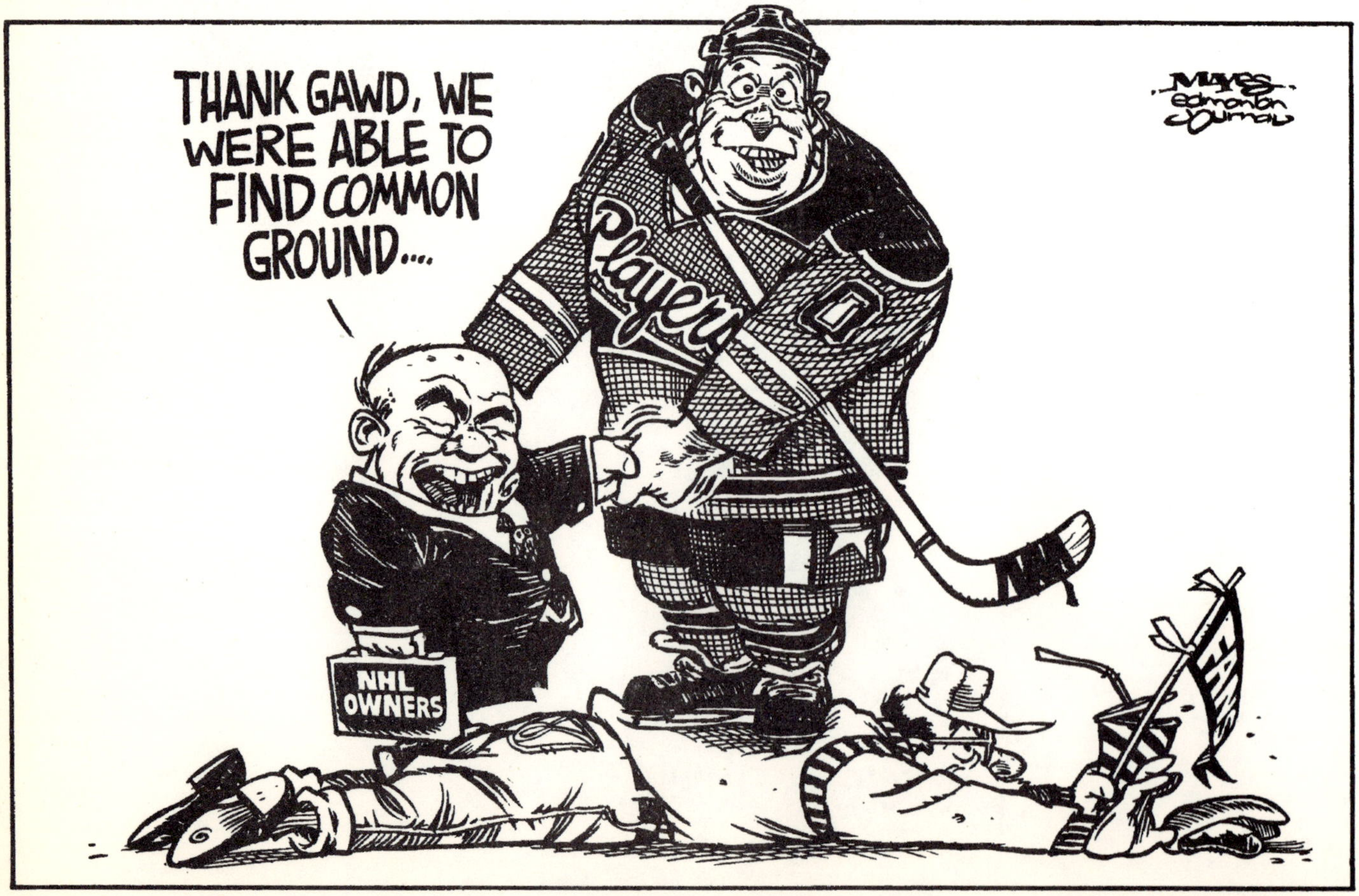
THANK GAWD, WE WERE ABLE TO FIND COMMON GROUND....
Players
NHL OWNERS
MAYES Edmonton Journal

MAYES, *The Edmonton Journal*

CAM, *The Leader-Post*, Regina

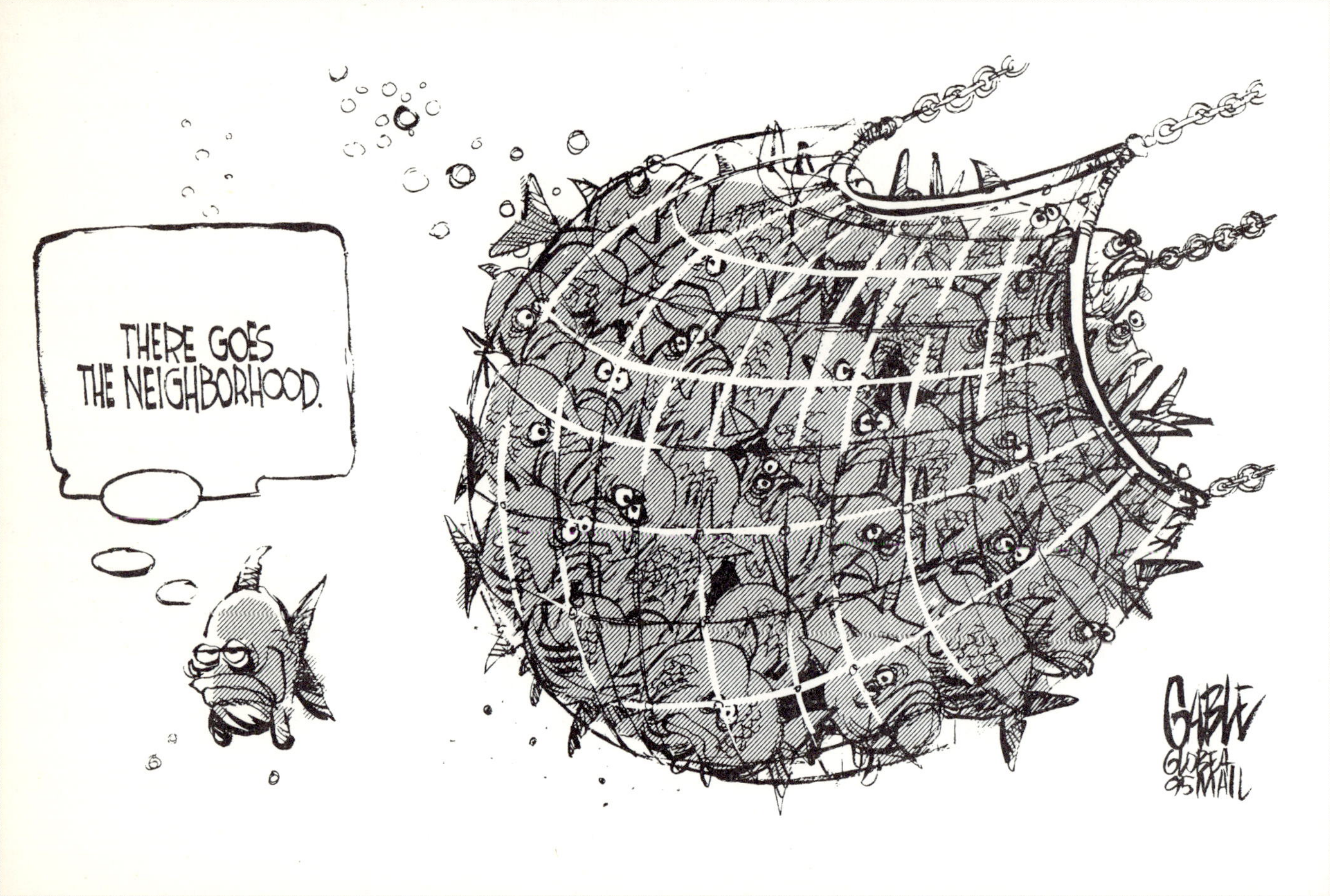
THERE GOES THE NEIGHBORHOOD.
GABLE
GLOBE & MAIL

# From Sea to Empty Sea
## With no cod to batter, we turned our attention to the NDP

Years from now, children, sitting at the kitchen table, will say, "Daddy, what did you do in the Great Fish War of '95?" Dads will turn red, mothers will blanch. "Eat your soy-meal fishstick substitute, dear," they will say nervously. "We'll talk about it when you get older."

By now, most Canadians have graciously forgiven Spain for that nasty little contretemps out beyond the Grand Banks. A pragmatic people, we have decided that a Rioja in the bottle is better than two slimy, bug-eyed fish in the sea.

Writing this in the summer of '95 we see only blue skies and clear sailing for Fisheries Minister Brian Turbot, who sort of won the sort of fish war. There is much speculation that he will replace Clyde Wells as premier of Newfoundland, a job that used to be as much fun as a barrel of salt cod… back when there were cod, and they weren't wearing the barrel. Salt, though, there's still plenty of that.

There is also the matter of the increasingly elusive West Coast salmon. If Captain Turbot solves that wee problem, well the sky is limitless. We could see him replacing Captain High Liner in every freezer in the land. We even see him as a potential prime minister. A Newfoundlander at 24 Sussex? Why not? These are the 90s! Is it too much to hope that Canadians are finally ready to accept a prime minister who speaks with an accent?

In other business, it is safe to say that the middle of the road shifted so far to the right that there is no longer a need to double-lane the Trans-Canada Highway. The New Democrats of Ontario got mowed down by a speeding golf cart driven by Mike Harris. In B.C., poor Mike Harcourt seems frozen on the yellow line waiting for a facefull of bumper at election time.

Jacques (Chainsaw) Parizeau did not find governing to be near as much fun as he'd hoped. But then, the poor chap was preoccupied with another project, as you will notice in another chapter.

Ralph (The Other Chainsaw) Klein continued to do what he promised to do, which is a precedent that is scaring the hell out of every other elected official. Not to mention the poor.

It was not a good time to be poor. But then, it never is.

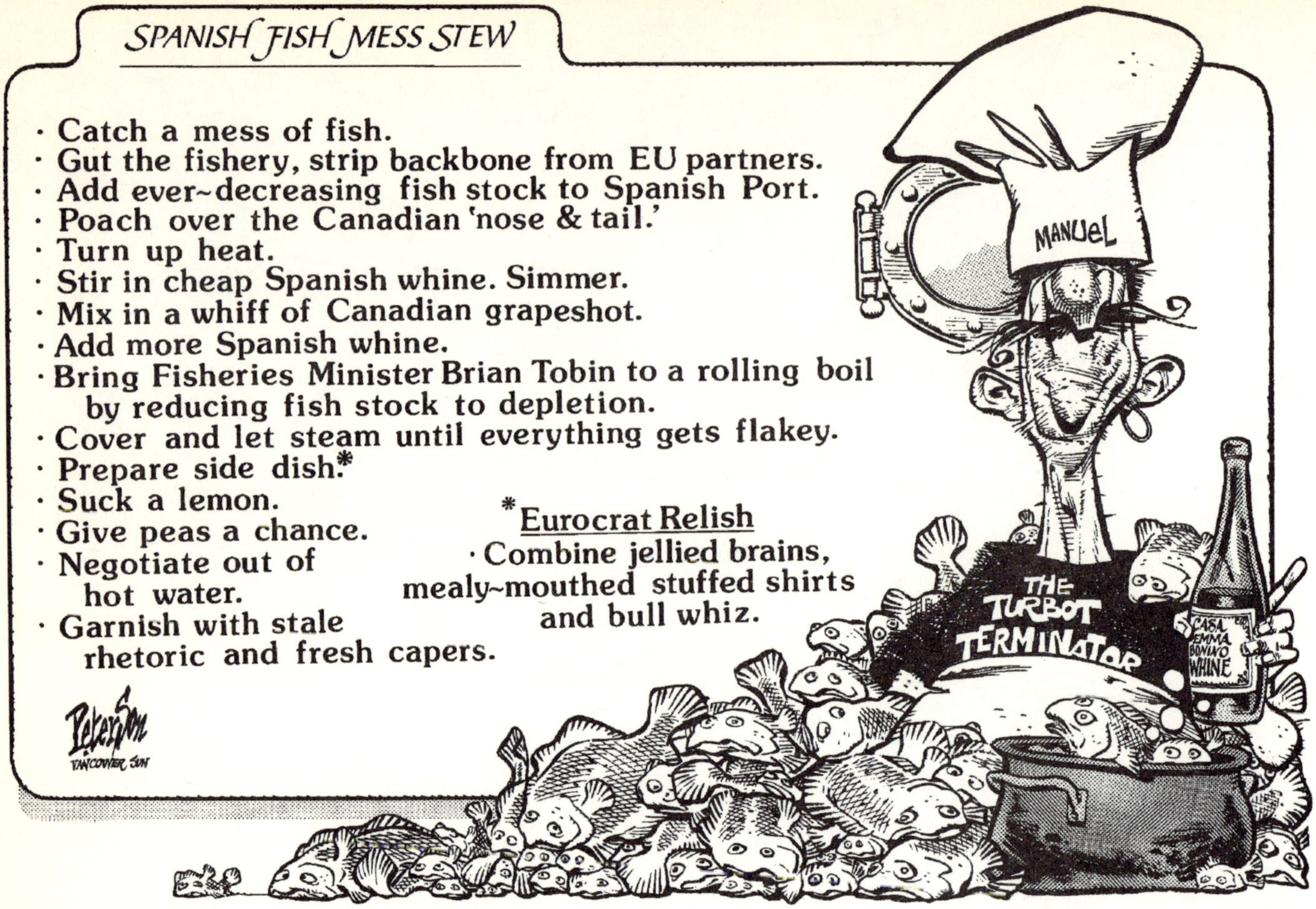
SPANISH FISH MESS STEW
· Catch a mess of fish.
· Gut the fishery, strip backbone from EU partners.
· Add ever~decreasing fish stock to Spanish Port.
· Poach over the Canadian 'nose & tail.'
· Turn up heat.
· Stir in cheap Spanish whine. Simmer.
· Mix in a whiff of Canadian grapeshot.
· Add more Spanish whine.
· Bring Fisheries Minister Brian Tobin to a rolling boil by reducing fish stock to depletion.
· Cover and let steam until everything gets flakey.
· Prepare side dish.*
· Suck a lemon.
· Give peas a chance.
· Negotiate out of hot water.
· Garnish with stale rhetoric and fresh capers.
*Eurocrat Relish
· Combine jellied brains, mealy~mouthed stuffed shirts and bull whiz.
MANUEL
THE TURBOT TERMINATOR
CASA EMMA BONINO WHINE
Peterson
VANCOUVER SUN

PETERSON, *The Vancouver Sun*

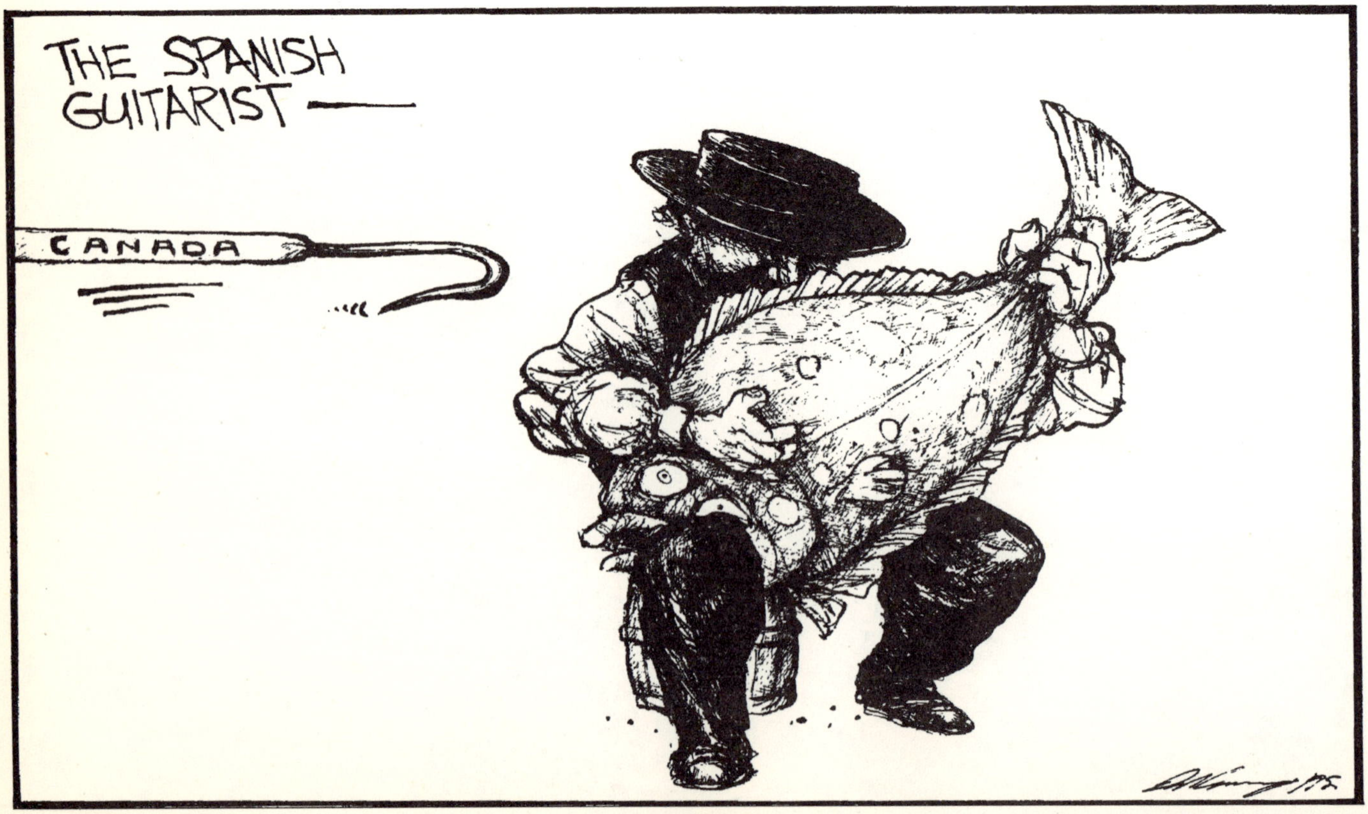
THE SPANISH GUITARIST —
CANADA

CUMMINGS, *The Winnipeg Free Press*

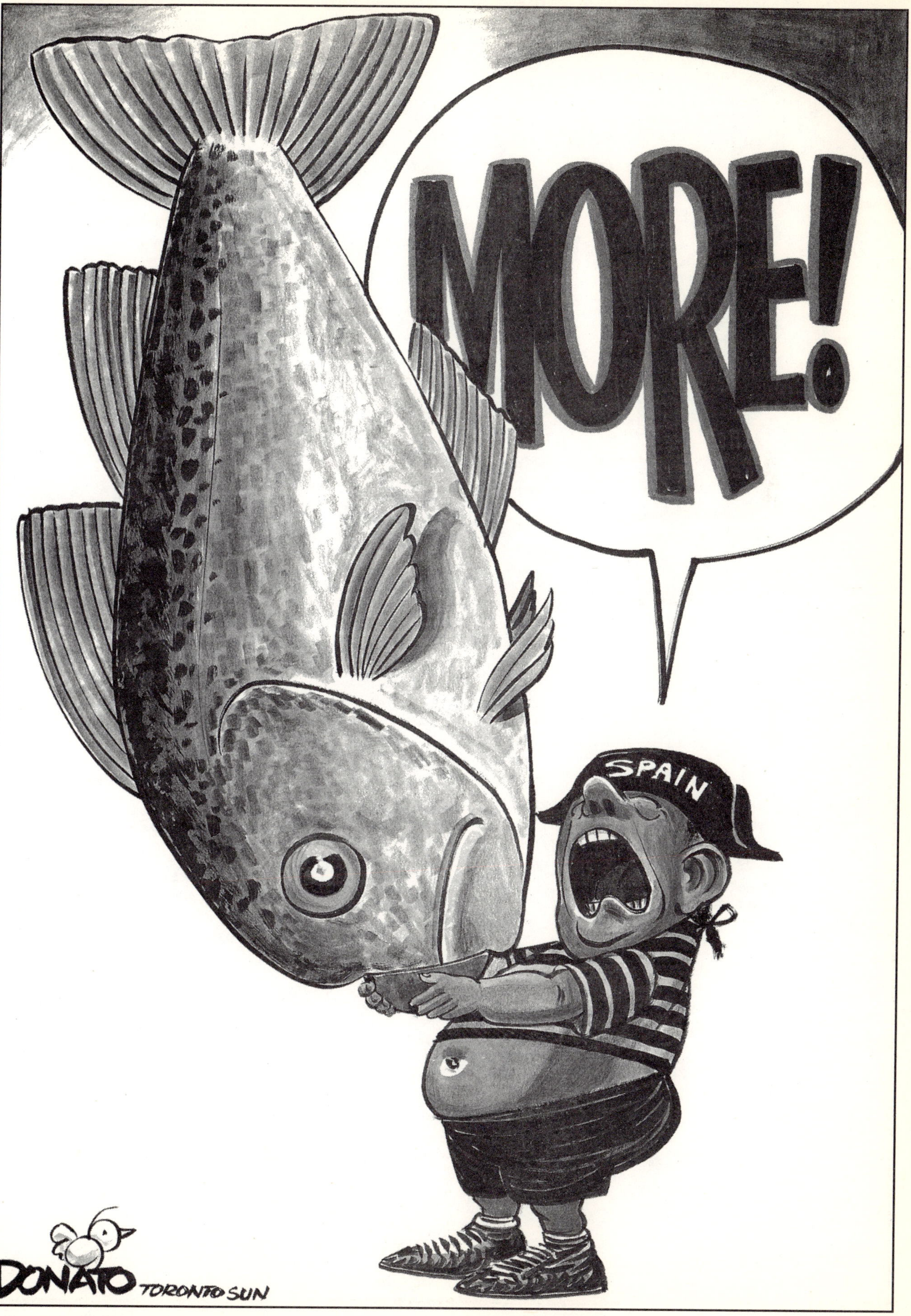
MORE!
SPAIN
DONATO TORONTO SUN

DONATO, *The Toronto Sun*

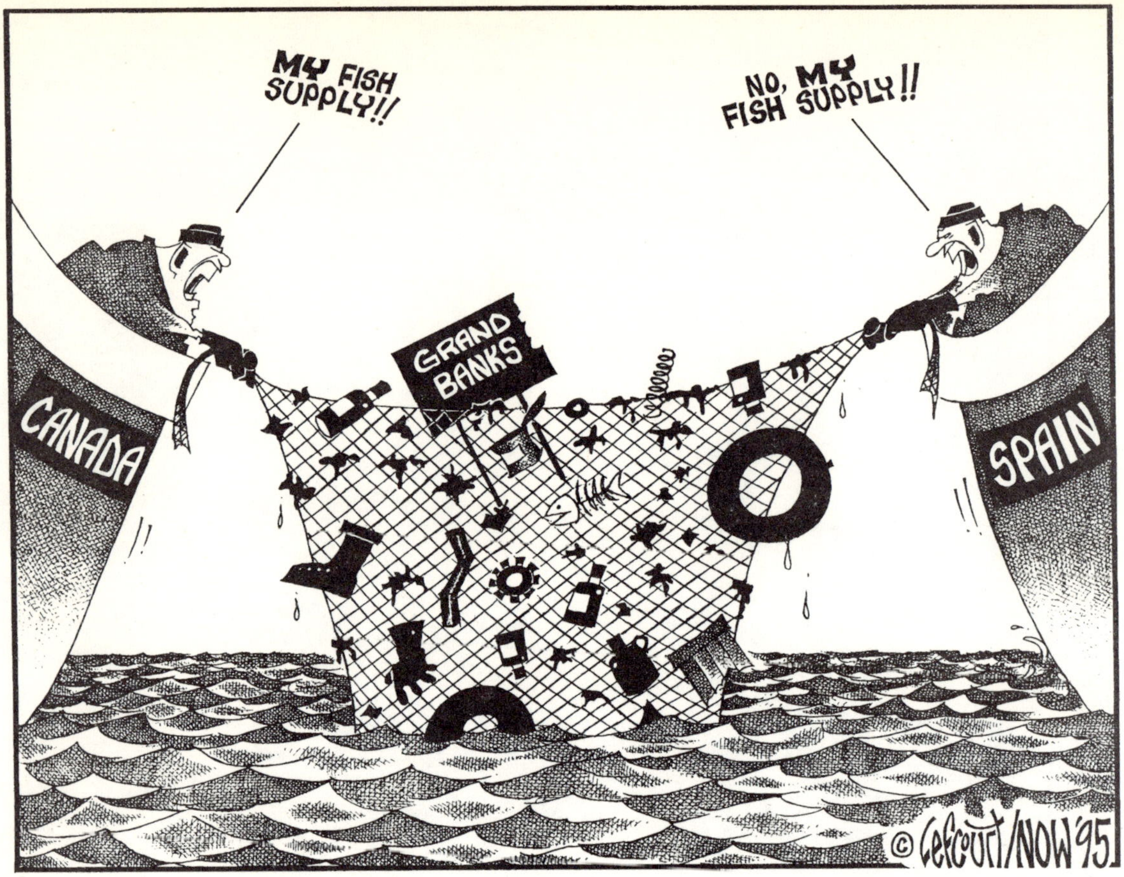
MY FISH SUPPLY!!
NO, MY FISH SUPPLY!!
GRAND BANKS
CANADA
SPAIN
© LEFCOURT/NOW '95

LEFCOURT, *NOW*, Toronto

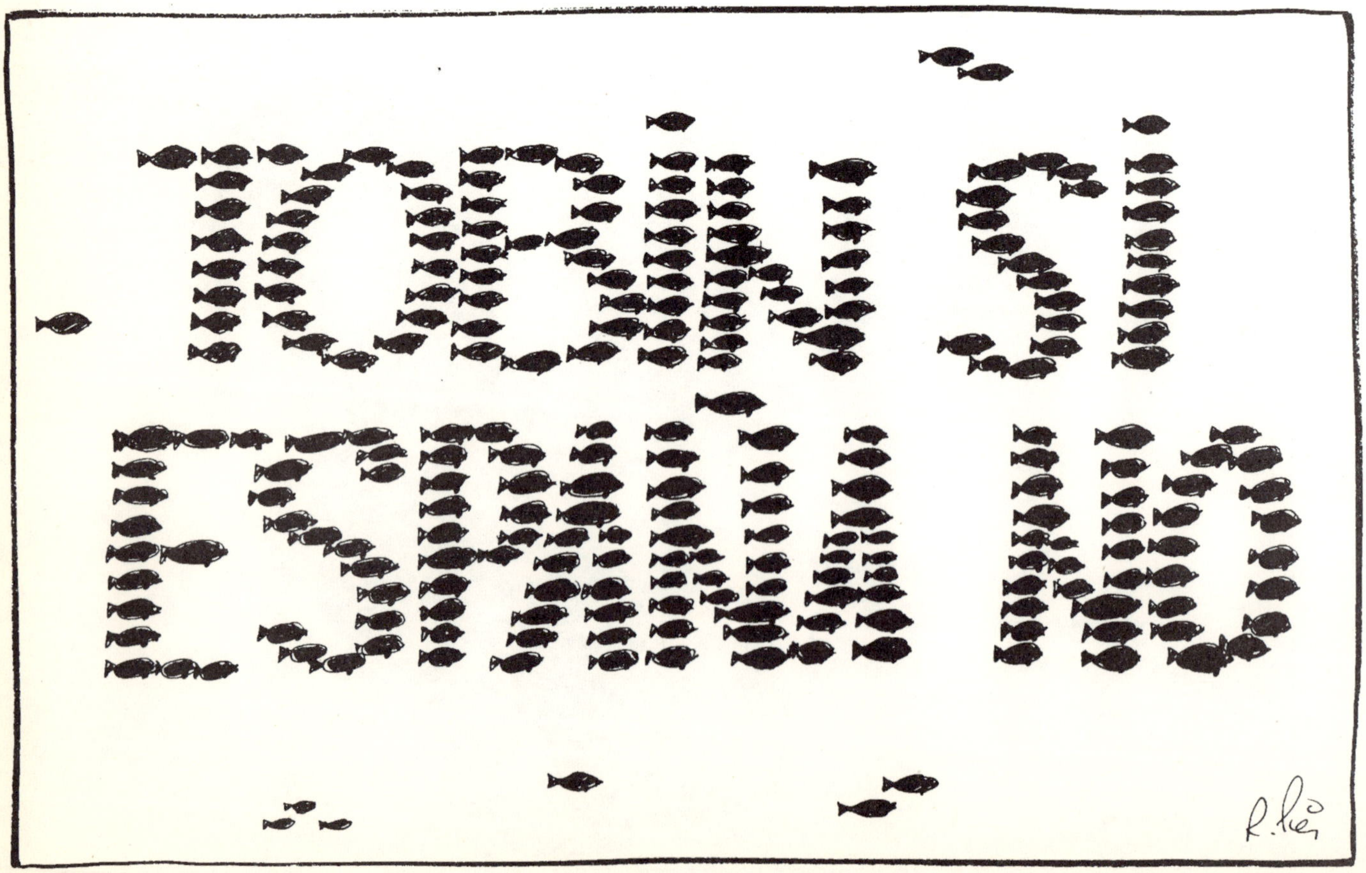
TOBIN SI
ESPAÑA NO

PIER, *Le Journal de Montréal*

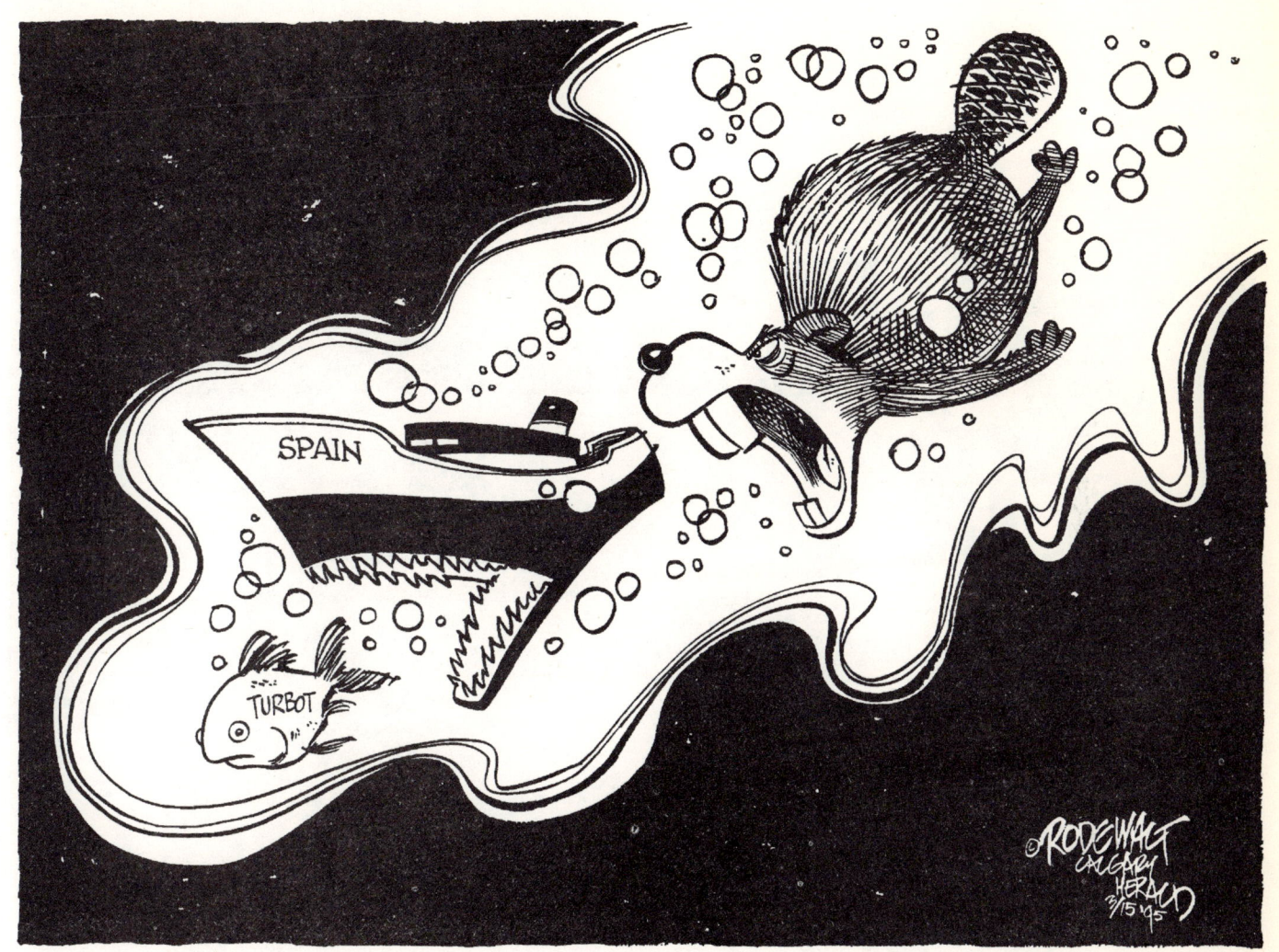

RODEWALT, *The Calgary Herald*

DUSAN, *The Toronto Star*

HARROP, *The Globe and Mail*

CORRIGAN, *The Toronto Star*

HARROP, *The Globe and Mail*

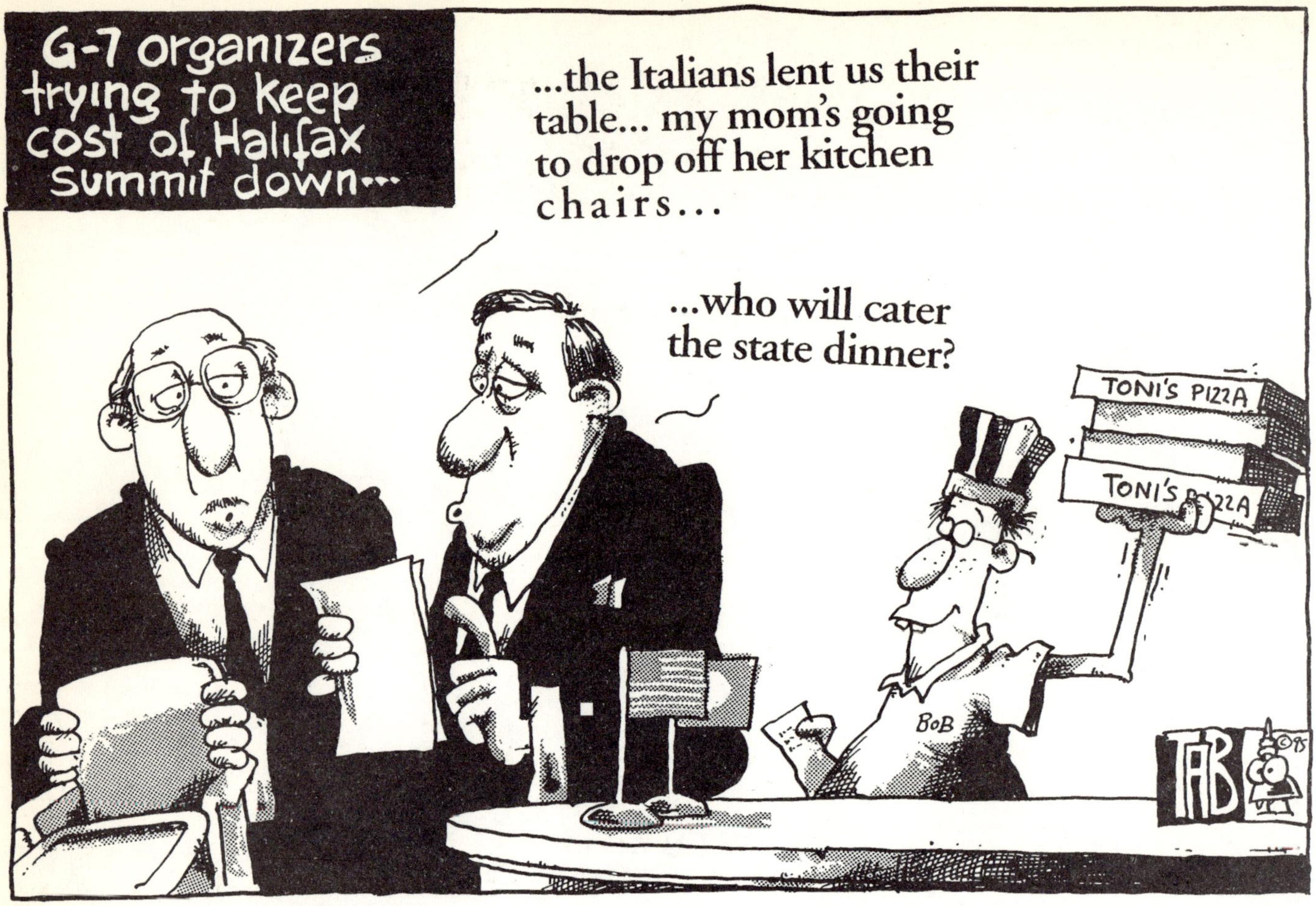
G-7 organizers trying to keep cost of Halifax summit down...
...the Italians lent us their table... my mom's going to drop off her kitchen chairs...
...who will cater the state dinner?
TONI'S PIZZA
TONI'S PIZZA
BOB
TAB ©95

TAB

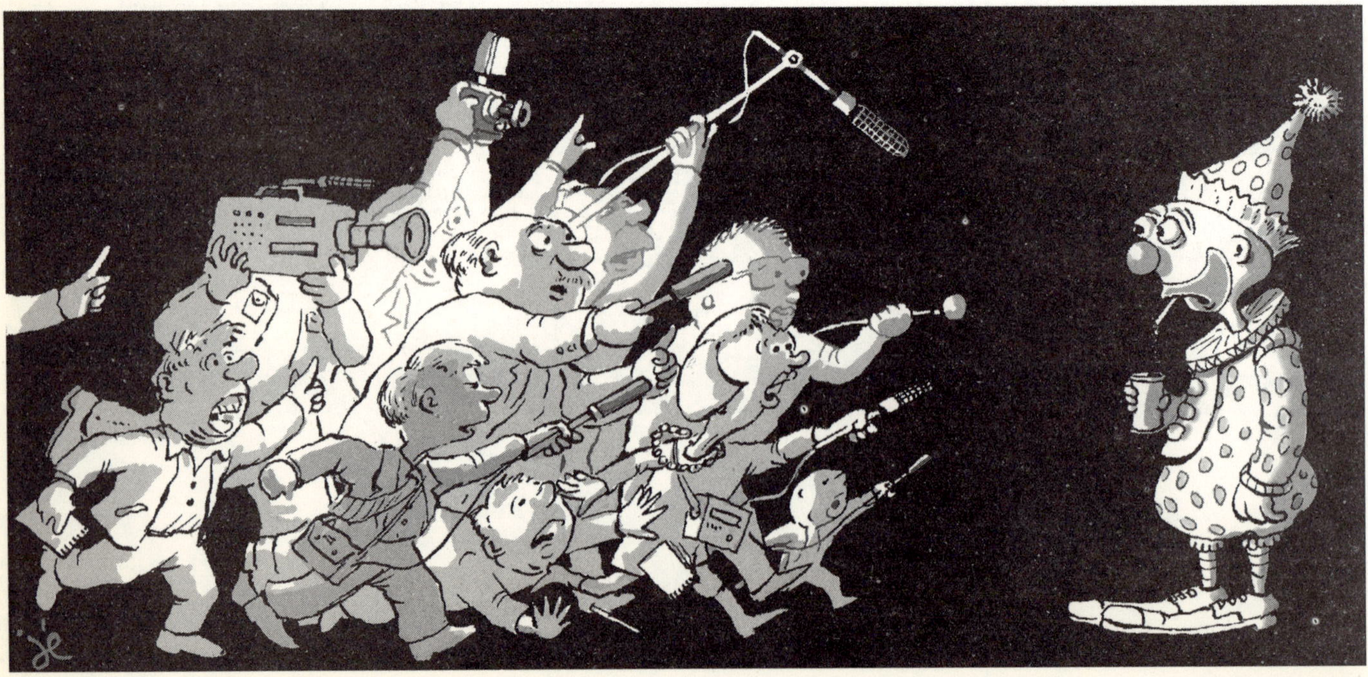

JÉ, *Frank*, unpublished

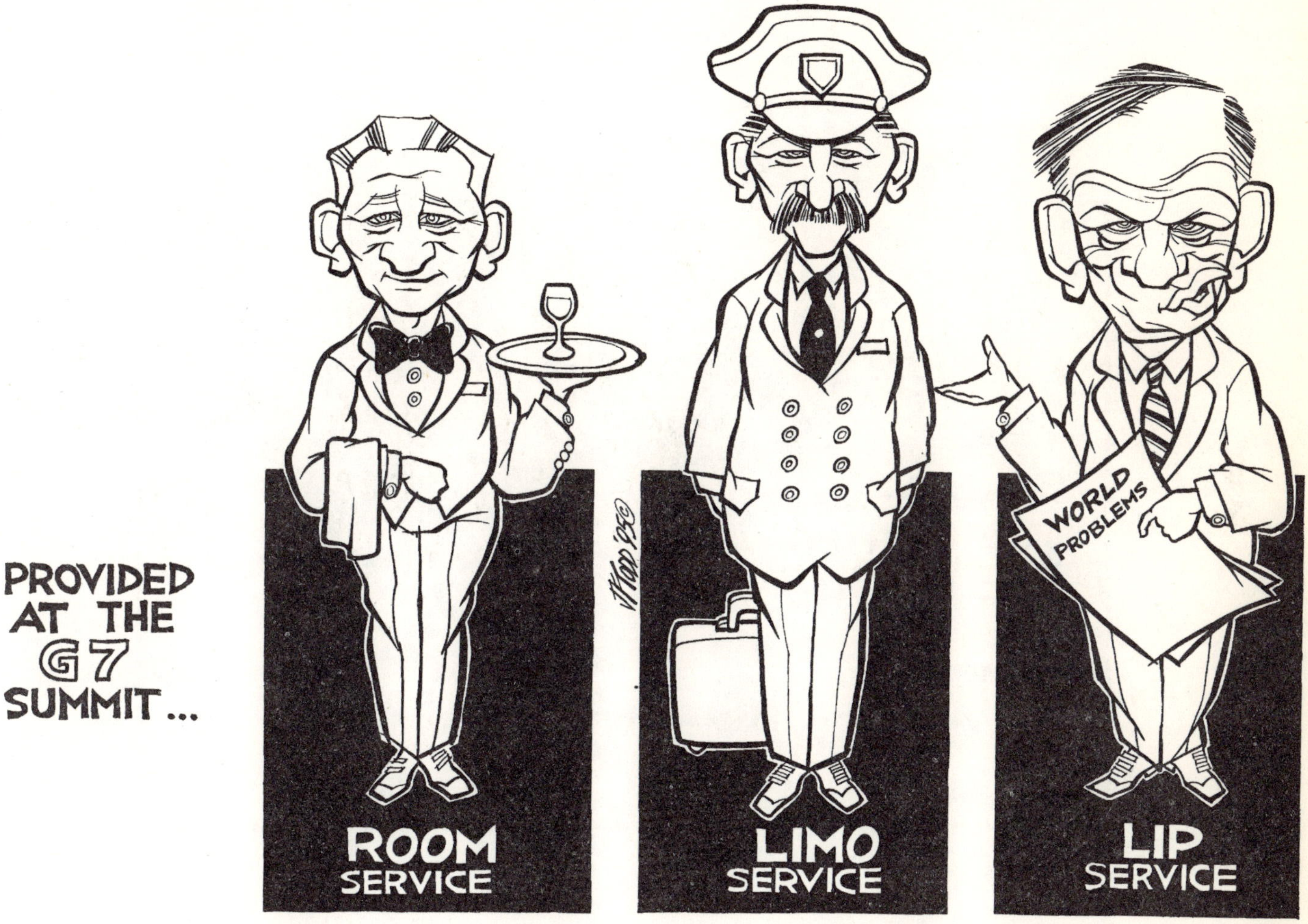
PROVIDED AT THE G7 SUMMIT...
ROOM SERVICE
LIMO SERVICE
WORLD PROBLEMS
LIP SERVICE

TODD

NEASE, *The Oakville Beaver*

LAST WEEK OF THE CAMPAIGN, AND BOB RAE COMES OUT SWINGING...

JENKINS, *The Globe & Mail*

CORRIGAN, *The Toronto Star*

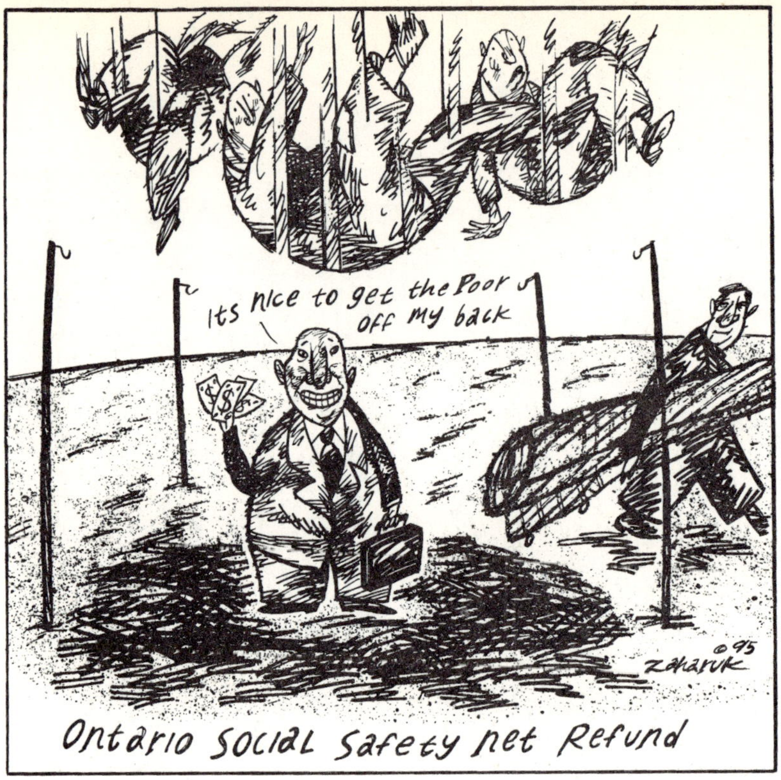
Its nice to get the Poor off my back
©95 Zaharuk
Ontario Social Safety net Refund

ZAHARUK, Union Art Services

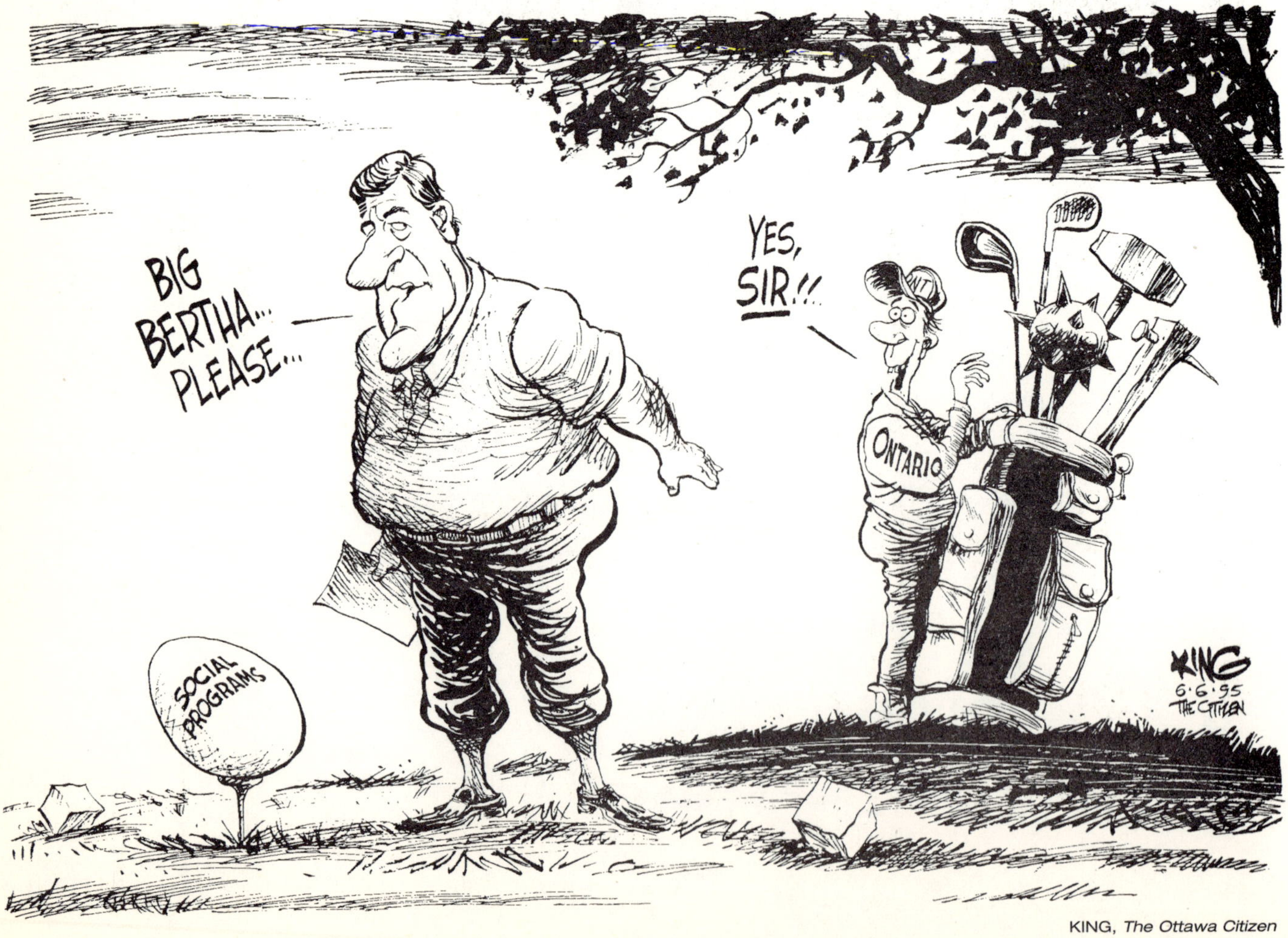
BIG BERTHA... PLEASE...
YES, SIR!!
ONTARIO
SOCIAL PROGRAMS
KING 6·6·95 THE CITIZEN

KING, *The Ottawa Citizen*

CAM, *The Leader-Post*, Regina

PETERSON, *The Vancouver Sun*

OLSON, *The Vancouver Courier*

OLSON, *The Vancouver Courier*

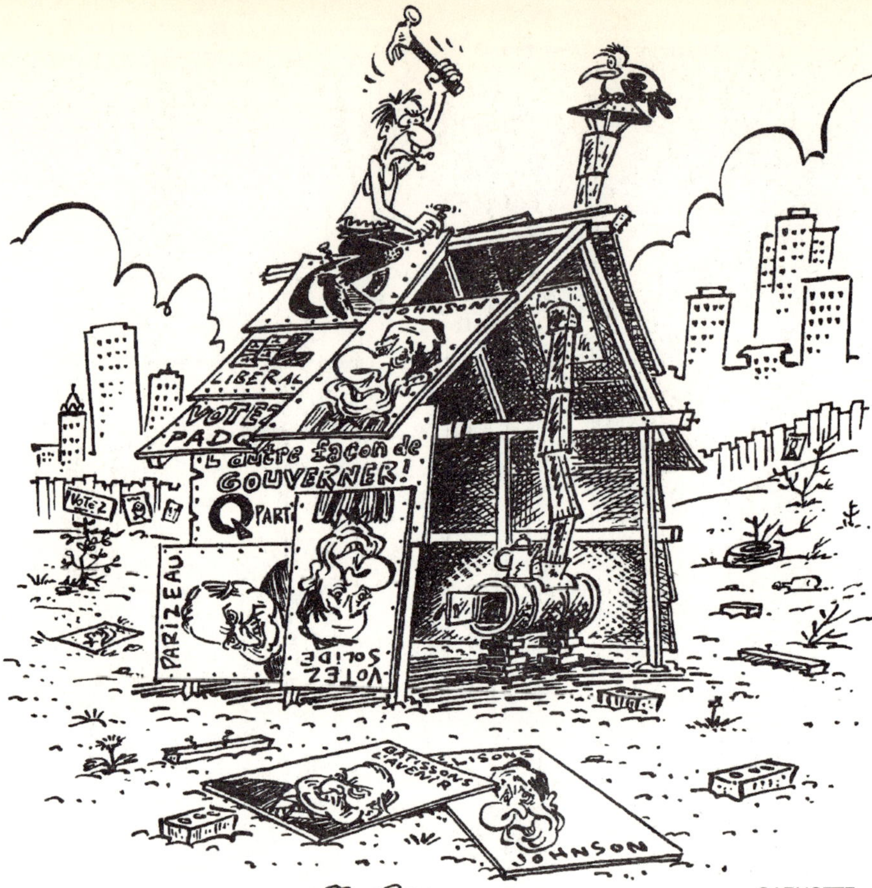
JOHNSON
LIBÉRAL
VOTEZ
PADO
L'autre façon de
GOUVERNER!
Q PARTI
PARIZEAU
VOTEZ SOLIDE
BATISSONS L'AVENIR
JOHNSON

GARNOTTE

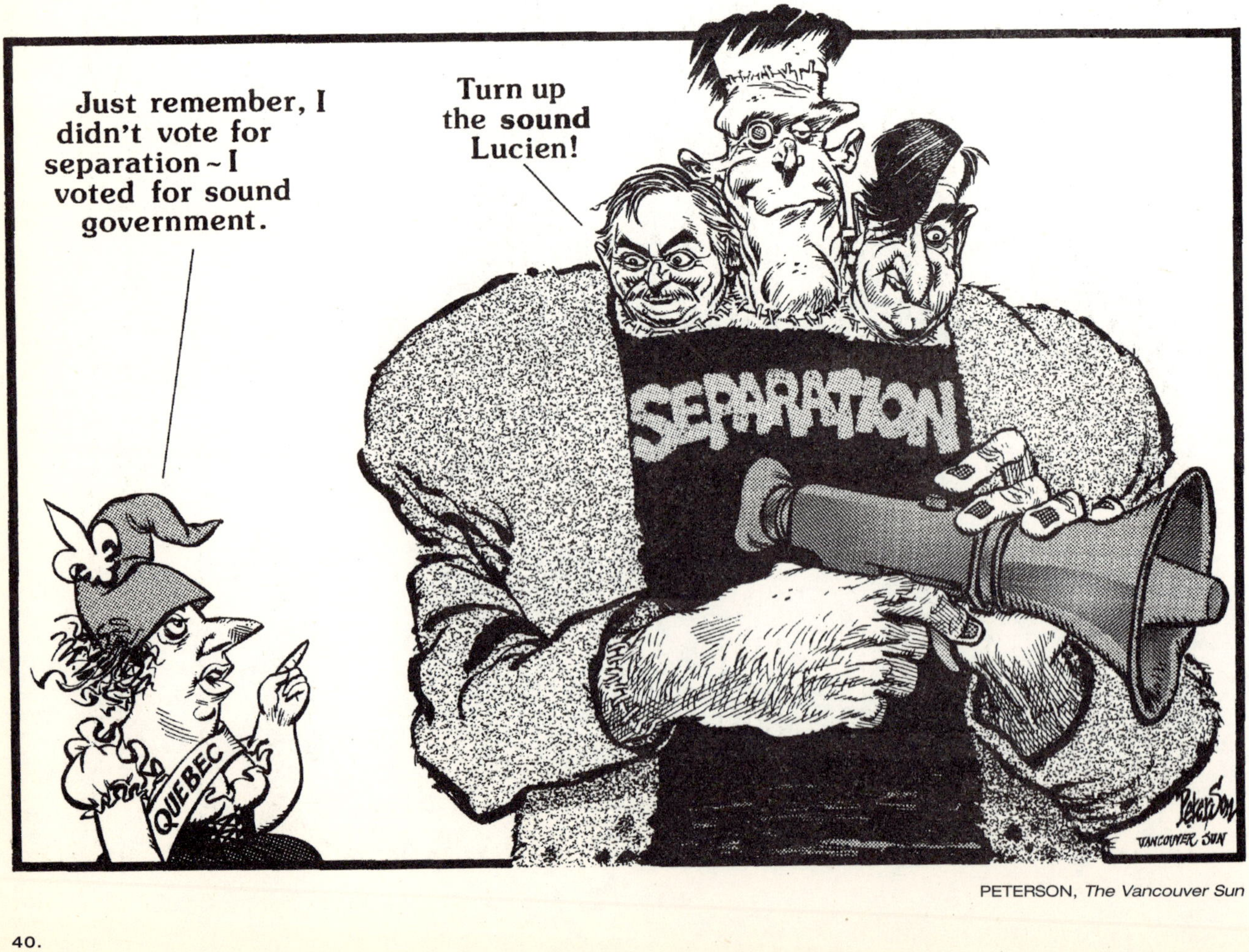
Just remember, I didn't vote for separation ~ I voted for sound government.
Turn up the sound Lucien!
SEPARATION
QUEBEC
VANCOUVER SUN

PETERSON, *The Vancouver Sun*

Indian affairs / next wicket

PIER, Le Journal de Montréal

This is art... but *this* is a mess!

GARNOTTE, Nouvelles CSN, Montreal

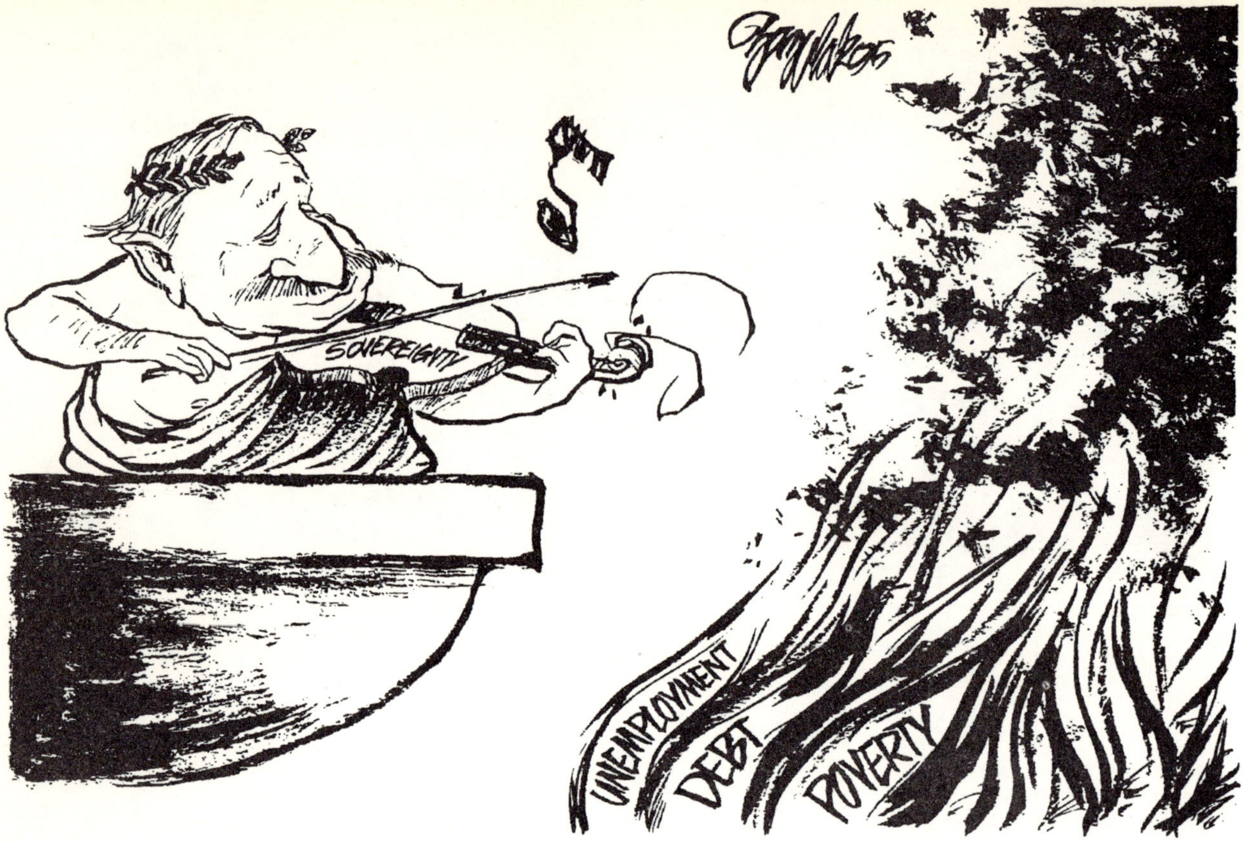
SOVEREIGNTY
UNEMPLOYMENT
DEBT
POVERTY

ZAZULAK, *The Hill Times*, Ottawa

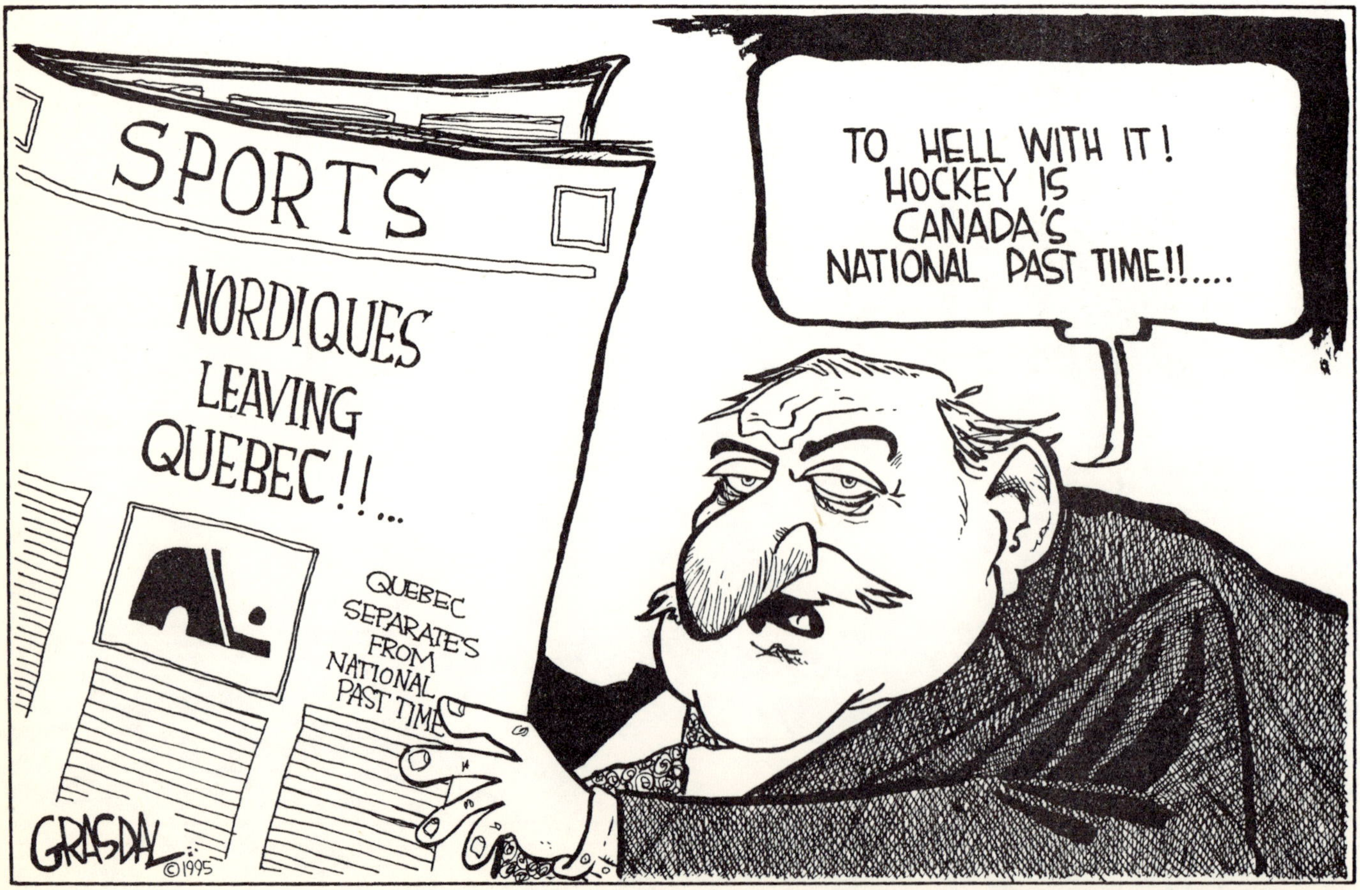
SPORTS
NORDIQUES LEAVING QUEBEC!!...
QUEBEC SEPARATE'S FROM NATIONAL PAST TIME
TO HELL WITH IT! HOCKEY IS CANADA'S NATIONAL PAST TIME!!....
GRASDAL ©1995

GRASDAL, *The Edmonton Journal*, Edmonton

NEASE, *The Oakville Beaver*

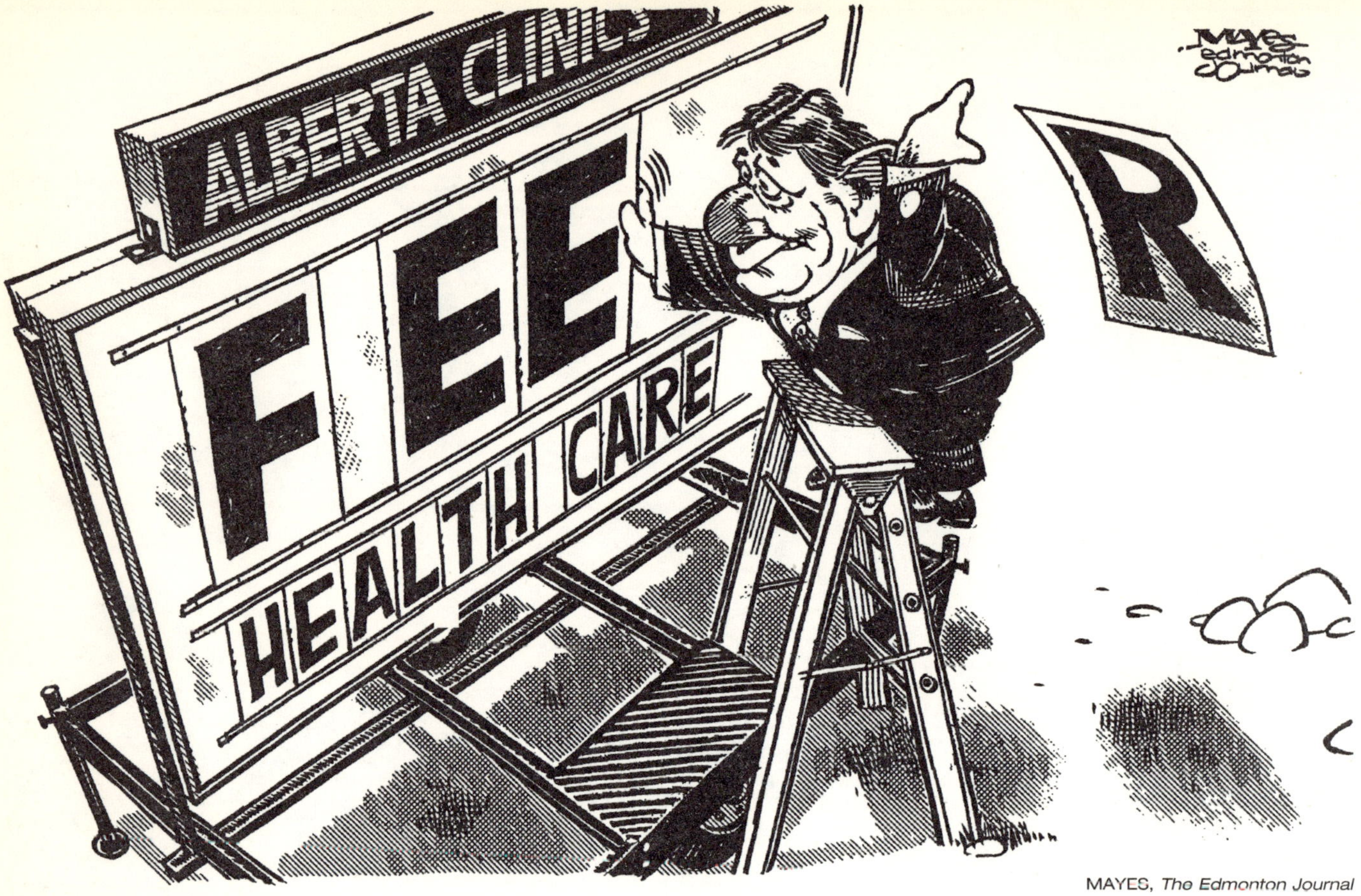

MAYES, *The Edmonton Journal*

GRASDAL, *The Edmonton Journal*

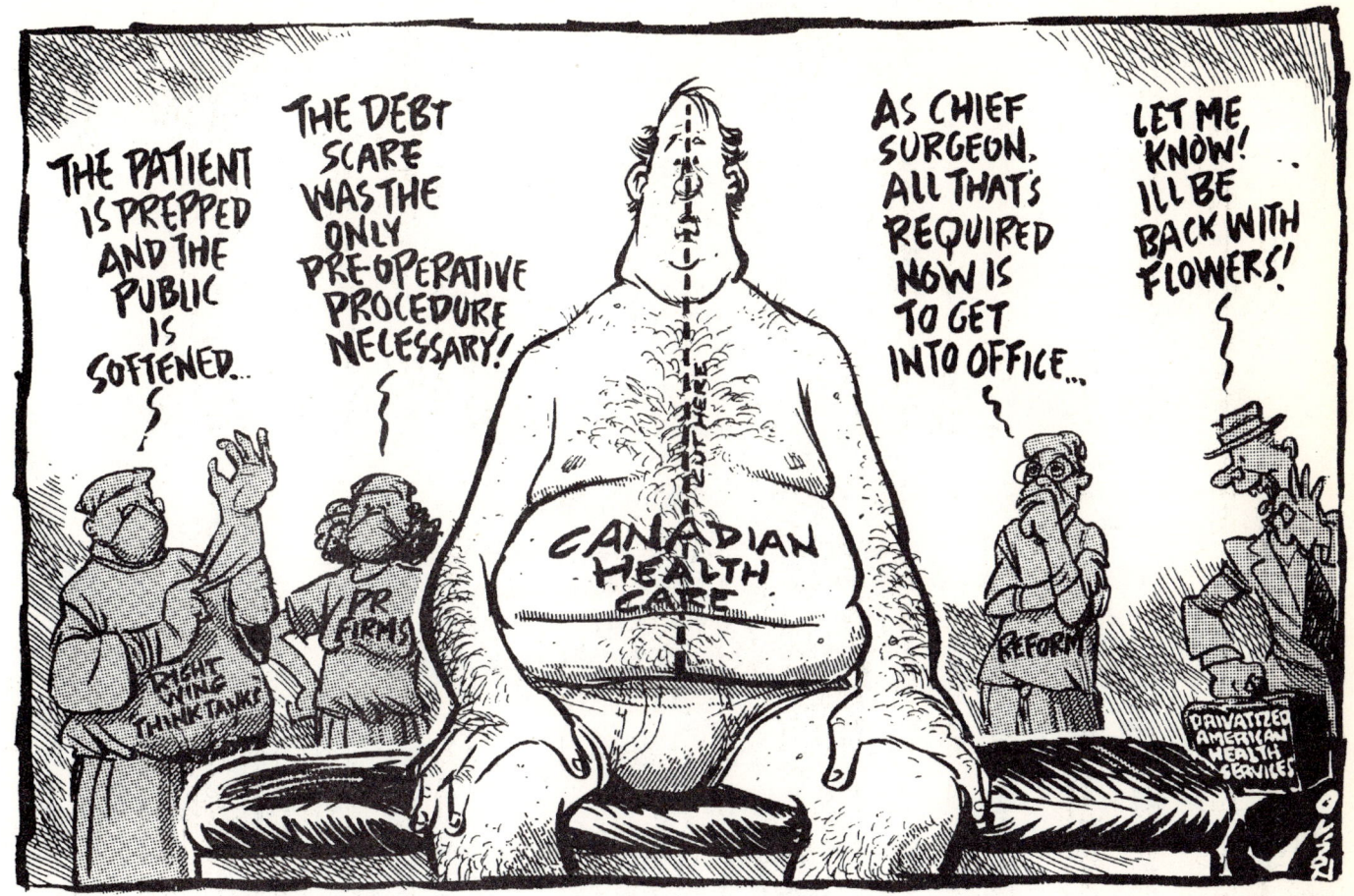

OLSON, *The Vancouver Courier*

CONSTABLE, Union Art Services

JÉ, Frank

RODEWALT, *The Calgary Herald*

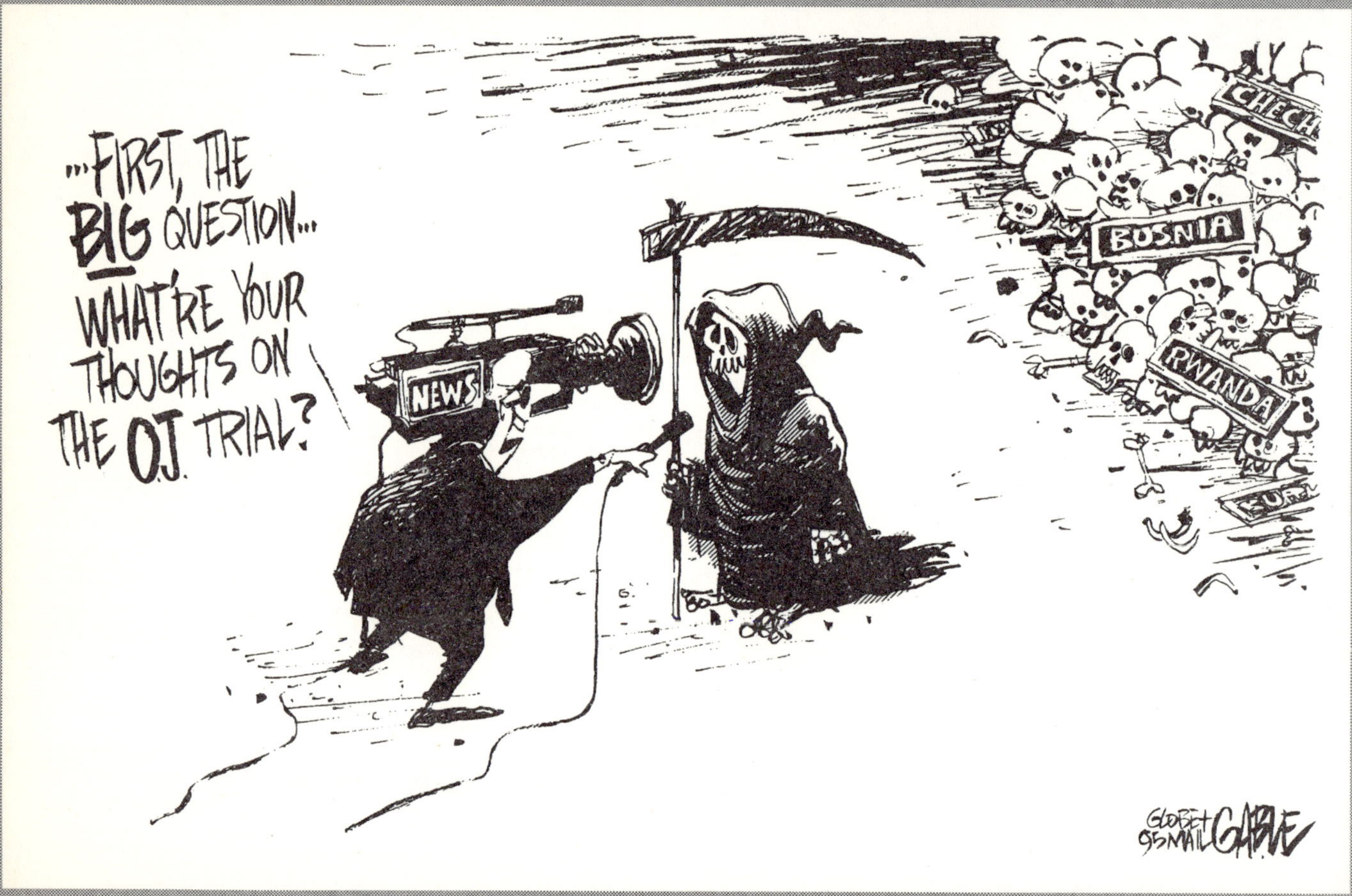
...FIRST, THE BIG QUESTION... WHAT'RE YOUR THOUGHTS ON THE O.J. TRIAL?
NEWS
BOSNIA
RWANDA
GLOBE+MAIL 95 GABLE

**Portfoolio 11**

# The World and Stuff
## War, mayhem and the creaking of a billion bedsprings

Thank heavens for the 50th anniversary of the end of the Second World War! Without this bit of celebration and the knowledge that madness does pass, you'd have to lock up the razor blades before you delved any deeper into international affairs. About the only thing keeping Bosnia from exploding into a really big war was a relative handful of peacekeepers, and the cowardice and feigned indifference of much of the rest of the world. Meanwhile, Chechnya, which is giving separatism a really bad name, looked an awful lot like Afghanistan to many nervous Russians.

In Haiti the U.S. played puppet master—say what you will about the U.S., they have been careful to pick their spots. "No big wars for us, thanks, we gave at the Persian Gulf"—and that was sufficient challenge for a time. That and lobbing hollow threats at Bosnia from a safe distance. If there is a safe distance from Bosnia.

In Cuba, the U.S. policy—"Okay, give 'em Florida, but that's it!"—is working splendidly. There is some fear among southern Senators, though, that Canada will be the next domino to fall for Cuba's communist charms. Frankly, we doubt it. Aside from sugar, rum, sun, cigars and a whole lot of '54 Chevies, Cuba just doesn't have a lot to offer. Canada would never sell its soul for a country with such a small Gross Domestic Product (unless maybe it's interested in a Candu reactor).

China, now that's another story. The prime minister likes China. He likes trade. Oh, sure, there are minor ideological problems to iron out. Canada remains soft on arbitrary detention, occasional massacres and other human rights...er...lapses. The strategy is to get these regimes hooked on the fine family of Canadian products. Once they play hockey, once they've tasted Canadian beer, once their secret police eavesdrop on enemies of the state using crystal-clear Canadian telecommunications technology, why, they'll be putty in our hands.

Now, all is not bleak. The world population conference proved just how many people love their neighbours, enthusiastically, frequently, and with a bouncing bundle of consequences.

NEASE, *The Oakville Beaver*

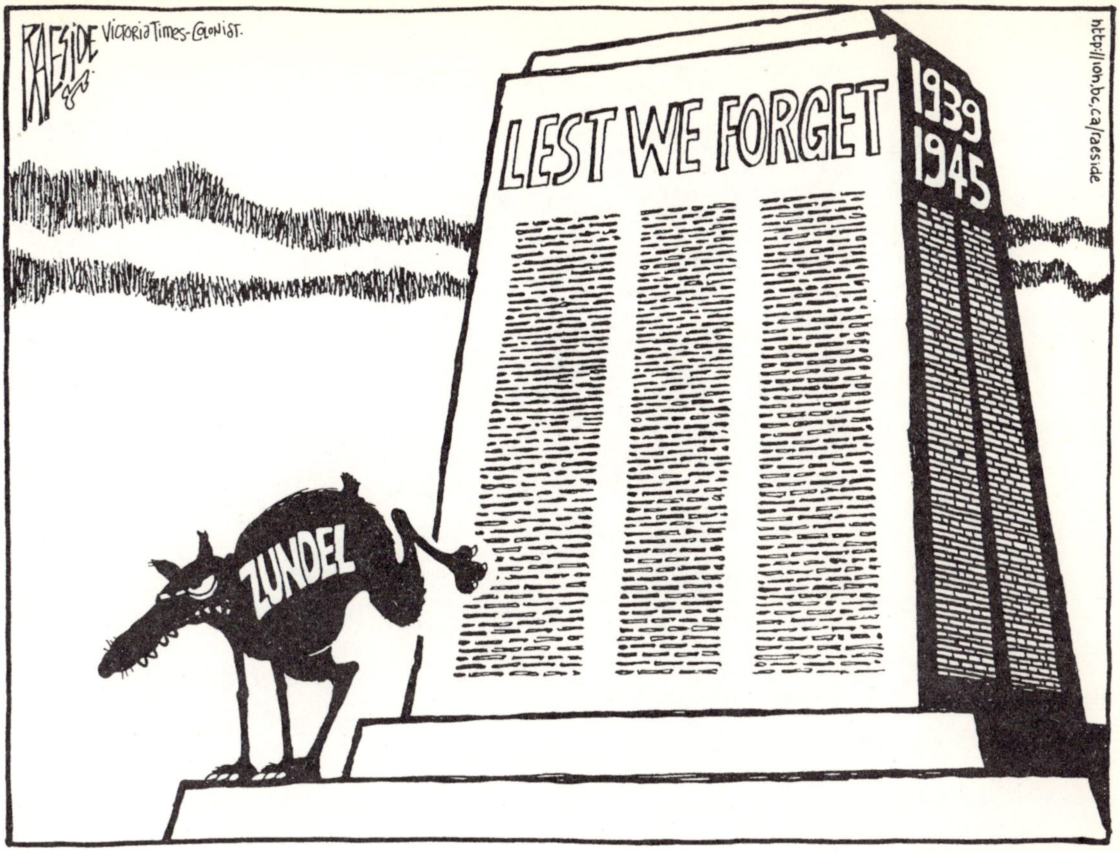
RAESIDE Victoria Times-Colonist.
LEST WE FORGET
1939
1945
http://ion.bc.ca/raeside
ZUNDEL

RAESIDE, *The Times-Colonist*, Victoria

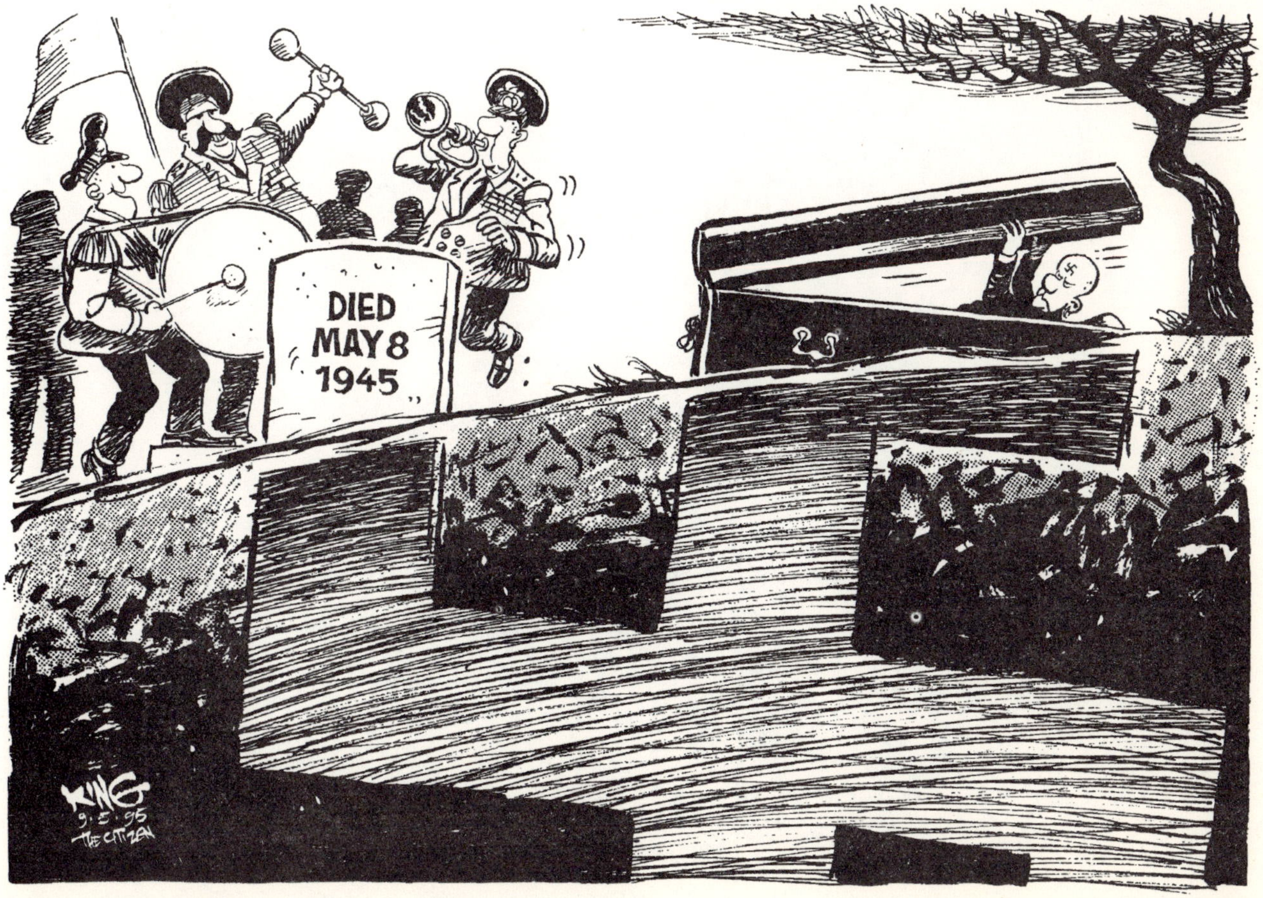
DIED
MAY 8
1945
KING
9.5.95
THE CITIZEN

KING, *The Ottawa Citizen*

CUMMINGS, *The Winnipeg Free Press*

DEWAR, *The Ottawa Sun*

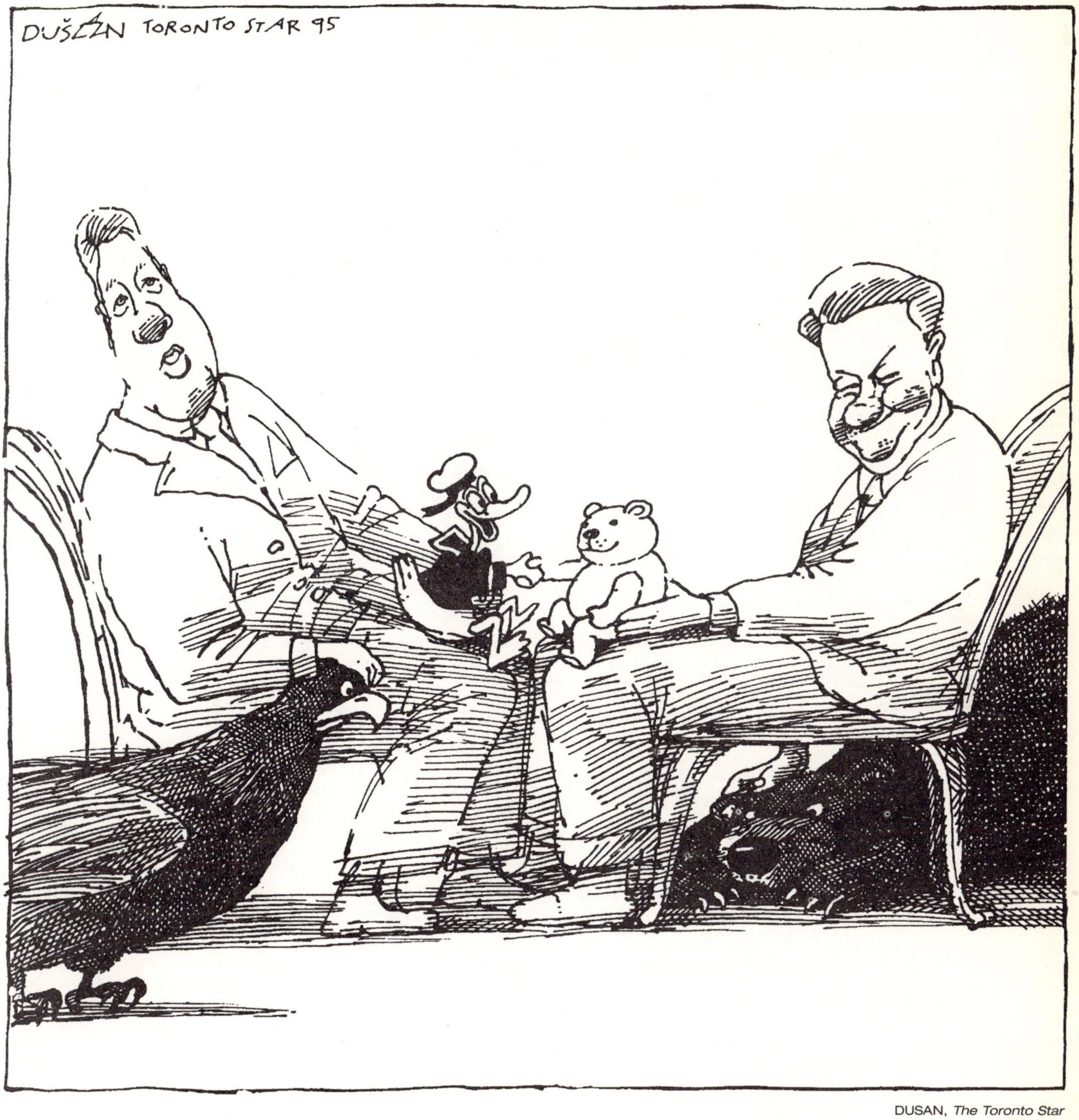
DUŠAN TORONTO STAR 95

DUSAN, *The Toronto Star*

BADO, *Le Droit*, Ottawa

EDWARDS

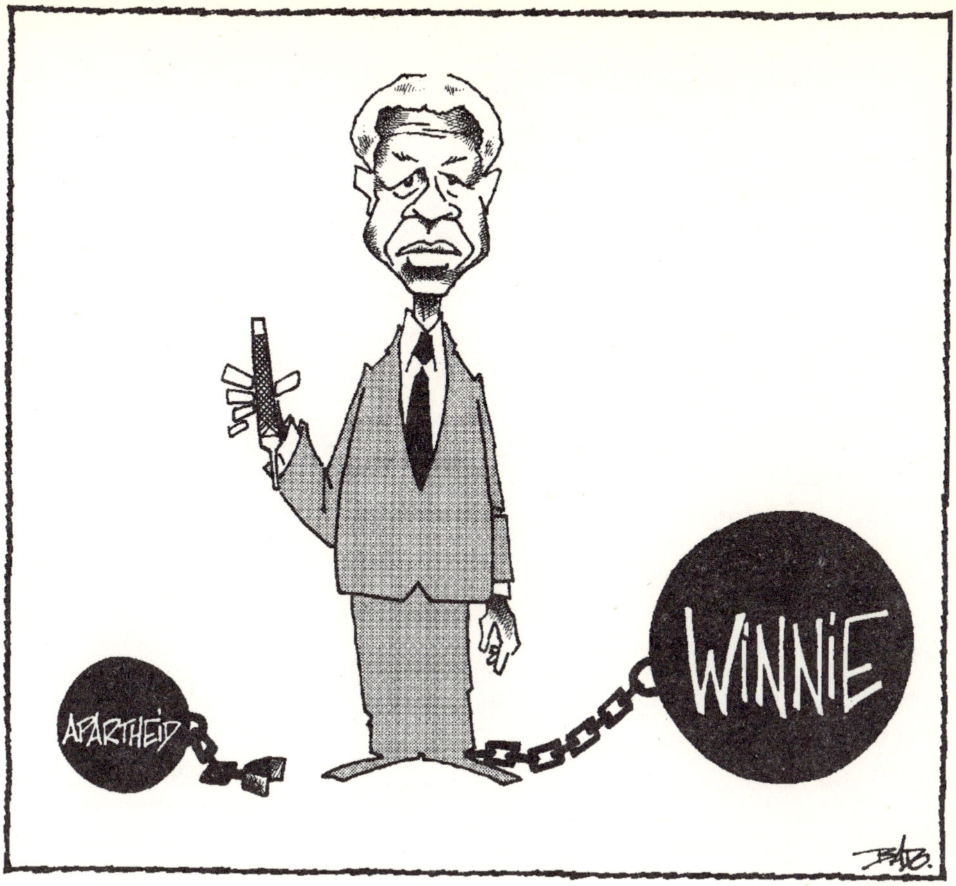
APARTHEID
WINNIE
BADO.

BADO, *Le Droit*, Ottawa

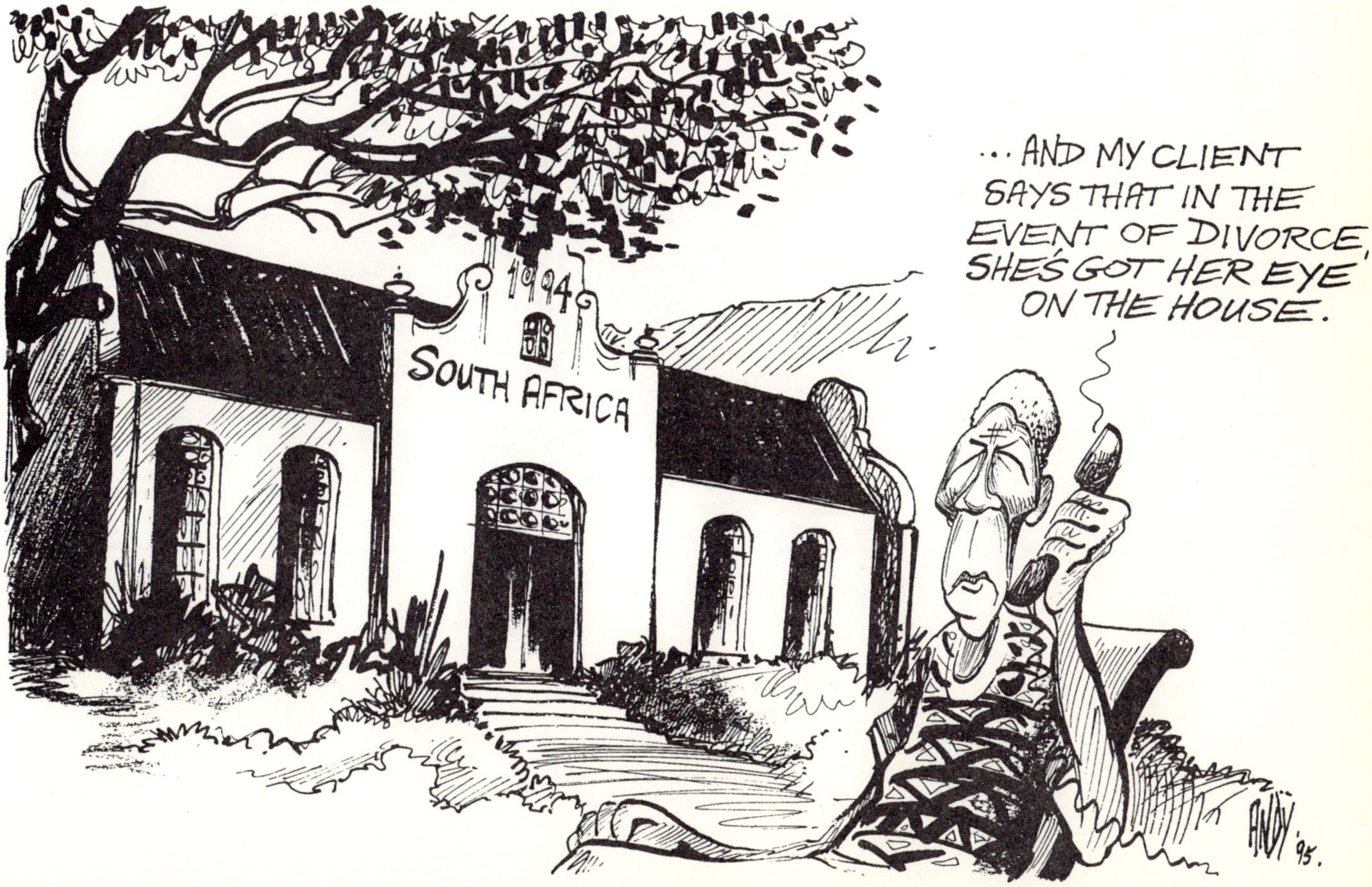
...AND MY CLIENT SAYS THAT IN THE EVENT OF DIVORCE, SHE'S GOT HER EYE ON THE HOUSE.
1994
SOUTH AFRICA
ANDY '95.

ANDY, Cartoonists & Writers Syndicate

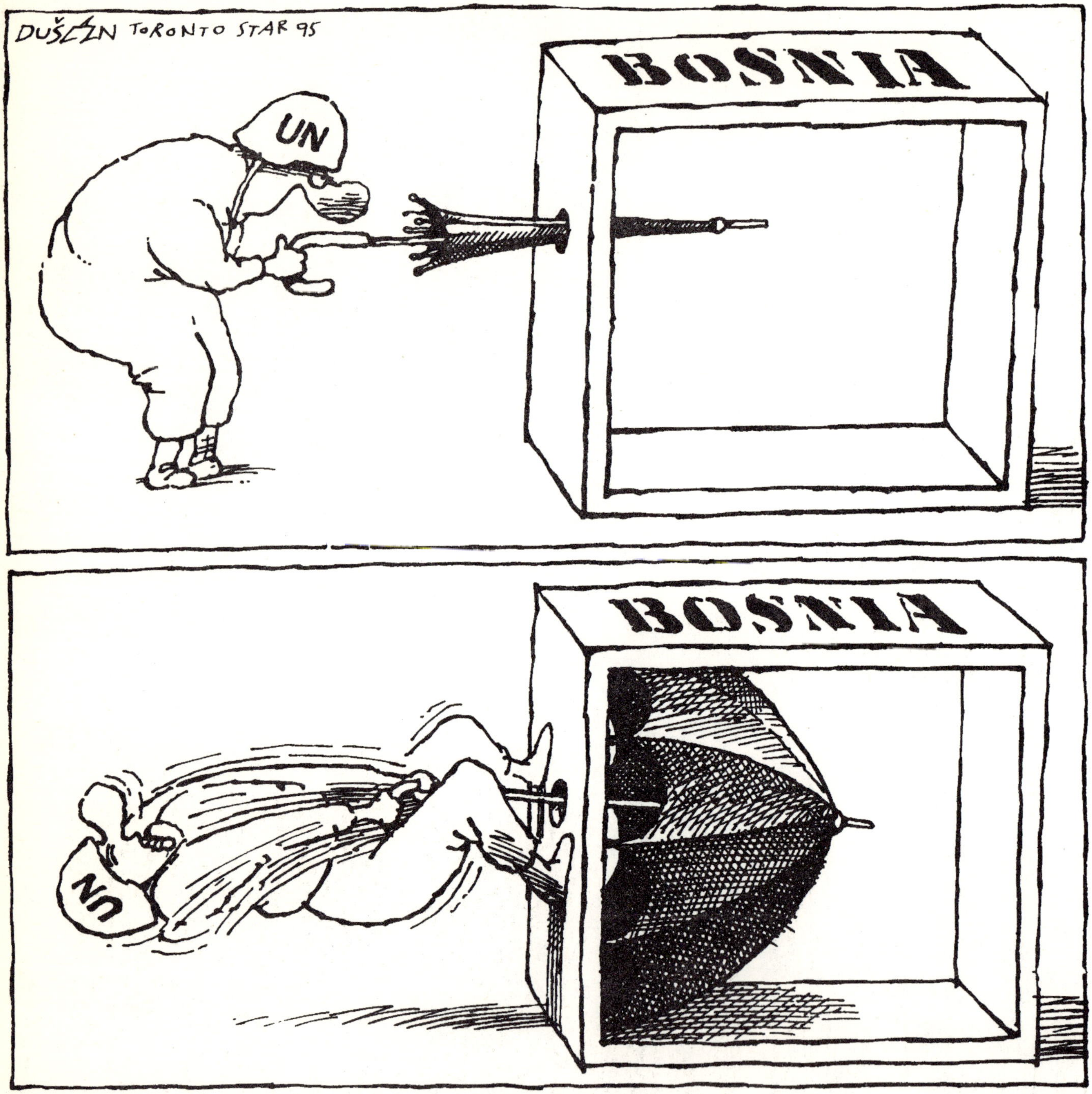
DUŠAN TORONTO STAR 95
BOSNIA
UN
BOSNIA
UN

DUSAN, *The Toronto Star*

CUMMINGS, *The Winnipeg Free Press*

MAYES, *The Edmonton Journal*

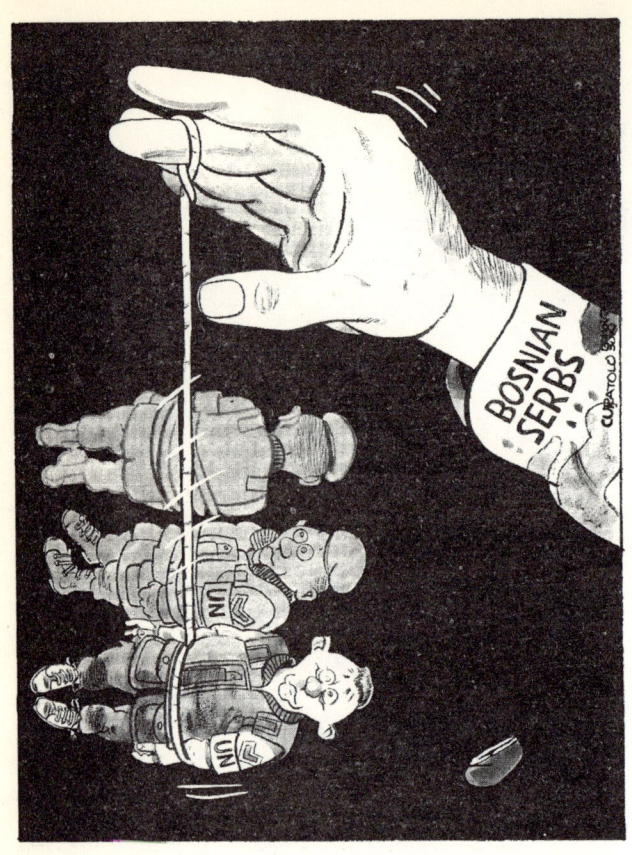

CURATOLO, *The Edmonton Sun*

TODD

AISLIN, *The Gazette*, Montreal

PETERSON, *The Vancouver Sun*

MURPHY, *The Province*, Vancouver

CUMMINGS, *The Winnipeg Free Press*

BORIS ET LA MOUCHE TCHÉTCHÈNE

CHAPLEAU, *Le Devoir*, Montreal

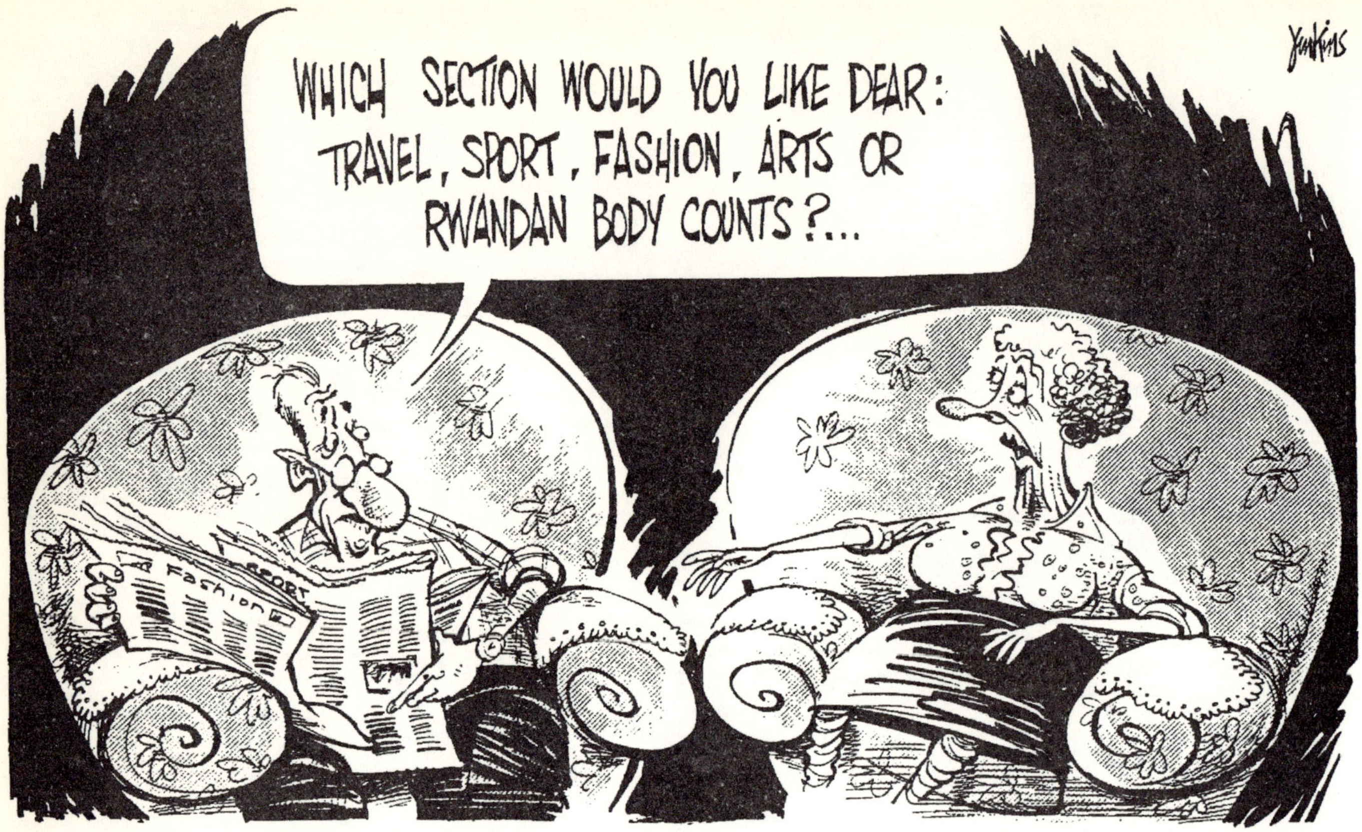

WHICH SECTION WOULD YOU LIKE DEAR: TRAVEL, SPORT, FASHION, ARTS OR RWANDAN BODY COUNTS?...
Fashion
SPORT
JENKINS


JENKINS, *The Globe & Mail*

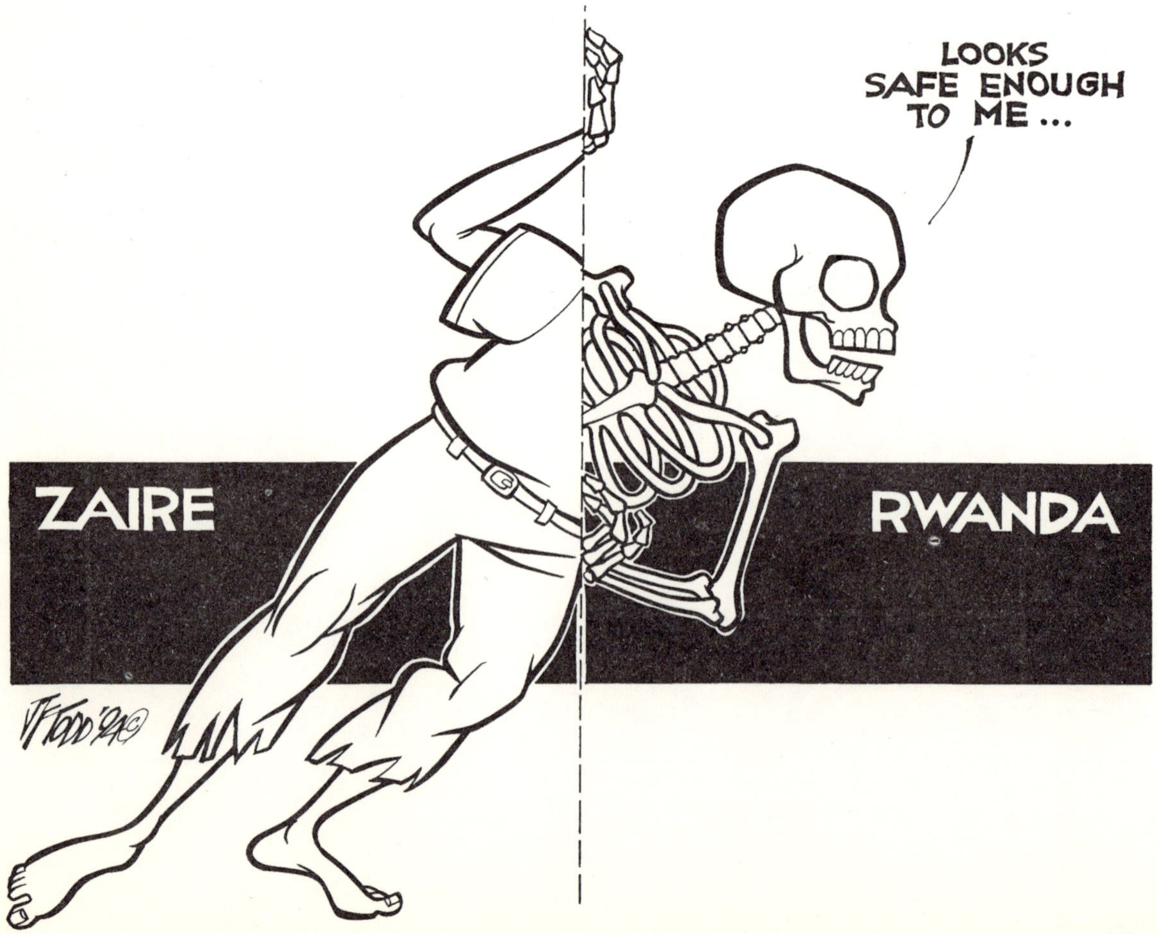

LOOKS SAFE ENOUGH TO ME...
ZAIRE
RWANDA


TODD

HUMOUR NOIR

CHAPLEAU, *Le Devoir*, Montreal

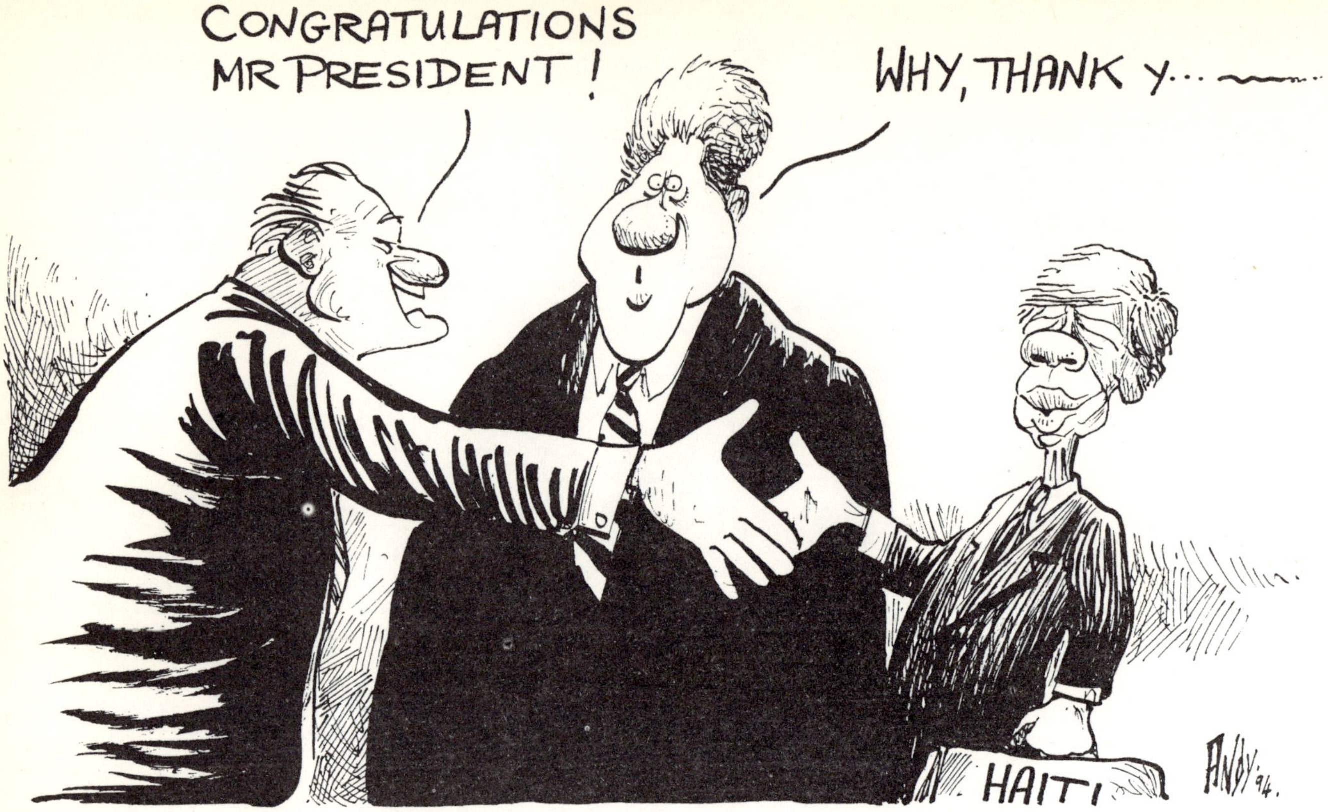
CONGRATULATIONS
MR PRESIDENT !
WHY, THANK Y...
HAITI
ANDY '94.

ANDY, Cartoonists & Writers Syndicate

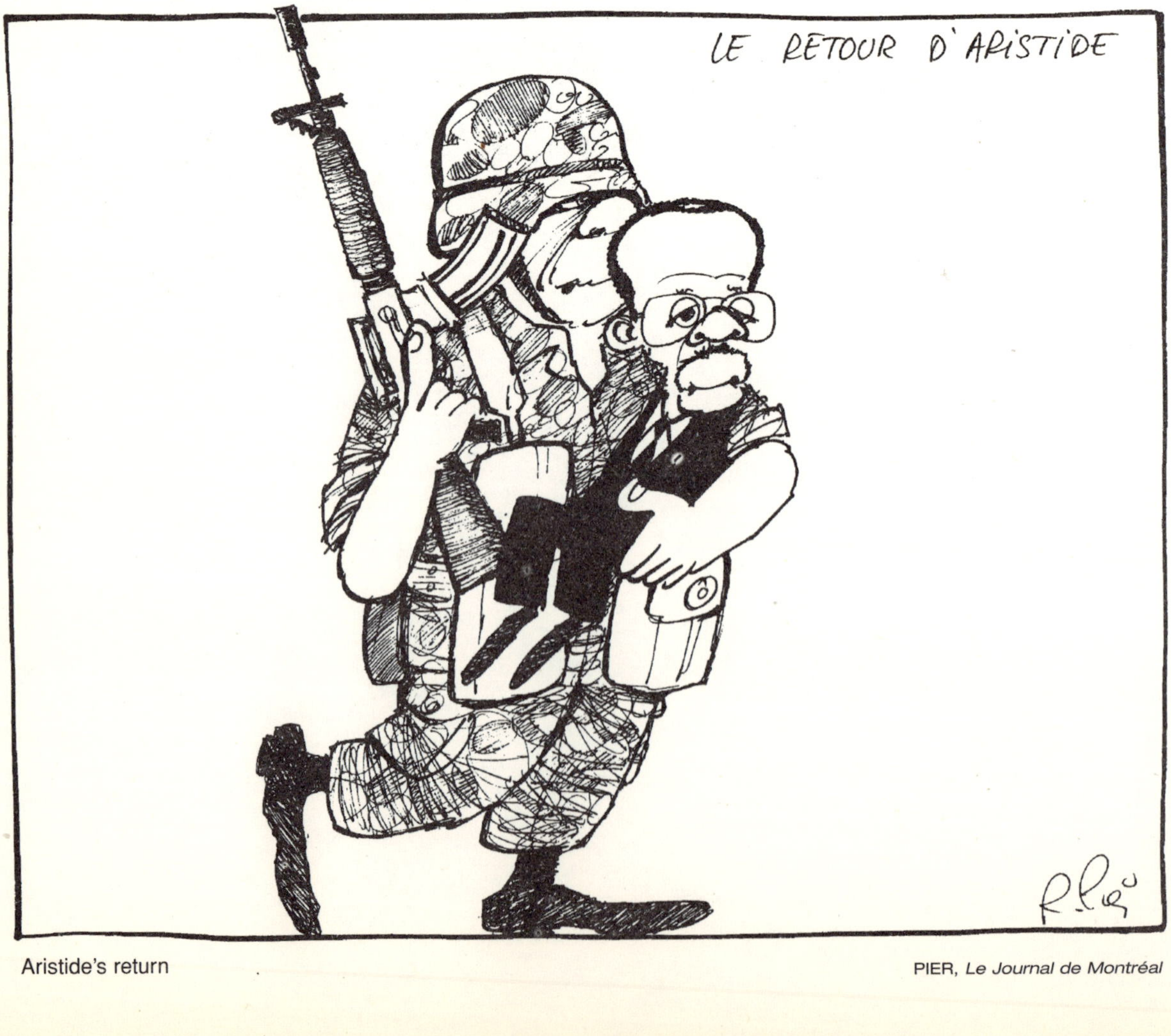
LE RETOUR D'ARISTIDE

Aristide's return

PIER, *Le Journal de Montréal*

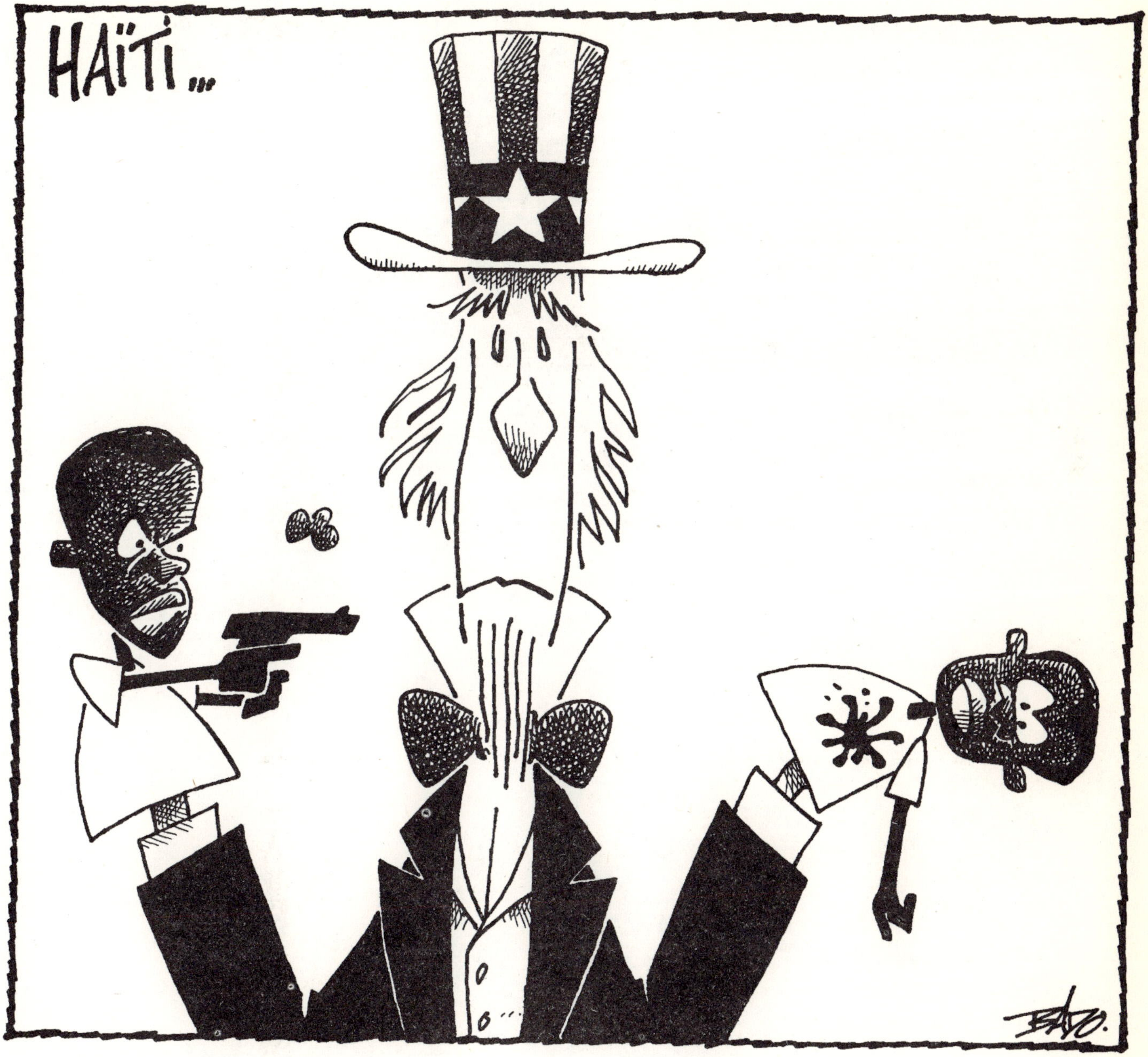
HAÏTI...
BADO.
BADO, *Le Droit*, Ottawa

RAESIDE, *The Times-Colonist*, Victoria

CHAPLEAU, *Le Devoir*, Montreal

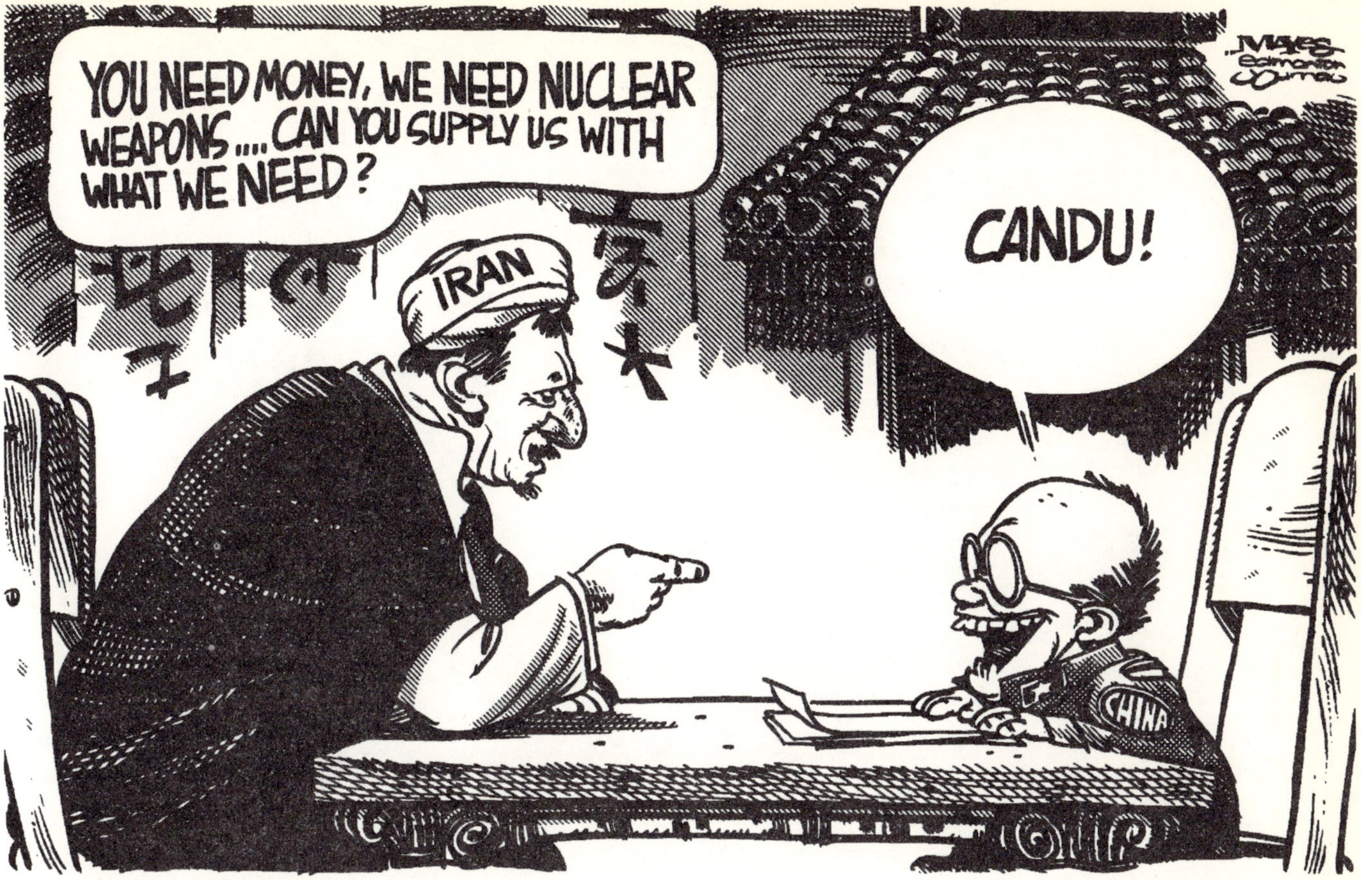
YOU NEED MONEY, WE NEED NUCLEAR WEAPONS....CAN YOU SUPPLY US WITH WHAT WE NEED?
IRAN
CANDU!
CHINA

MAYES, *The Edmonton Journal*

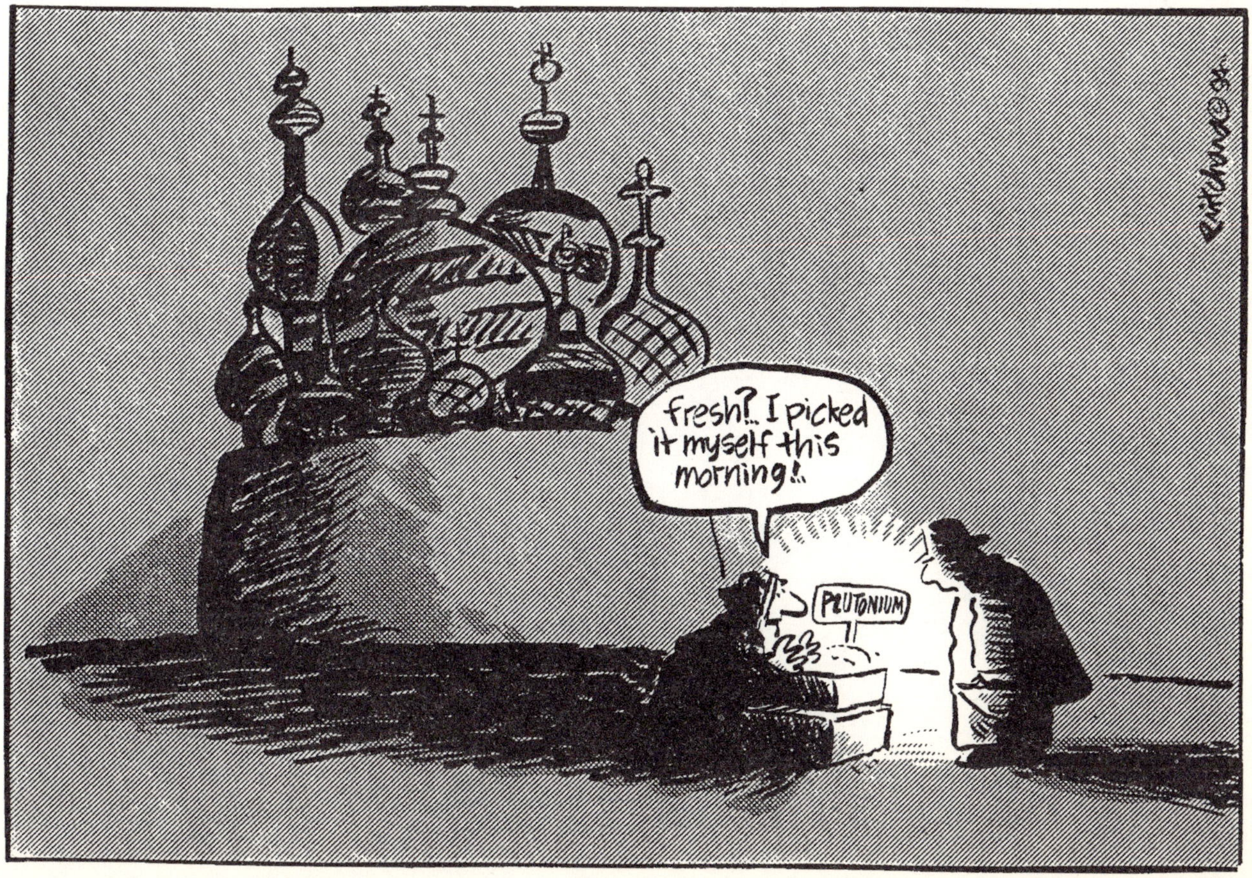
fresh?.. I picked it myself this morning!..
PLUTONIUM

PRITCHARD

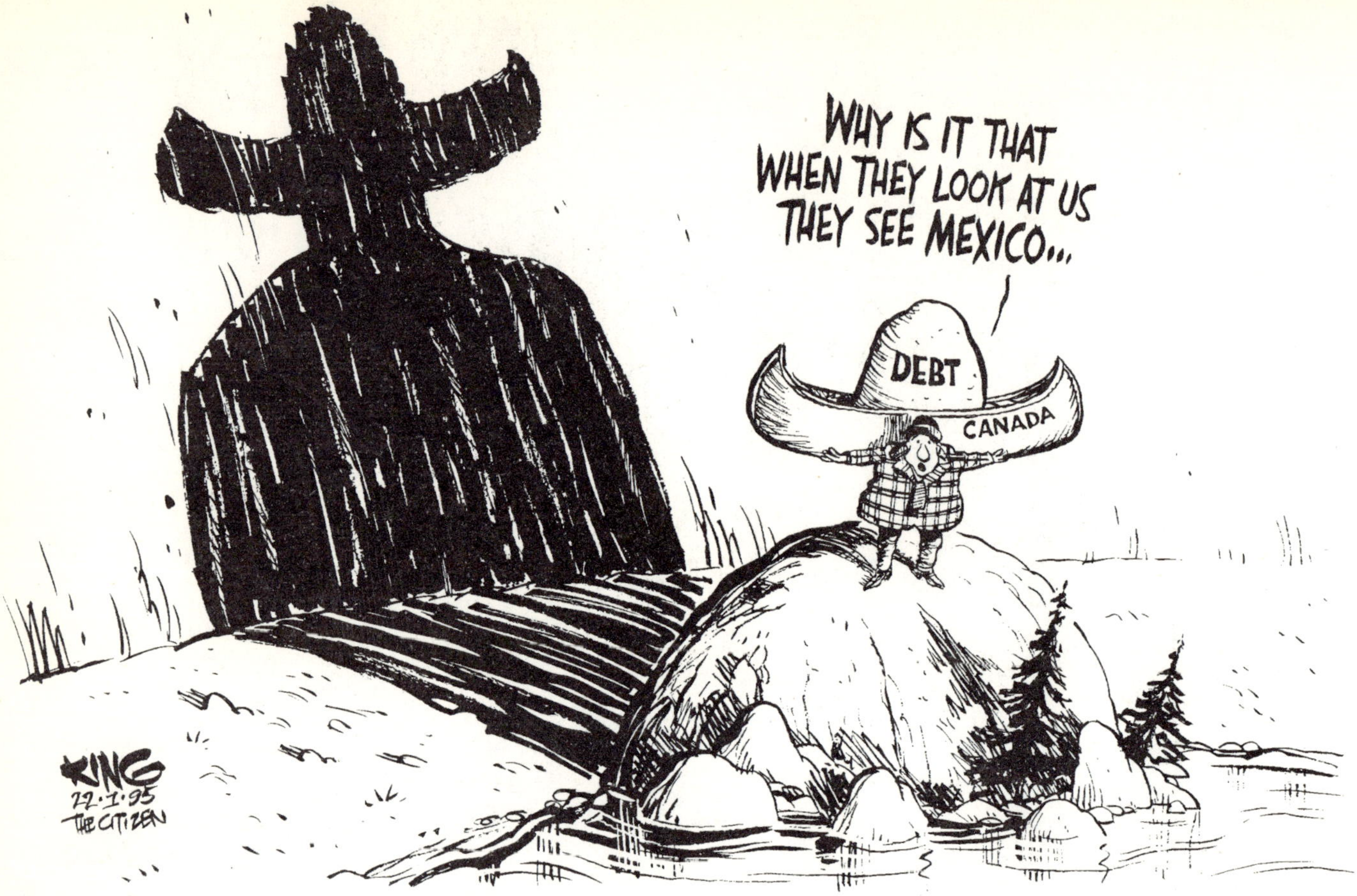
WHY IS IT THAT
WHEN THEY LOOK AT US
THEY SEE MEXICO...
DEBT
CANADA
KING
22·1·95
THE CITIZEN

KING, *The Ottawa Citizen*

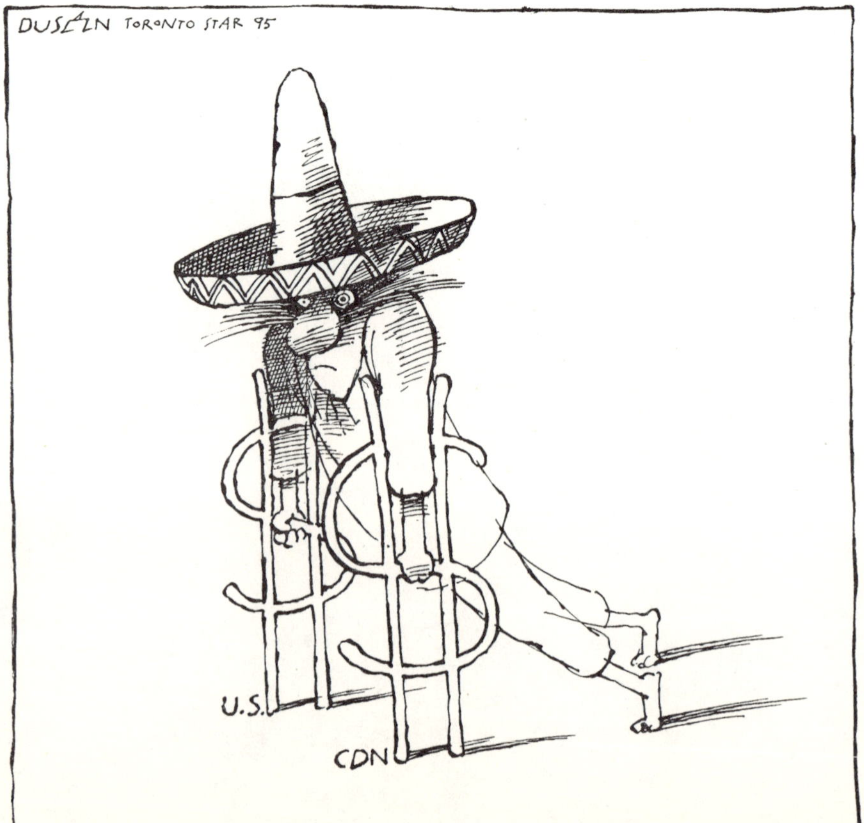
DUSAN TORONTO STAR 95
U.S.
CDN

DUSAN, *The Toronto Star*

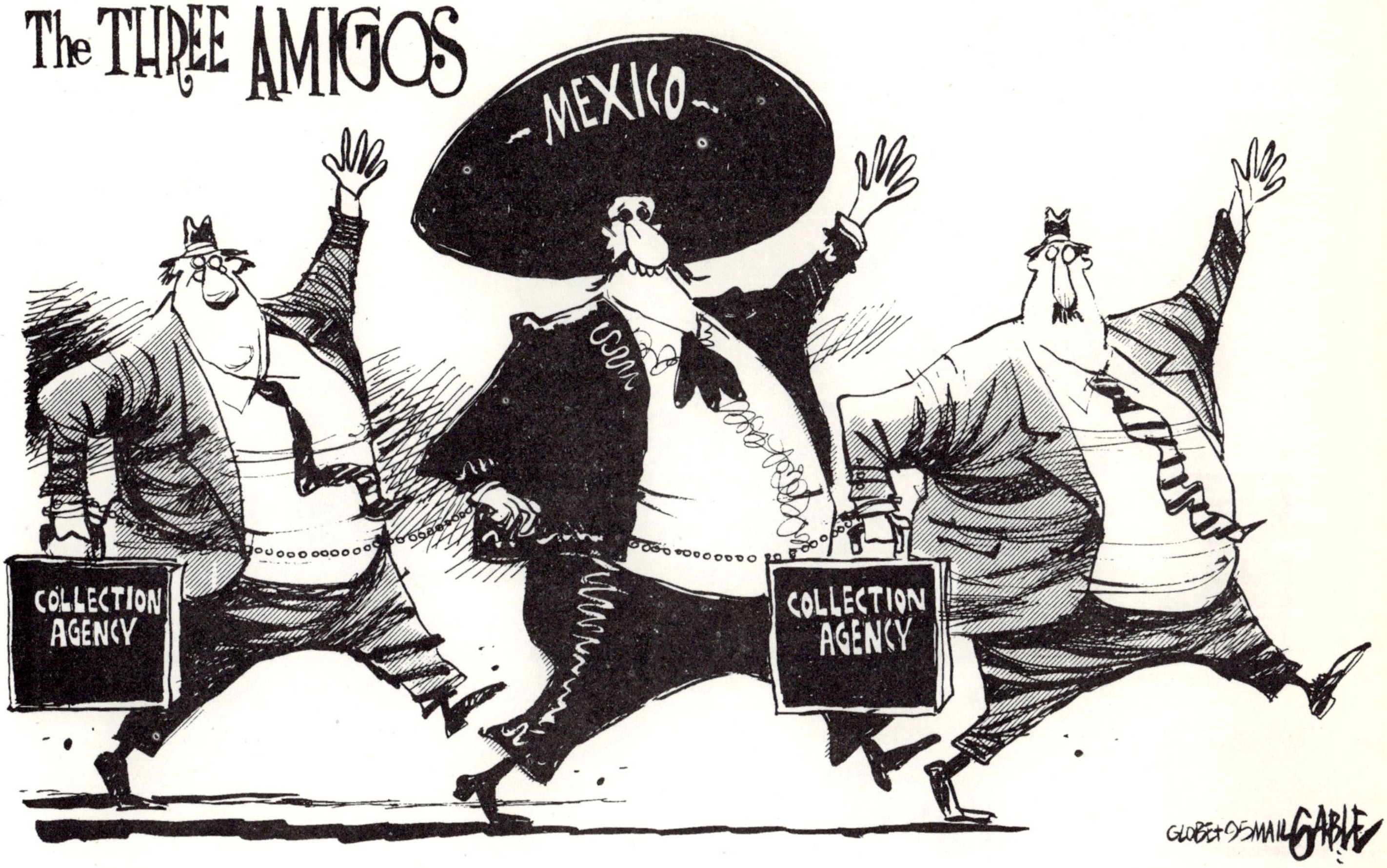
The THREE AMIGOS
MEXICO
COLLECTION AGENCY
COLLECTION AGENCY
GLOBE+95MAIL GABLE

GABLE, *The Globe & Mail*

PETERSON, *The Vancouver Sun*

MAYES, *The Edmonton Journal*

NEASE, *The Oakville Beaver*

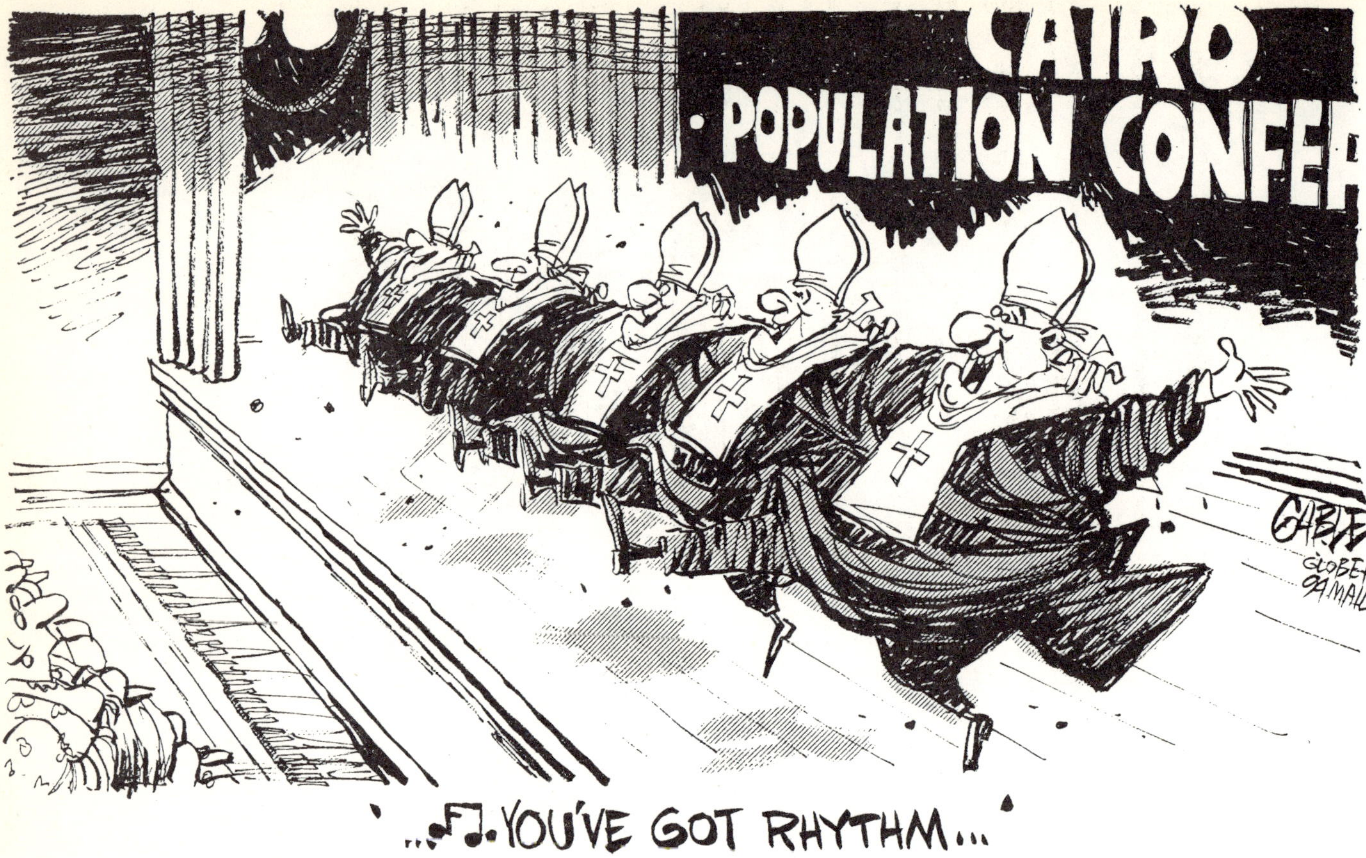
CAIRO
POPULATION CONFER
GABLE GLOBE & MAIL
...♫ YOU'VE GOT RHYTHM...

GABLE, *The Globe & Mail*

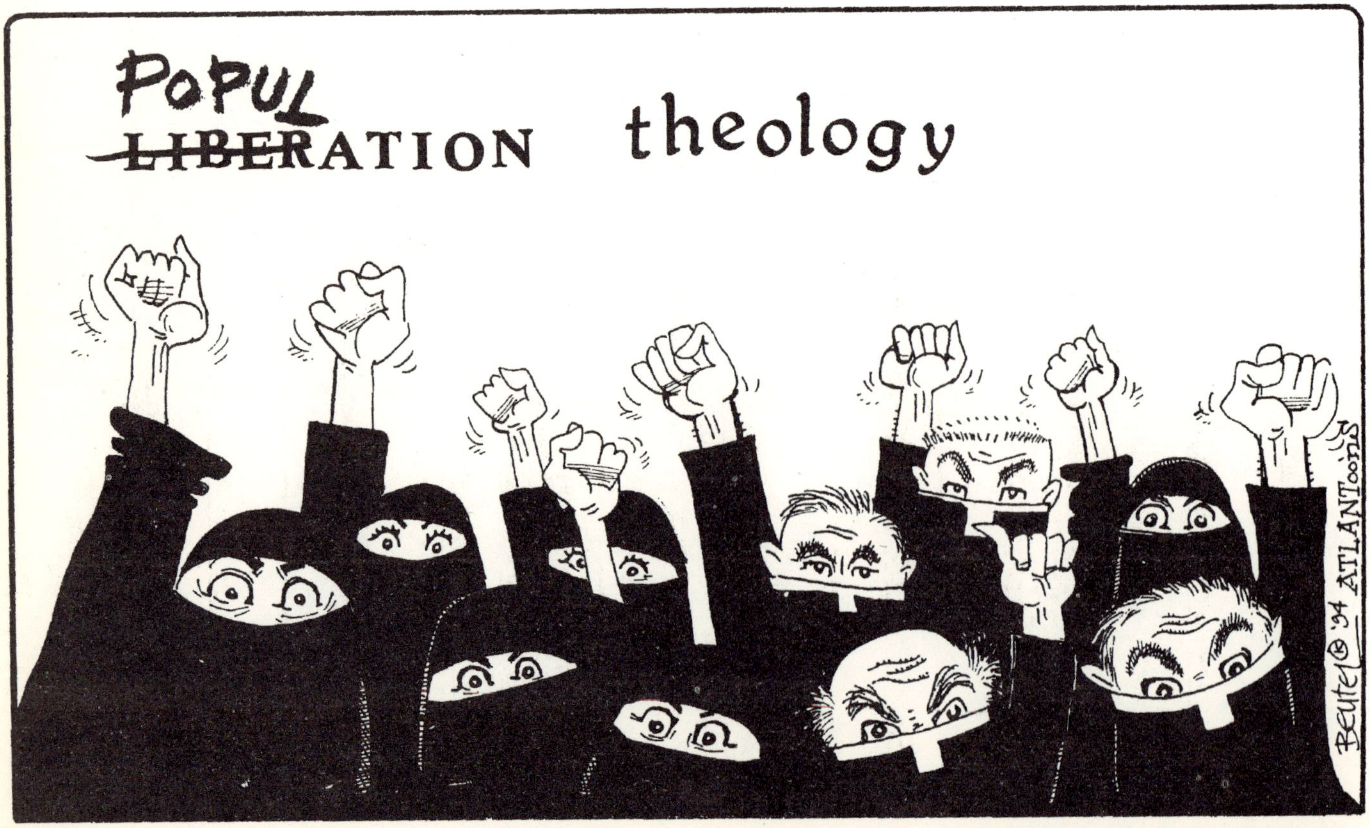
POPUL
LIBERATION theology
BEUTEL '94 ATLANToons

BEUTEL, the *Telegraph-Journal*, Saint John

MURPHY, *The Province*, Vancouver

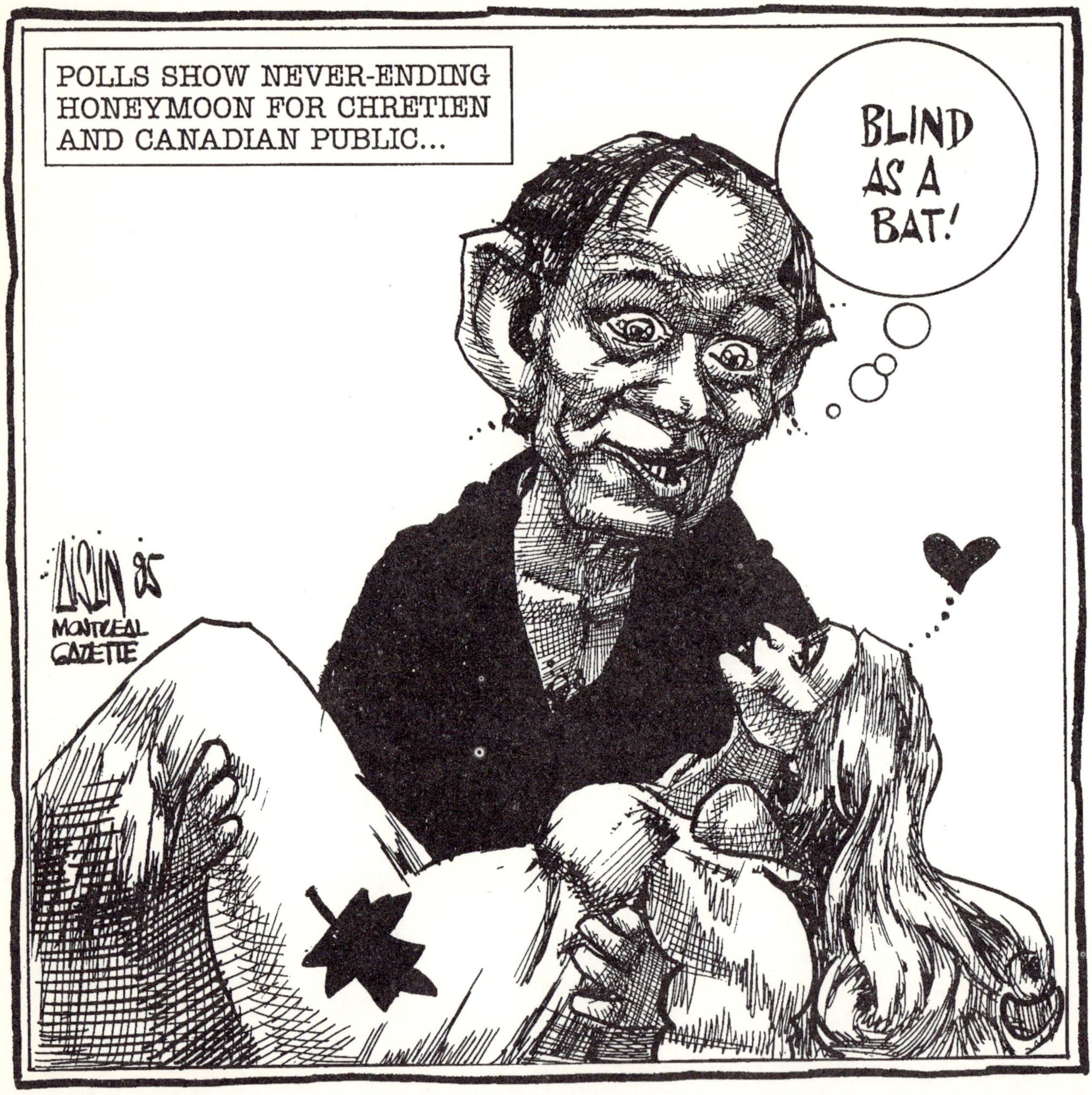
POLLS SHOW NEVER-ENDING HONEYMOON FOR CHRETIEN AND CANADIAN PUBLIC...
BLIND AS A BAT!
AISLIN 95
MONTREAL GAZETTE

Portfoolio 11

# Political Life (and other oxymorons)

You might think that Lucien Bouchard, having lost a leg to a ghastly flesh-eating disease, would have earned a few moments of grace, and perhaps he did. Cartoonists briefly held their fire, at least until it was clear (from his staged return to public life) that he neither needed nor wanted to be treated as a political invalid. So enough of the kid glove treatment—in the endless saw-off between federalism and sovereignty, it is the quality of his ideas that will determine whether Lucien Bouchard has a leg to stand on.

Meantime, life was pretty much unchanged for the other major party leaders. Preston Manning—Newt Lite to his American friends—continued to preach the politics of drastically reduced government. Strangely enough, the politician who best followed that ideal was Prime Minister Jean Chretien, who raised doing nothing in government to an art form. The public opinion polls called this Chretien's record-breaking political honeymoon. Frankly, though most Canadians have trouble picturing Uncle Jean "that way." More likely, he's just catching up on his sleep, which is fine by us. Wake us after the referendum.

Of course, not all was quiet. There was the Gun Debate, which many Canadians mistakenly believed was sponsored by the National Rifle Association or the Reform Party. In fact, it was just the Liberals playing smart politics. Most Canadians don't own a gun and never will, but if they weren't occupied debating the value of gun registration, they might have noticed that the Liberals hadn't changed the GST, improved day care or gotten the unemployment rate down to acceptable levels. They might have noticed that the little Liberal dustbunny, Rosanne Skoke, was still crawling under beds searching out homosexuals. And they might have realised that the Canada pension plan is broke while the MPs' pension plan is still wonderfully plump, and that the Senate is filling with Liberals. They might suspect that Governor General Romeo LeBlanc was not chosen to warm Government House merely because of his Acadian roots.

One thing they couldn't miss though, was the gruesome antics of the late Airborne Regiment, which were thoughtfully photographed and videotaped. There was a lot of that going around. Nor could the budget go unnoticed. All we know is that Finance Minister Paul Martin made the bond-raters *very* happy. If there is a video of that, we don't ever want to see it.

CUMMINGS, *The Winnipeg Free Press*

GARNOTTE, unpublished

CORRIGAN, The Toronto Star

OLSON, *The Vancouver Courier*

MURPHY, *The Province*, Vancouver

ZAZULAK, *The Hill Times*, Ottawa

NEASE, *The Oakville Beaver*

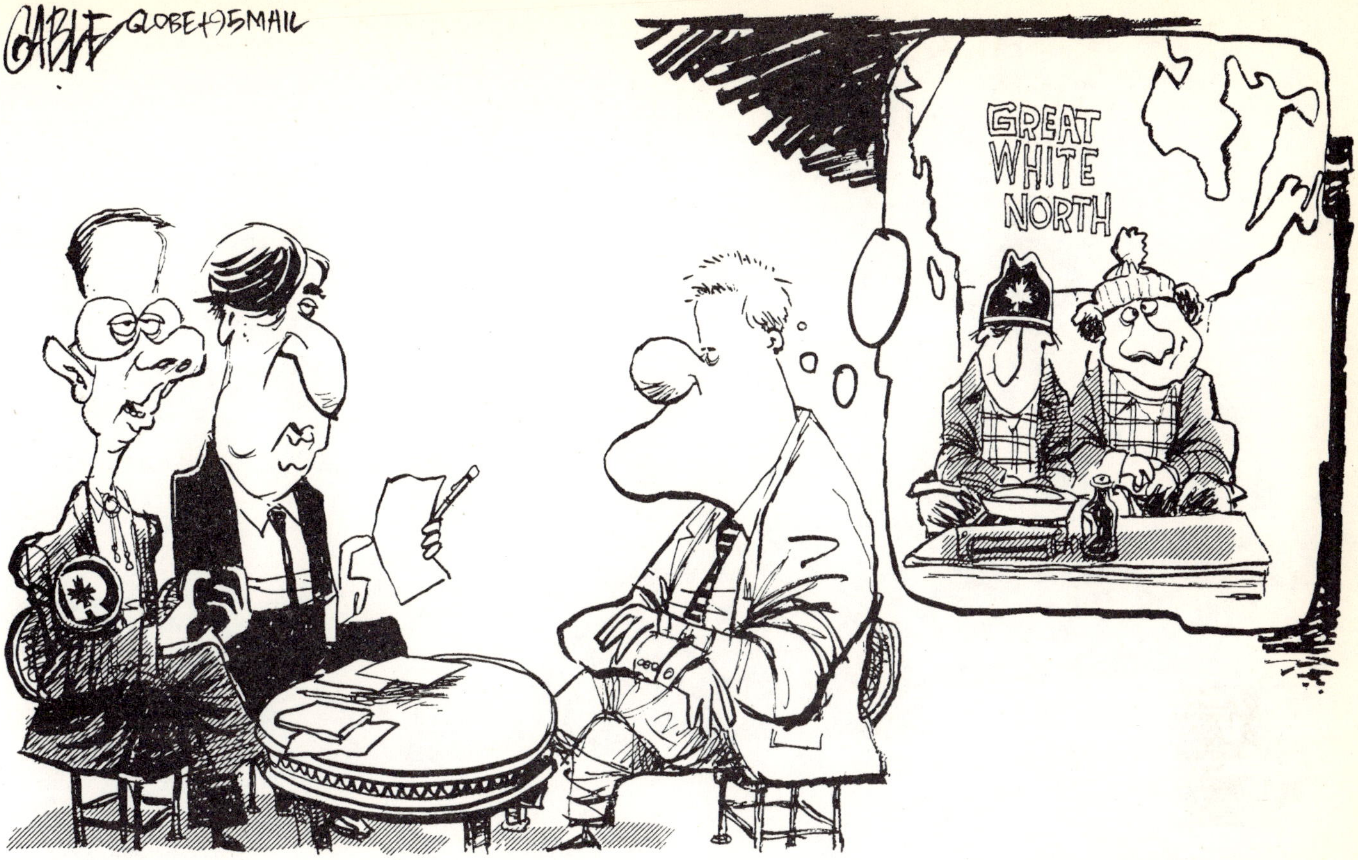
GABLE GLOBE+95MAIL
GREAT WHITE NORTH

GABLE, *The Globe & Mail*

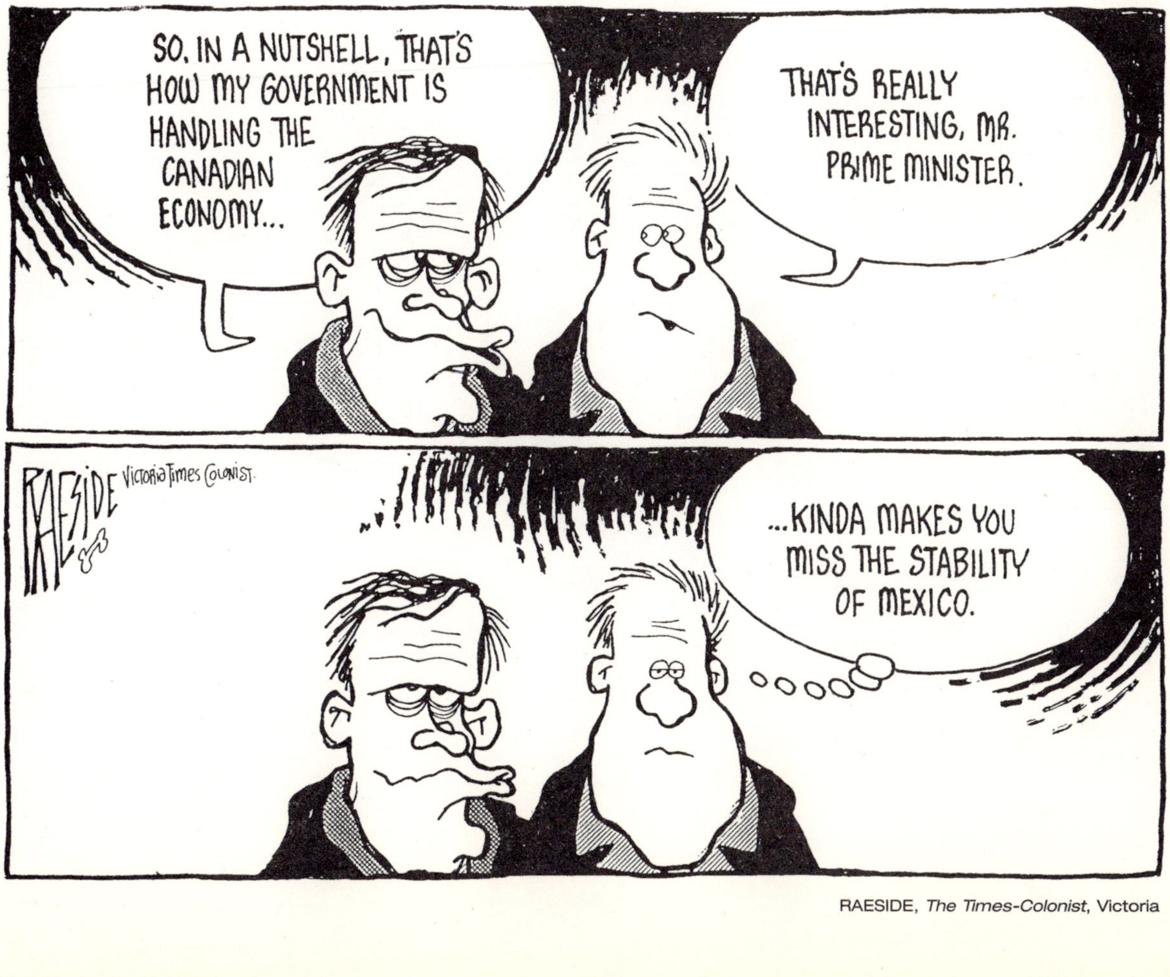
SO, IN A NUTSHELL, THAT'S HOW MY GOVERNMENT IS HANDLING THE CANADIAN ECONOMY...
THAT'S REALLY INTERESTING, MR. PRIME MINISTER.
RAESIDE Victoria Times Colonist
...KINDA MAKES YOU MISS THE STABILITY OF MEXICO.

RAESIDE, *The Times-Colonist*, Victoria

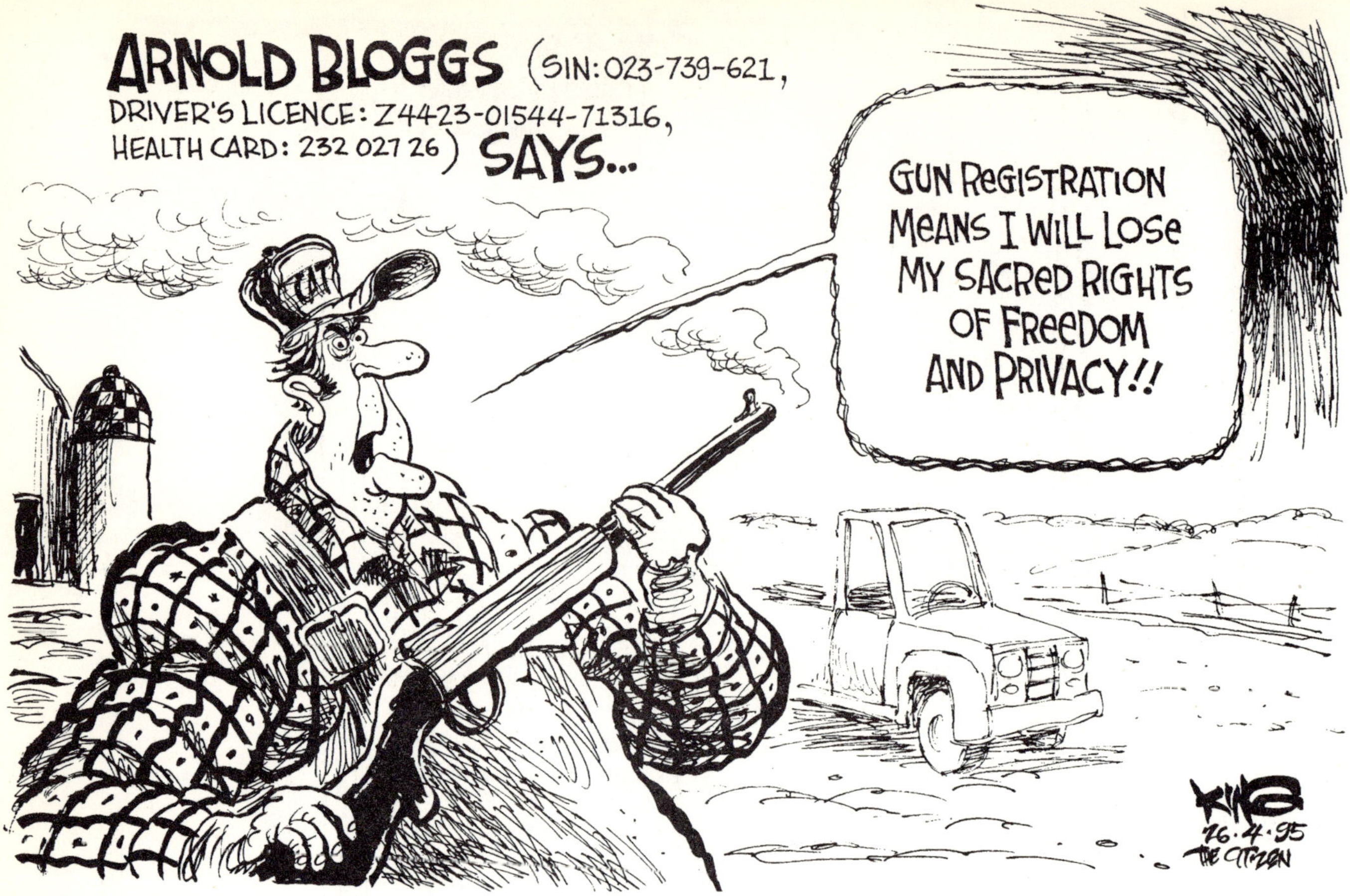
ARNOLD BLOGGS (SIN: 023-739-621,
DRIVER'S LICENCE: Z4423-01544-71316,
HEALTH CARD: 232 027 26) SAYS...
GUN REGISTRATION MEANS I WILL LOSE MY SACRED RIGHTS OF FREEDOM AND PRIVACY!!
CAT
KING 26·4·95 THE CITIZEN

KING, *The Ottawa Citizen*

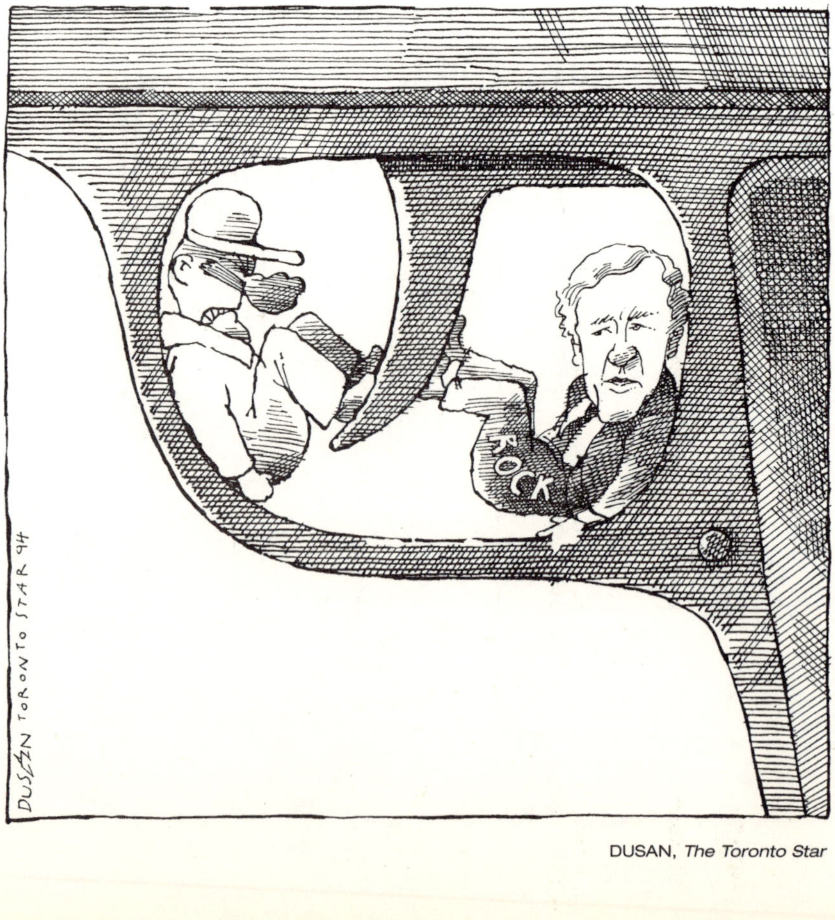
ROCK
DUSAN TORONTO STAR 94

DUSAN, *The Toronto Star*

MACLEAN, *The Vancouver Sun*

BARDAL

MURPHY, *The Province*, Vancouver

PRITCHARD

RAESIDE, *The Times-Colonist*, Victoria

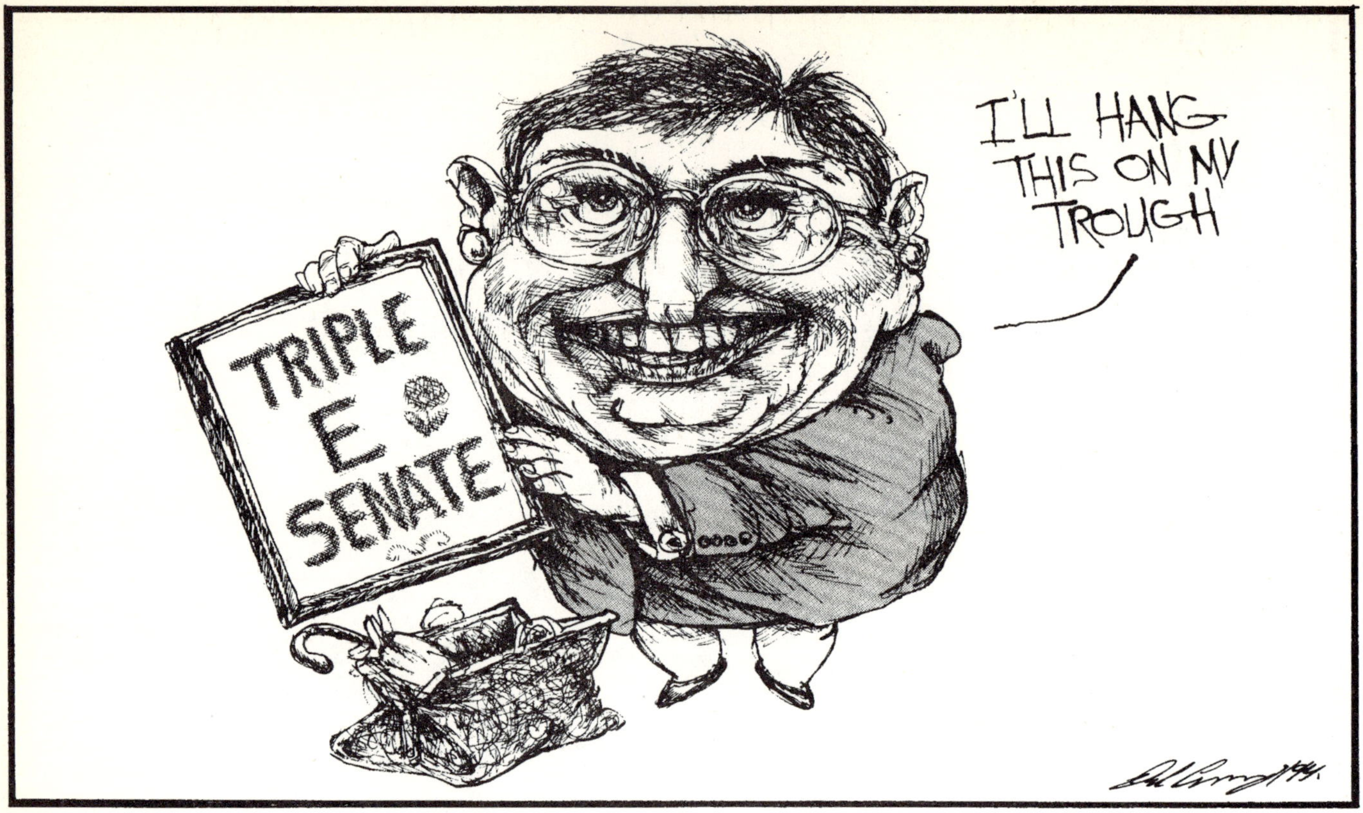
I'LL HANG THIS ON MY TROUGH
TRIPLE E SENATE

CUMMINGS, *The Winnipeg Free Press*

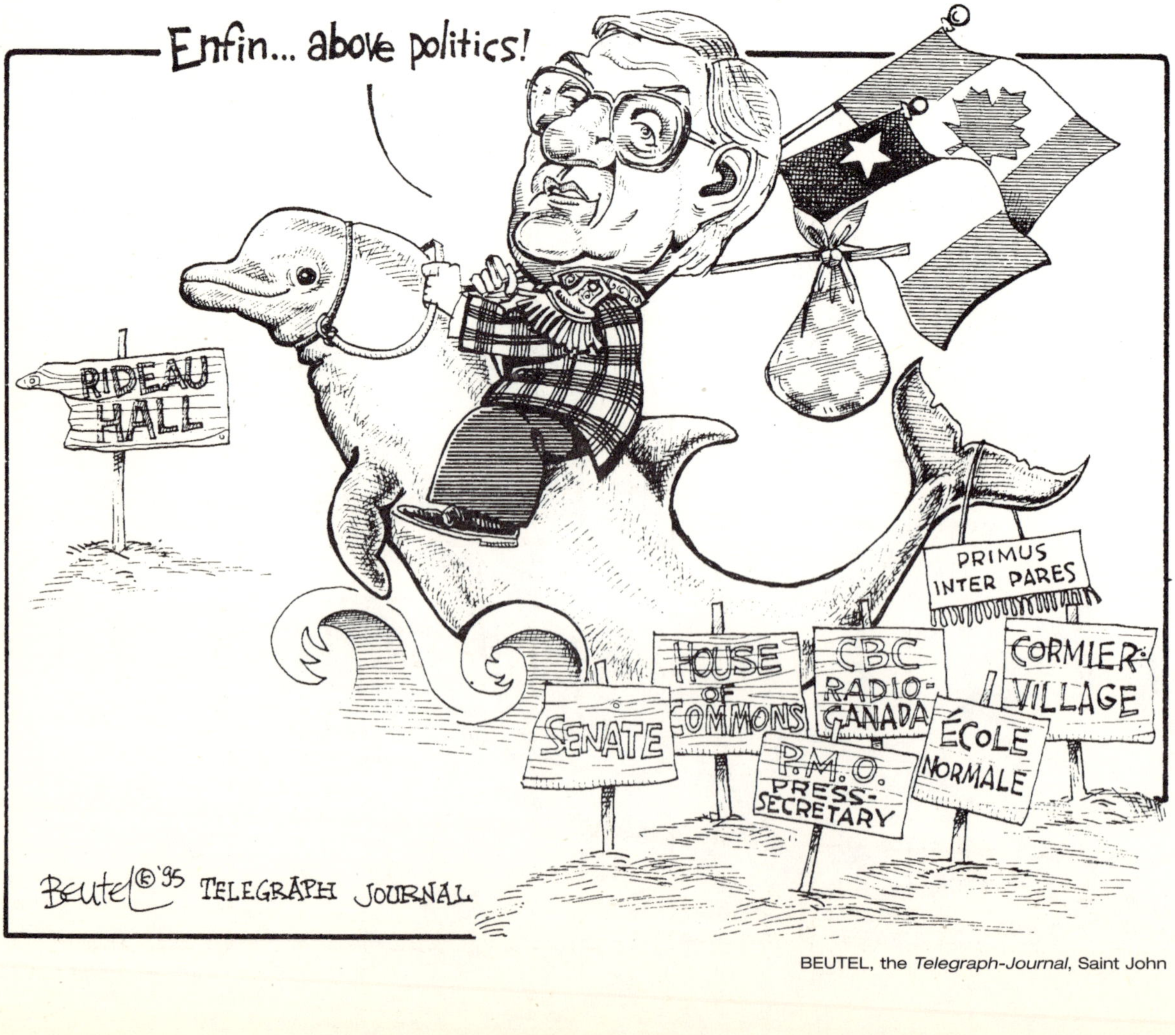
Enfin... above politics!
RIDEAU HALL
PRIMUS INTER PARES
HOUSE OF COMMONS
CBC RADIO-CANADA
CORMIER-VILLAGE
SENATE
ÉCOLE NORMALE
P.M.O. PRESS-SECRETARY
BEUTEL ©'95 TELEGRAPH JOURNAL

BEUTEL, the *Telegraph-Journal*, Saint John

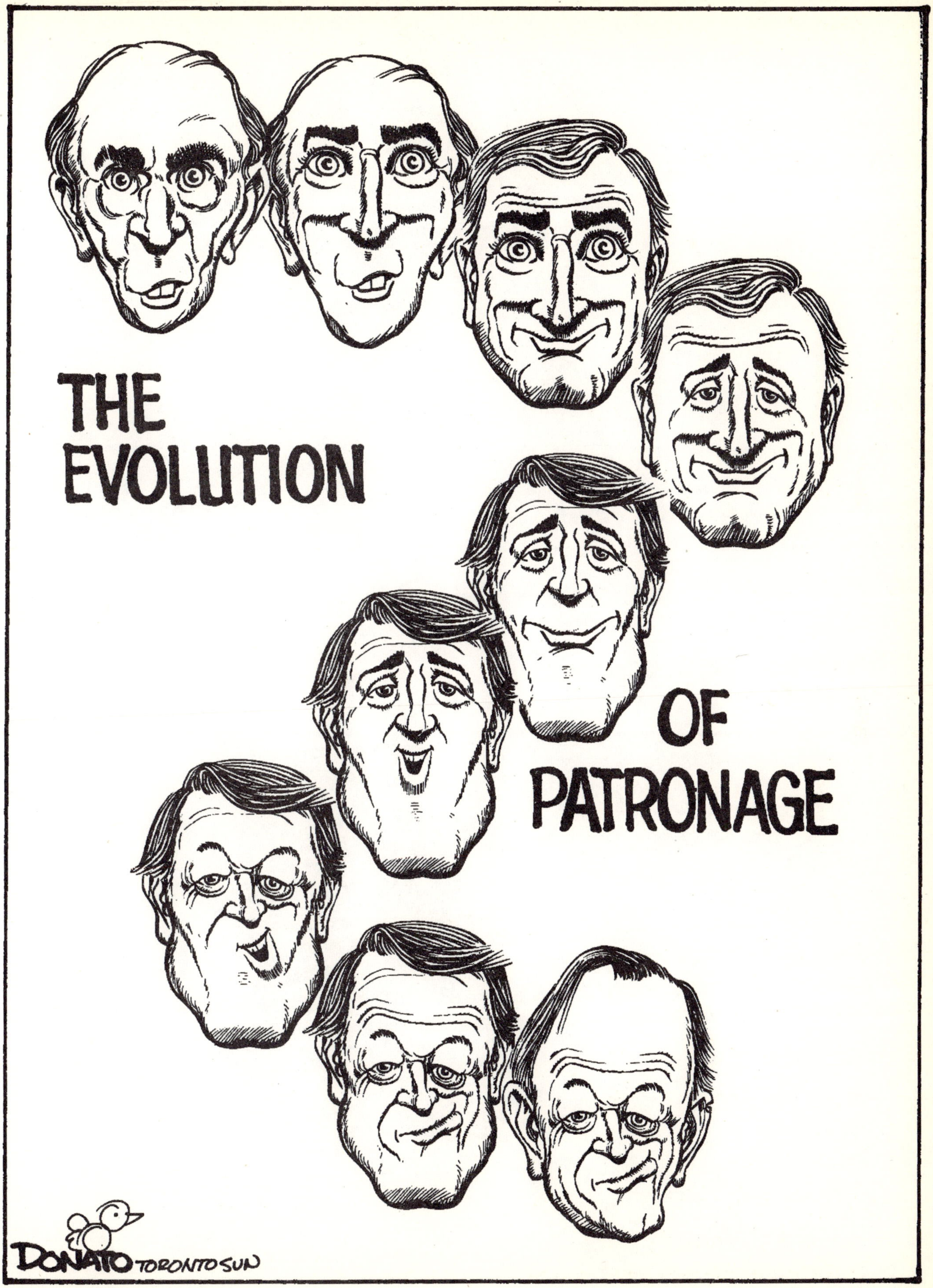
THE EVOLUTION
OF PATRONAGE
DONATO TORONTO SUN

DONATO, *The Toronto Sun*

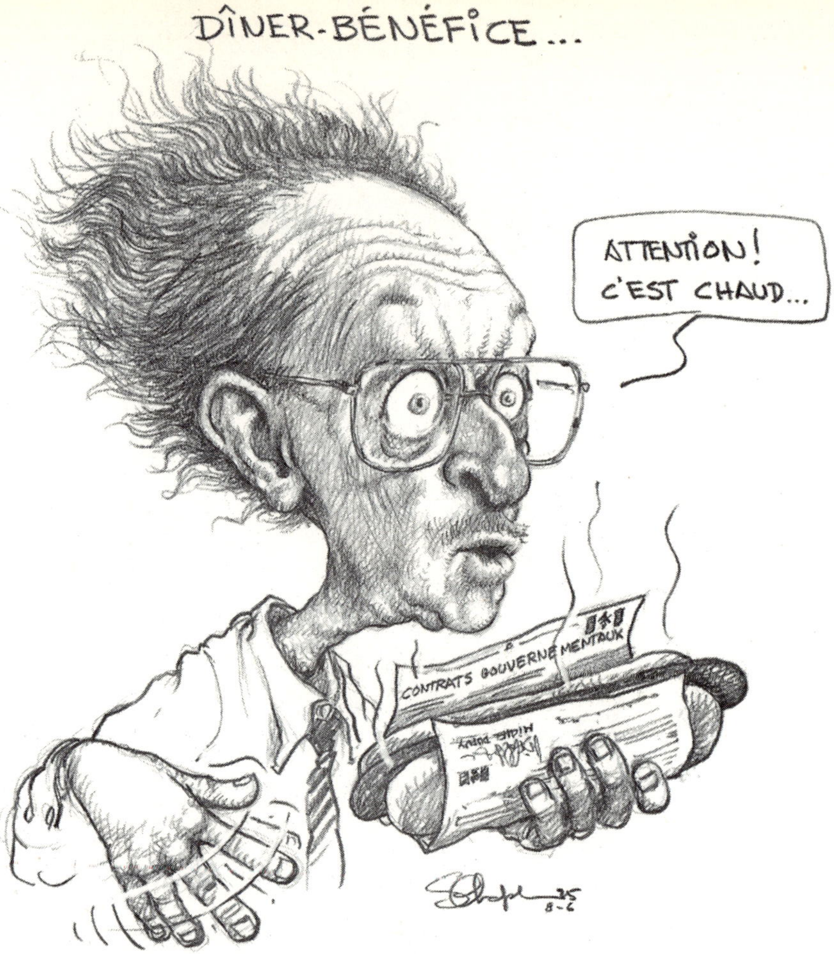
DÎNER-BÉNÉFICE...
ATTENTION! C'EST CHAUD...
CONTRATS GOUVERNEMENTAUX

Careful! It's hot!

CHAPLEAU, *Le Devoir*, Montreal

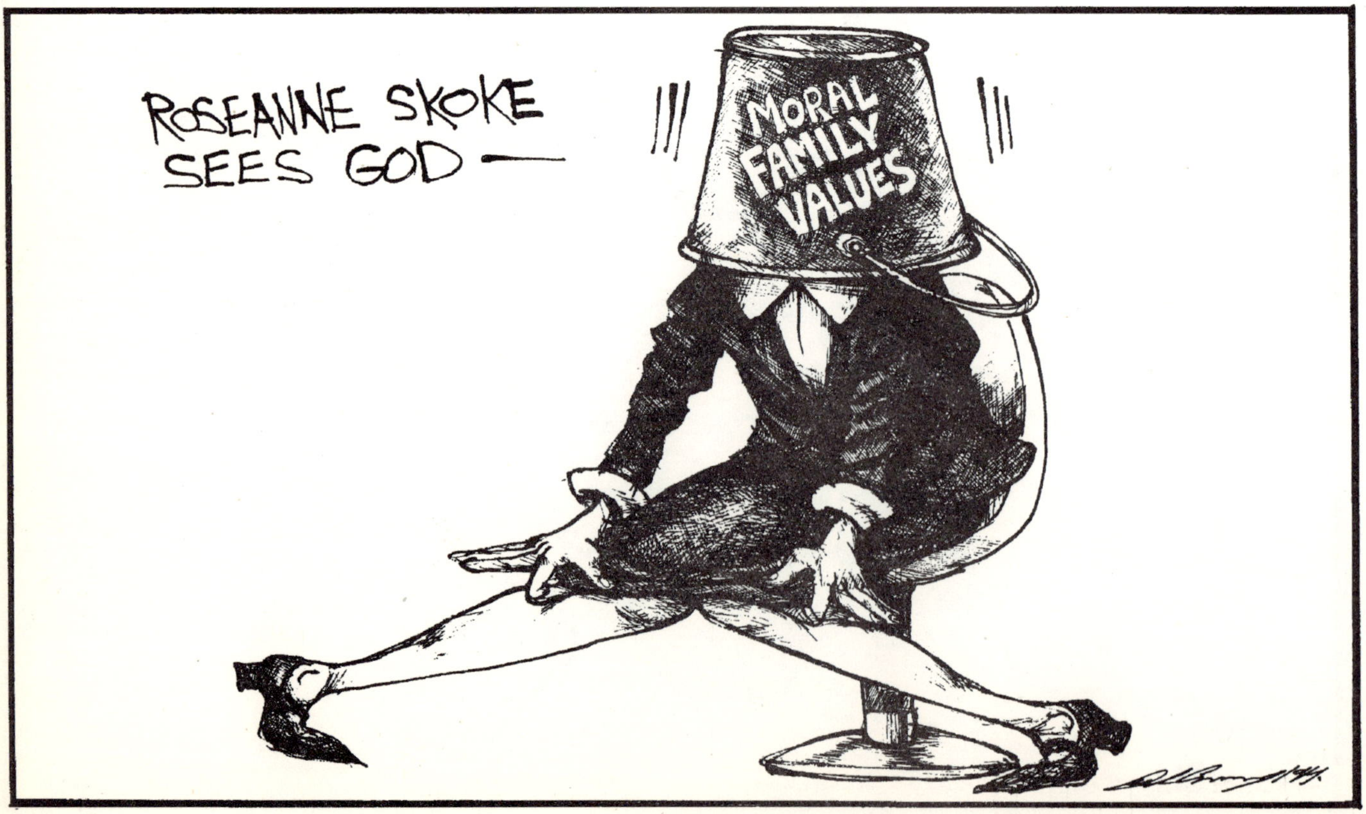
ROSEANNE SKOKE SEES GOD —
MORAL FAMILY VALUES

CUMMINGS, *The Winnipeg Free Press*

MOU, *The Daily News*, Halifax

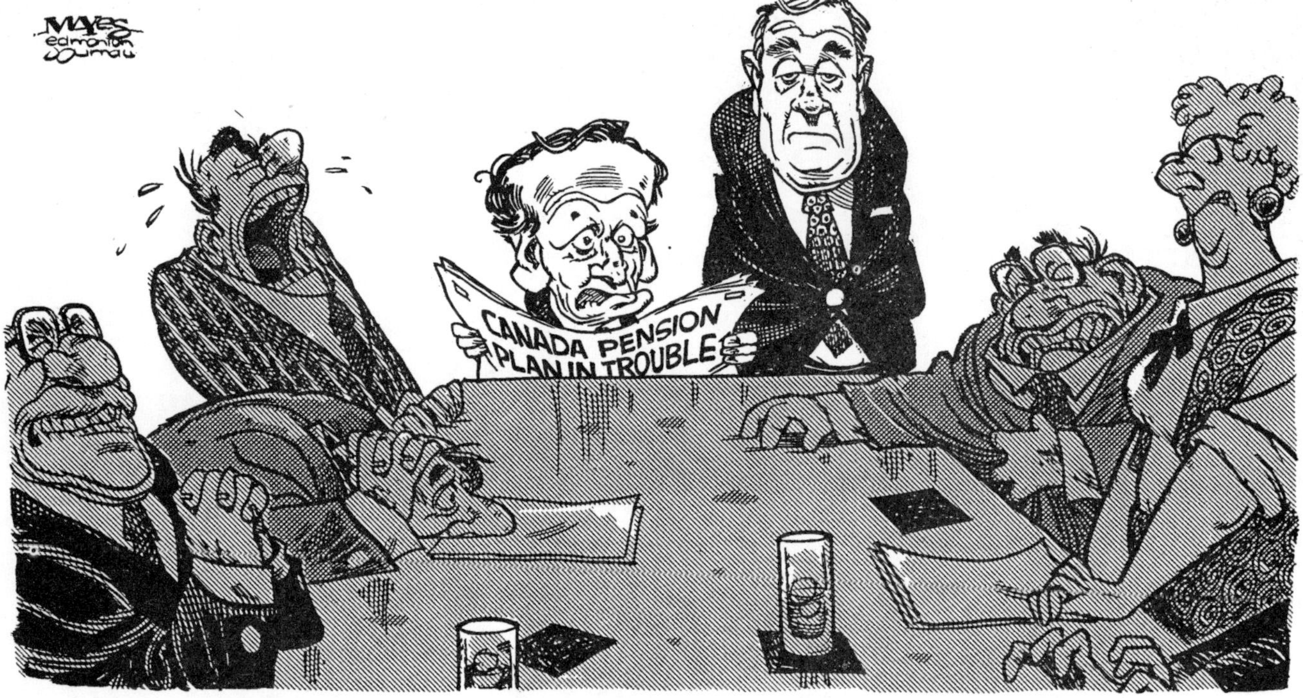
MAYES
edmonton journal
CANADA PENSION PLAN IN TROUBLE

"*RELAX, EVERYONE*.... WHEN PAUL SAID OUR MPs' PENSION PLAN WAS BANKRUPT TOO —— .. HE MEANT ***MORALLY***."

MAYES, *The Edmonton Journal*

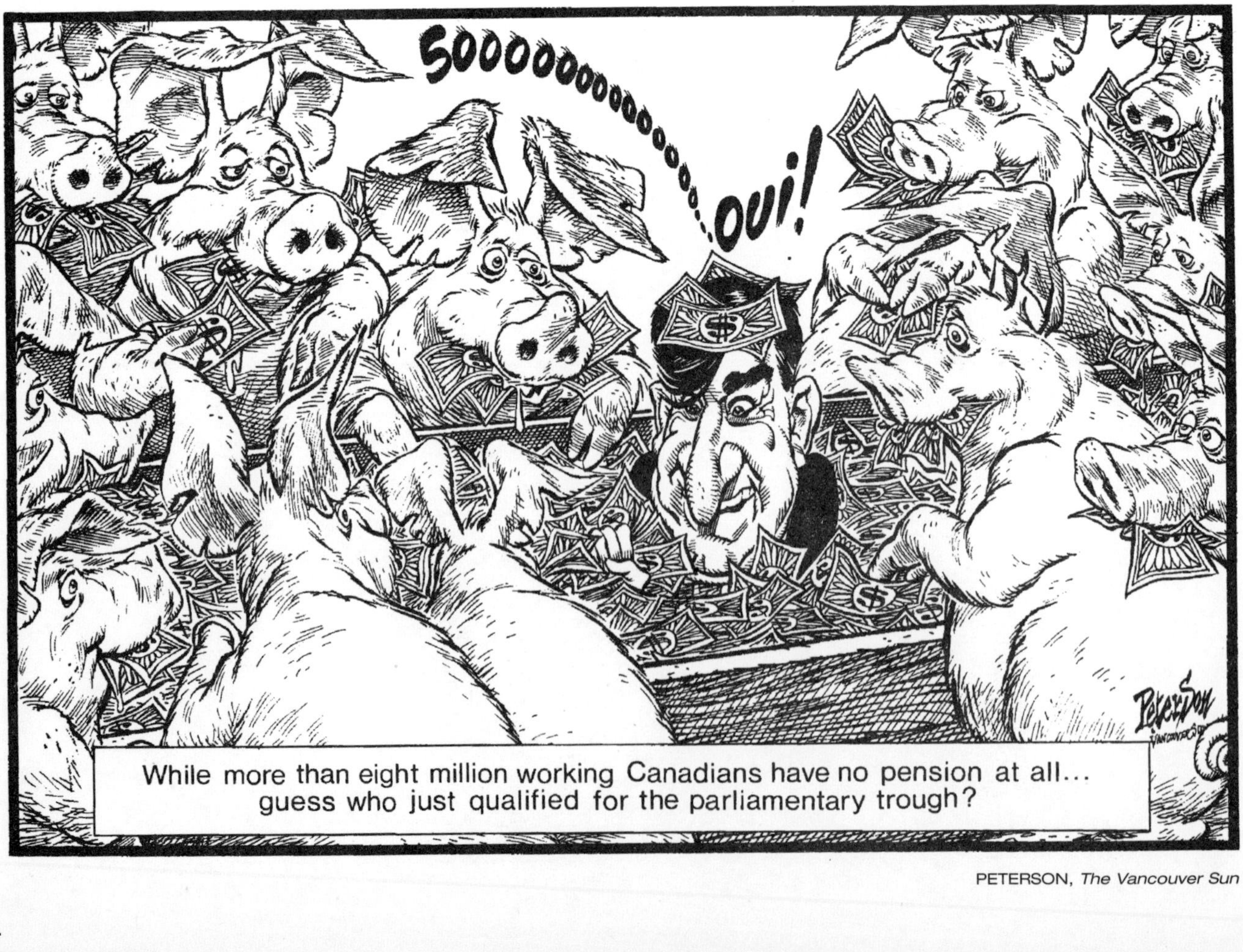
SOOOOOOOOOOOOOOOOOO....OUI!
PETERSON
While more than eight million working Canadians have no pension at all...
guess who just qualified for the parliamentary trough?

PETERSON, *The Vancouver Sun*

RODEWALT, *The Calgary Herald*

BARDAL

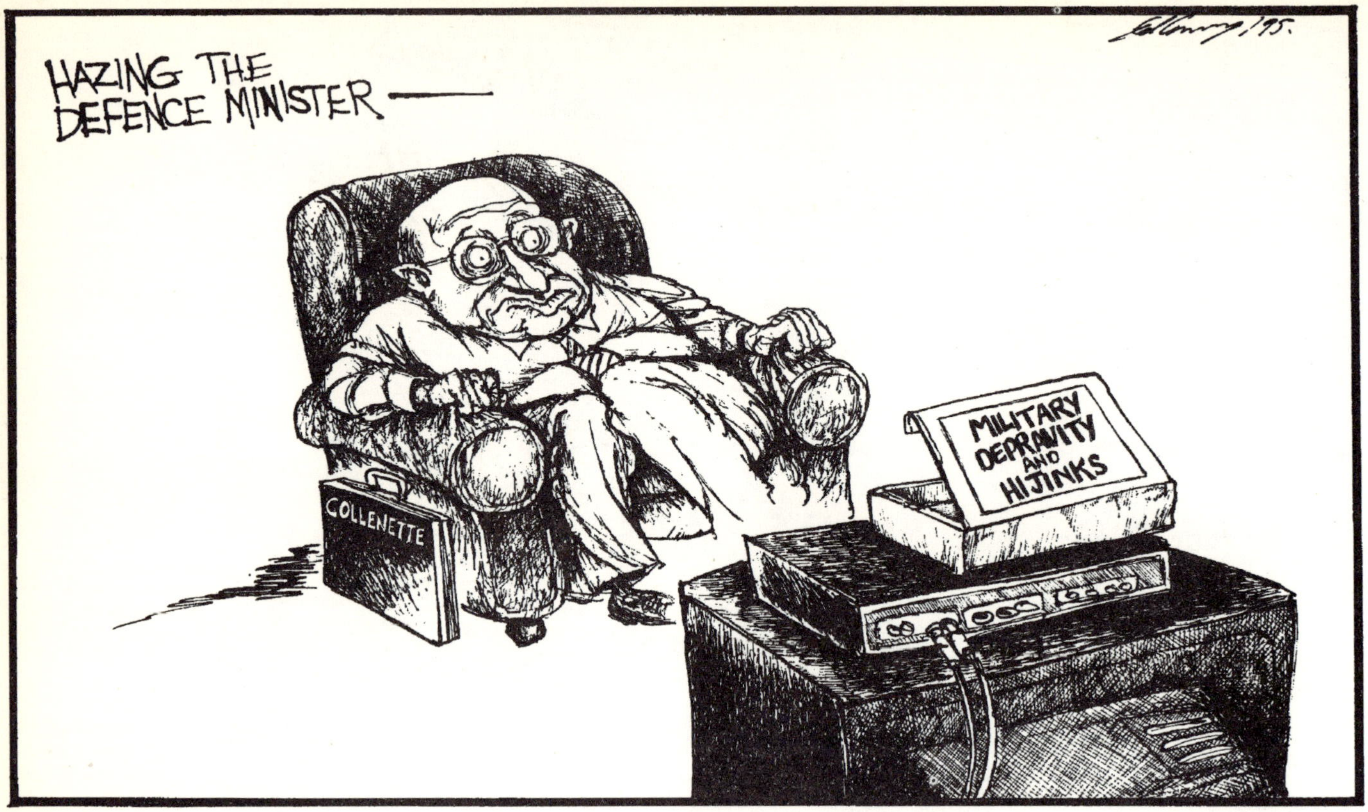
HAZING THE DEFENCE MINISTER——
COLLENETTE
MILITARY DEPRAVITY AND HIJINKS

CUMMINGS, *The Winnipeg Free Press*

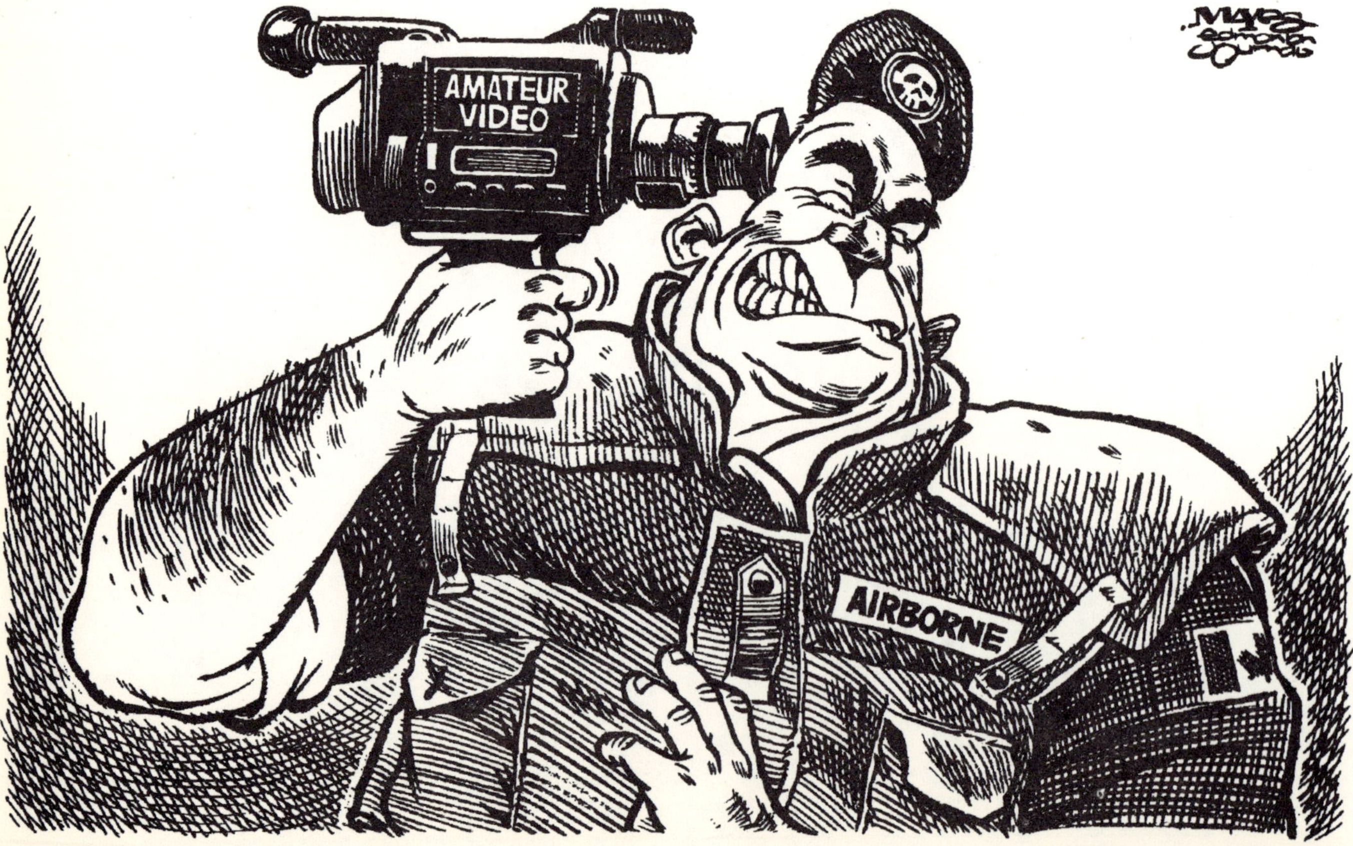
AMATEUR VIDEO
AIRBORNE

MAYES, *The Edmonton Journal*

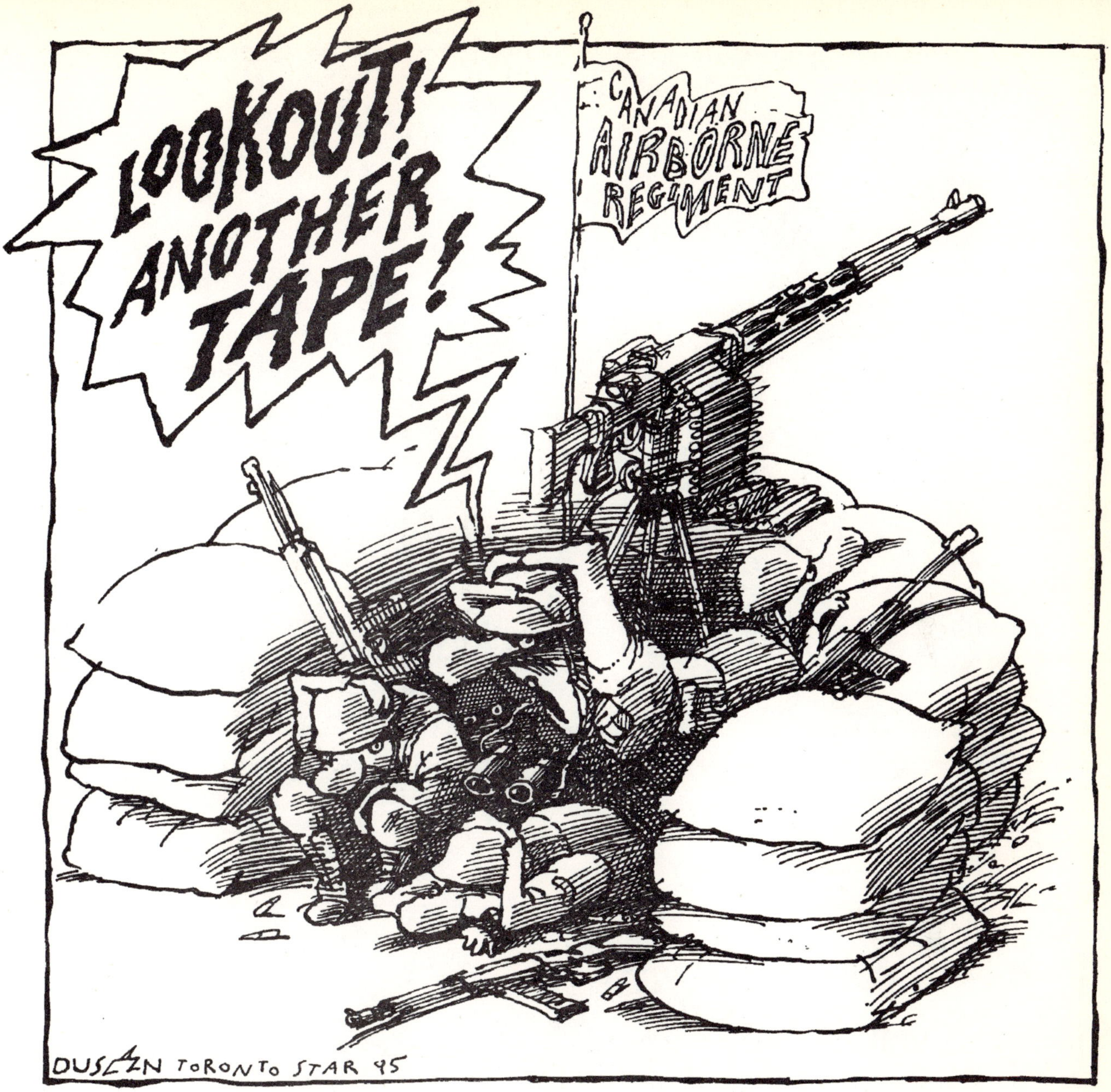
LOOKOUT! ANOTHER TAPE!
CANADIAN AIRBORNE REGIMENT
DUSAN TORONTO STAR 95

DUSAN, *The Toronto Star*

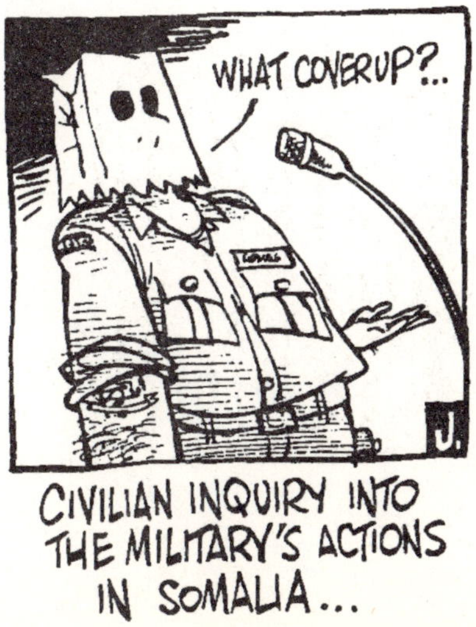
WHAT COVERUP?..
J.
CIVILIAN INQUIRY INTO THE MILITARY'S ACTIONS IN SOMALIA...

JENKINS, *The Globe & Mail*

"The deficit is angry today."

JÉ, *Frank*, unpublished

PRITCHARD

Paul Martin trying to wipe out the deficit

CHAPLEAU, *Le Devoir*, Montreal

AFTER YEARS OF MISMANAGEMENT, POOR JUDGMENT, AND RECKLESS SPENDING, WE **MUST** DO THE RESPONSIBLE THING— MAKE **YOU** PAY.

RODEWALT, *The Calgary Herald*

I THINK I SAW IT MOVE......

CROW RATE

CUMMINGS, *The Winnipeg Free Press*

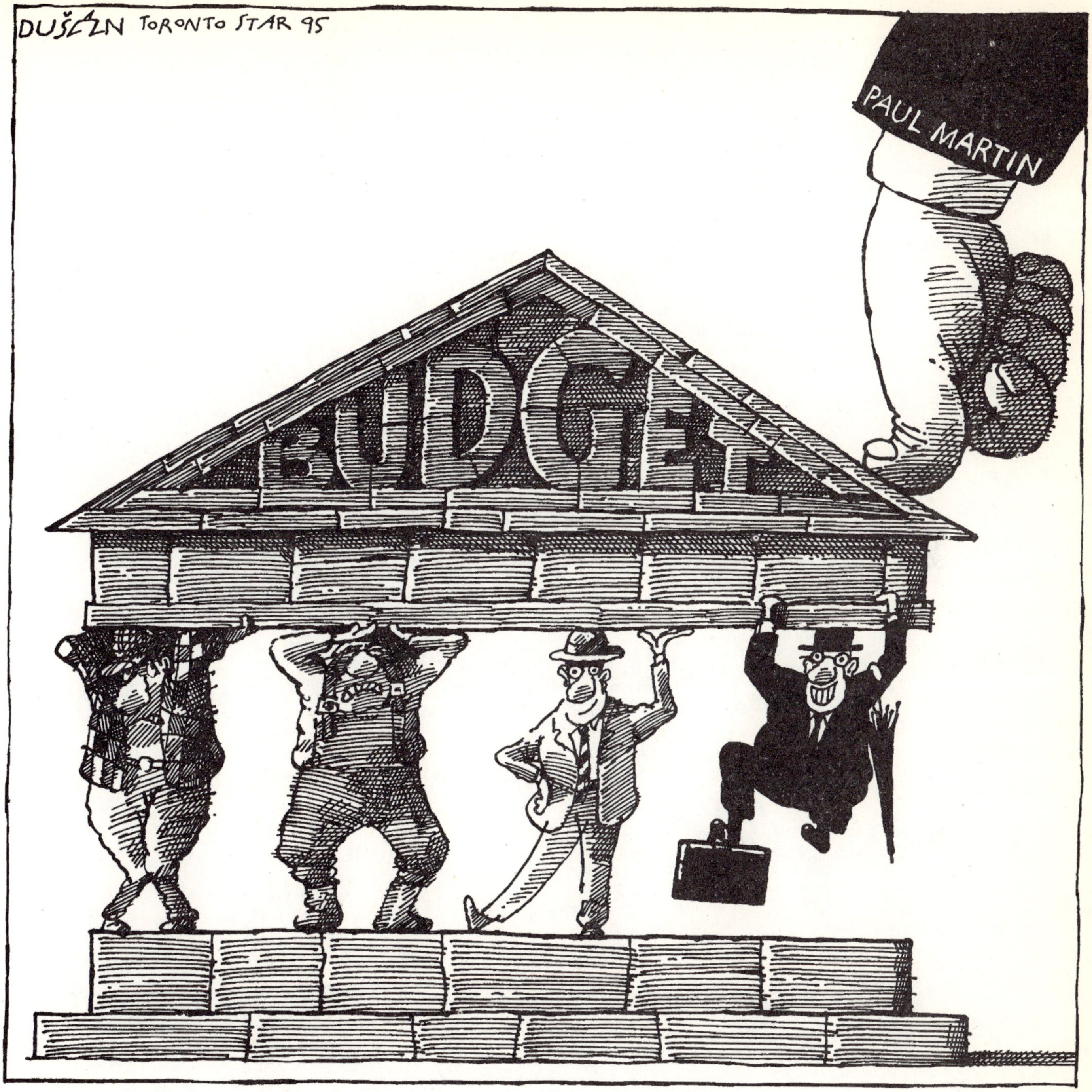
DUSAN TORONTO STAR 95
PAUL MARTIN
BUDGET

DUSAN, *The Toronto Star*

"A never ending visit to the dentist." Parizeau

**Portfoolio 11**

# Referendumb and dumber

It was Premier Jacques Parizeau who warned the rest of Canada that it was better to let Quebec go or the unresolved issue of separation would linger "like a never-ending trip to the dentist." It was also the premier who then spent many excruciating hours in the dental chair himself for a series of *pied-ectomies* (the surgical removal of one's foot from one's mouth).

*Non*, all was not well in the sovereignty camp in the early days of 1995. Although he was determined to hold a spring referendum, he was gently persuaded by his loyal lieutenant, Lucien Bouchard, that it would be prudent to wait. This sovereignty notion was just a new idea, see? It caught Quebecers by surprise, and they needed a bit more time to think about it. Yeah, that's the ticket. A beleaguered Parizeau must have thought Bouchard had carried his role as Leader of the Opposition into the provincial arena.

The two amigos were then to experience a *virage* on the road to Damascus, which is located just outside Trois-Pistoles. A softer semi-sovereignty-association was ordered by a chain-smoking angel who bore a striking resemblance to a departed Quebec premier. Parizeau learned to like this, too. And he was positively ecstatic when young Mario Dumont signed on for the referendum. Dumont, who wouldn't say he was a separatist, added a degree of ambivalent ambiguity unseen since the prime of Robert Bourassa.

With such tremendous clarity now surrounding the question, as this book goes to press, we're sure a definitive resolution is just around the next *virage*. You may spit and rinse. Don't forget to floss.

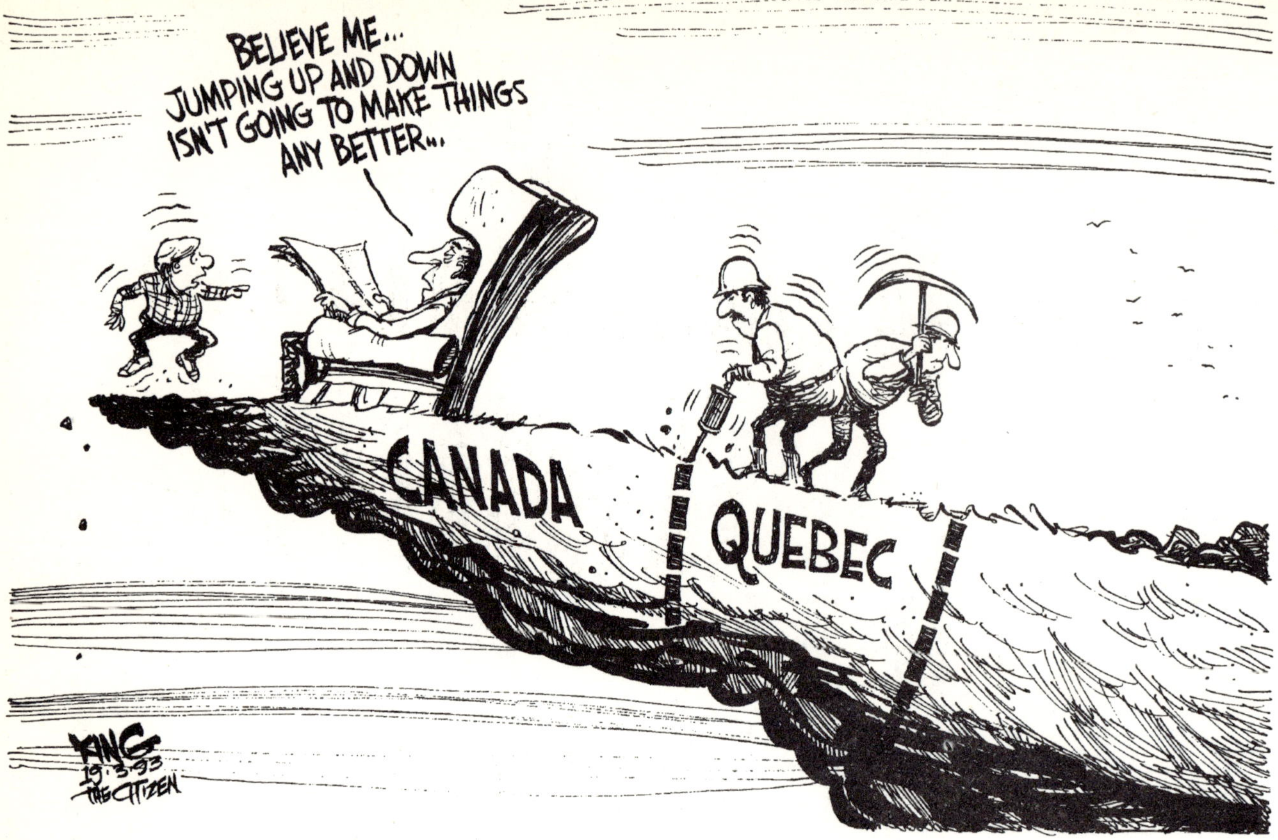
BELIEVE ME... JUMPING UP AND DOWN ISN'T GOING TO MAKE THINGS ANY BETTER...
CANADA
QUEBEC
KING 19.3.93 THE CITIZEN

KING, *The Ottawa Citizen*

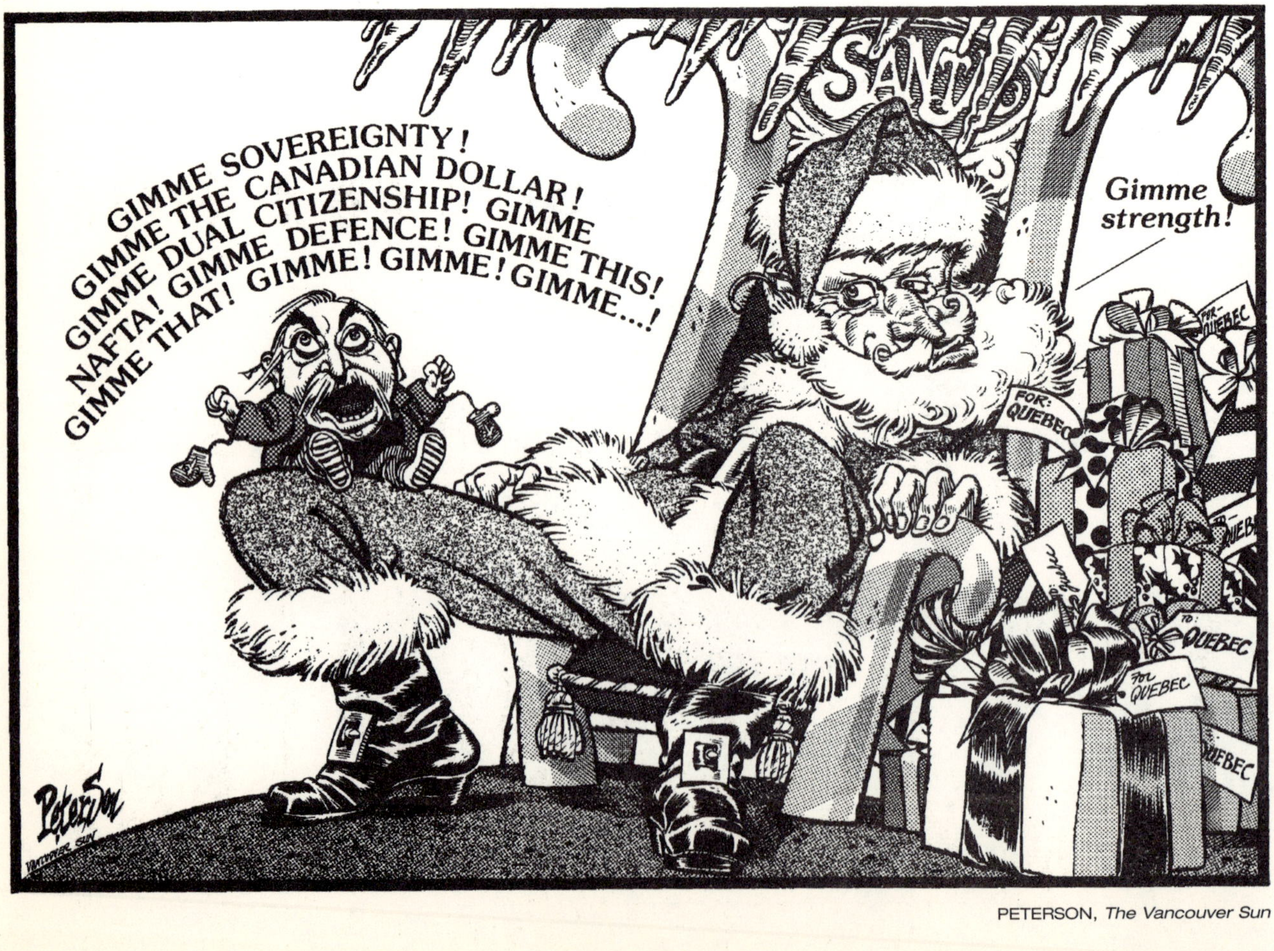
GIMME SOVEREIGNTY! GIMME THE CANADIAN DOLLAR! GIMME DUAL CITIZENSHIP! GIMME NAFTA! GIMME DEFENCE! GIMME THIS! GIMME THAT! GIMME! GIMME! GIMME...!
Gimme strength!
SANTA
FOR: QUEBEC
TO: QUEBEC
FOR QUEBEC
PETERSON

PETERSON, *The Vancouver Sun*

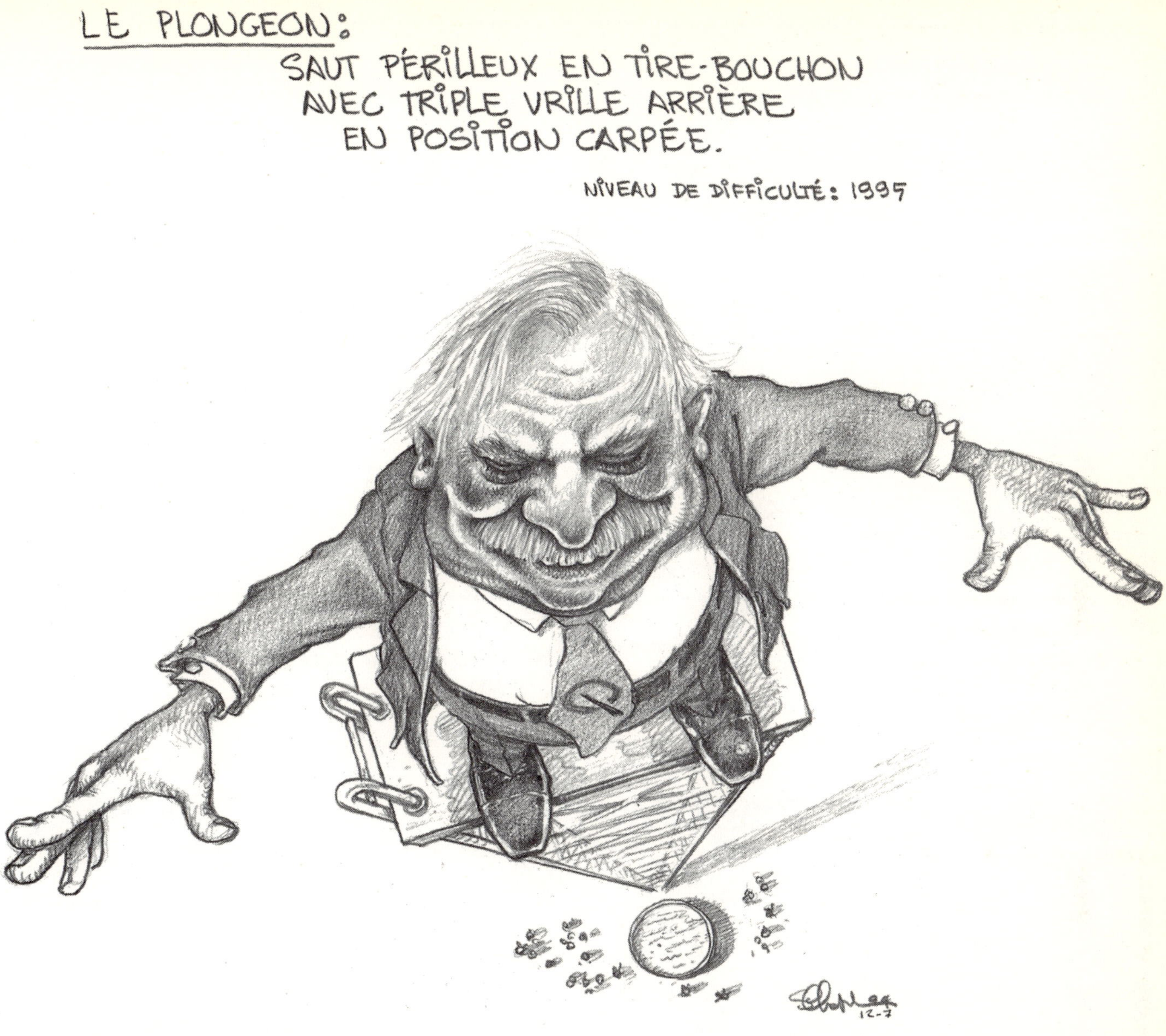
LE PLONGEON:
SAUT PÉRILLEUX EN TIRE-BOUCHON
AVEC TRIPLE VRILLE ARRIÈRE
EN POSITION CARPÉE.
NIVEAU DE DIFFICULTÉ: 1995

The High Dive: a triple axel followed by a double back somersault.
Degree of difficulty: 1995

CHAPLEAU, *Le Devoir*, Montreal

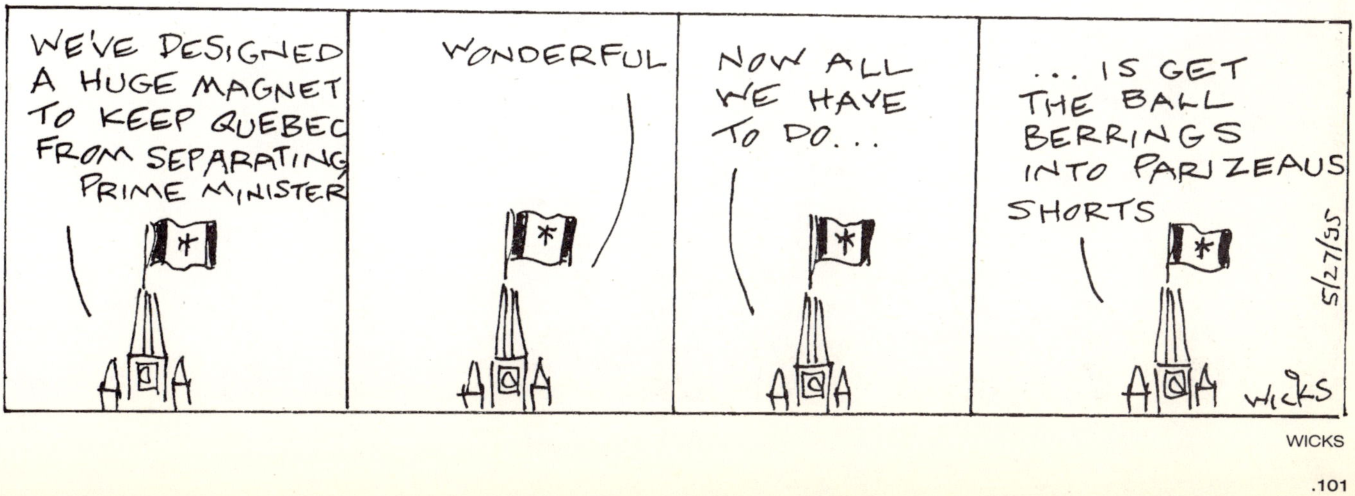
WE'VE DESIGNED A HUGE MAGNET TO KEEP QUEBEC FROM SEPARATING, PRIME MINISTER
WONDERFUL
NOW ALL WE HAVE TO DO...
... IS GET THE BALL BERRINGS INTO PARIZEAUS SHORTS
5/27/95
WICKS

WICKS

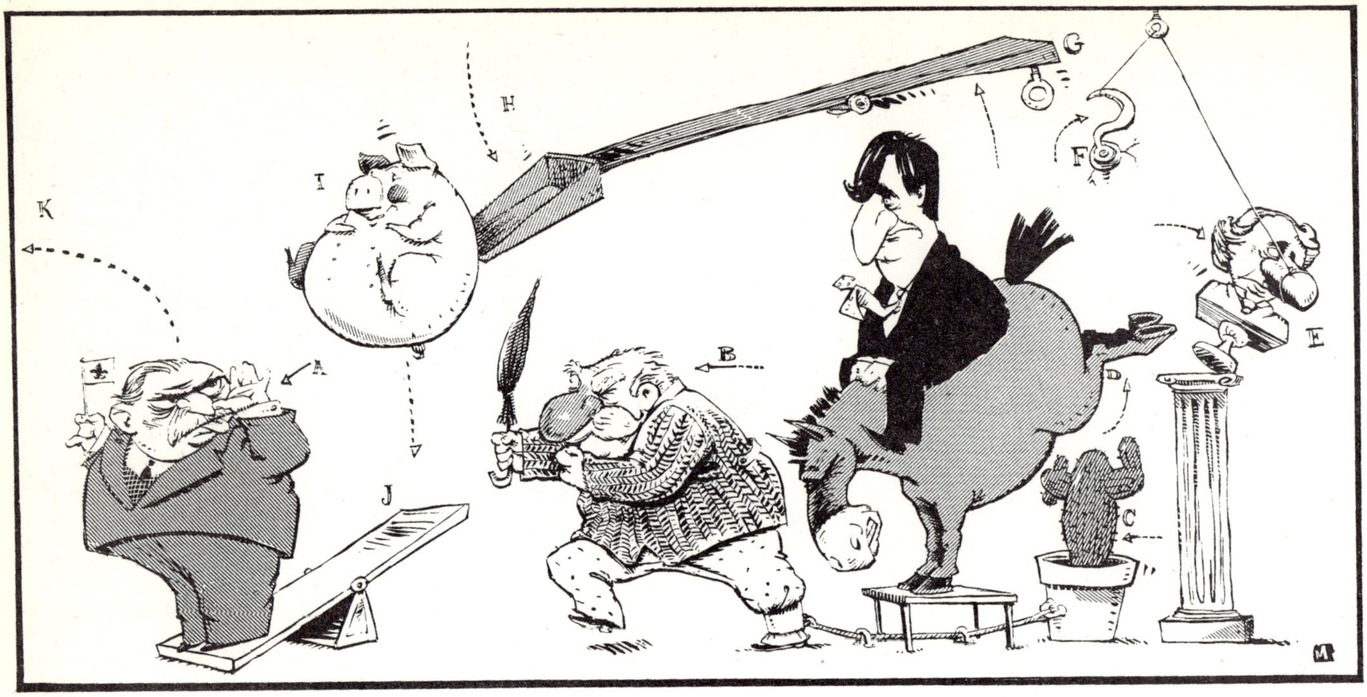
K
I
H
G
F
A
B
E
D
J
C

MURPHY, *The Province*, Vancouver

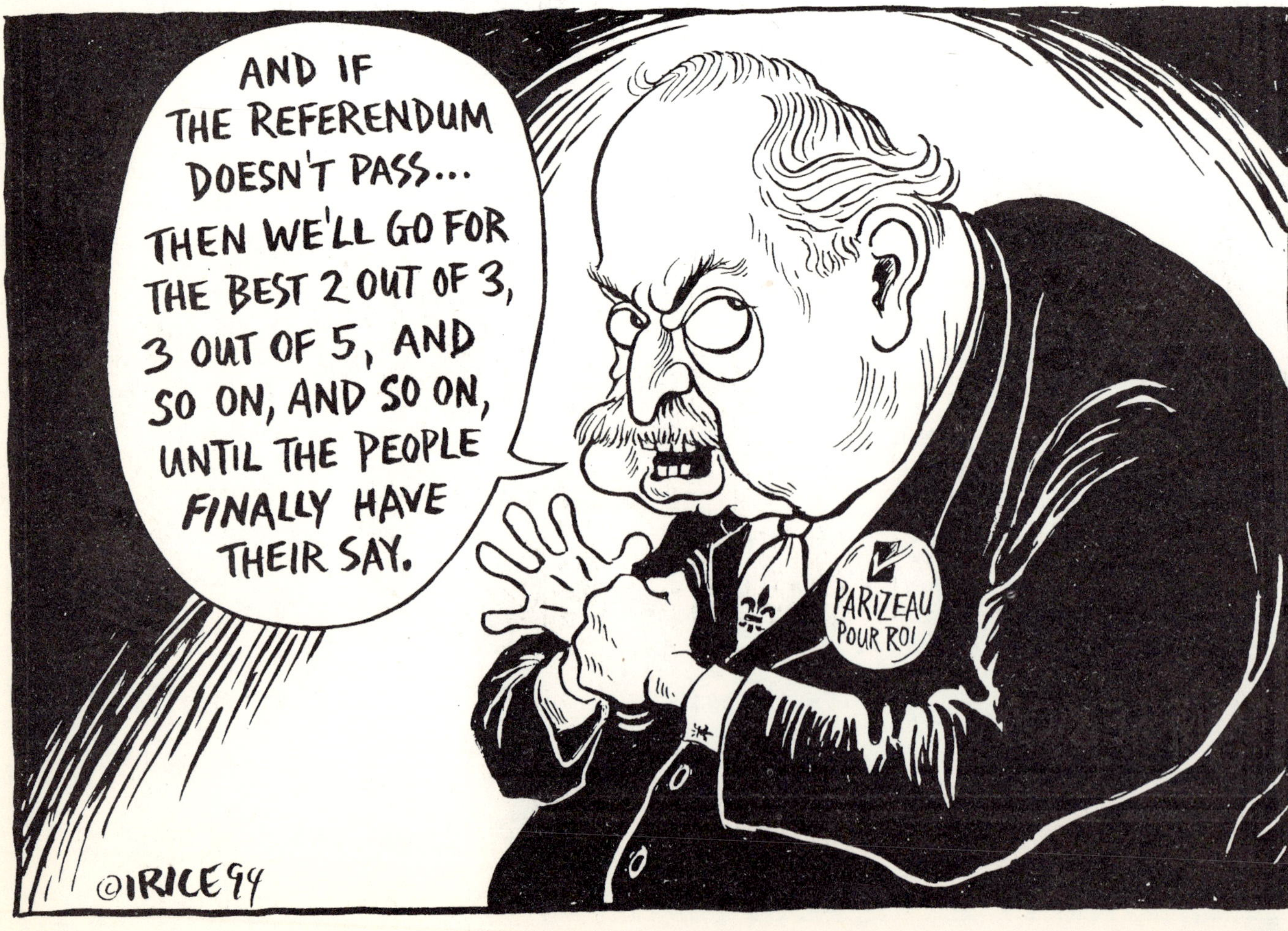
AND IF THE REFERENDUM DOESN'T PASS... THEN WE'LL GO FOR THE BEST 2 OUT OF 3, 3 OUT OF 5, AND SO ON, AND SO ON, UNTIL THE PEOPLE FINALLY HAVE THEIR SAY.
PARIZEAU POUR ROI
©RICE 94

RICE

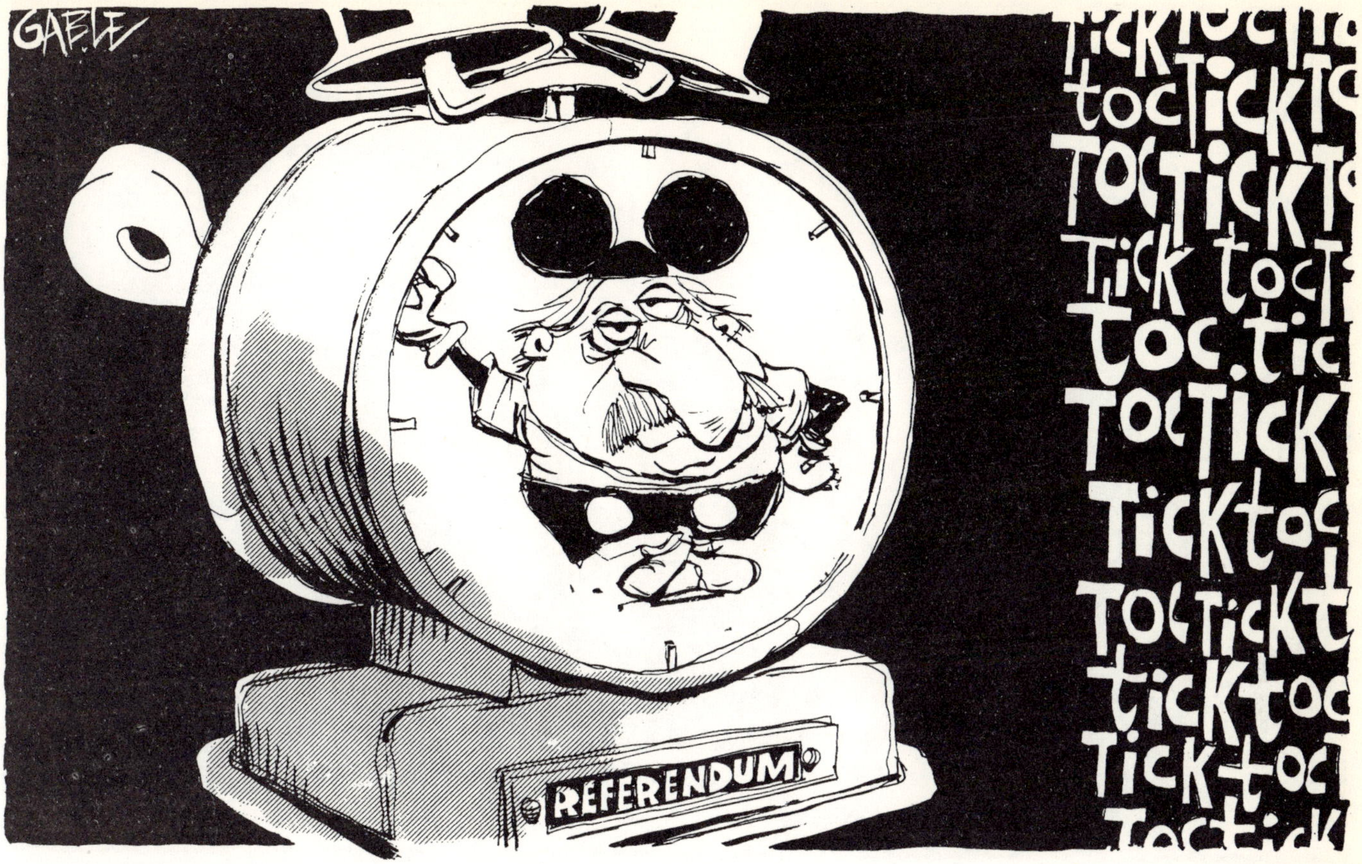
GABLE
REFERENDUM
TICK TOC TICK TOC TICK TOC TICK TOC TICK TOC TICK TOC TICK TOC TICK TOC

GABLE, *The Globe & Mail*

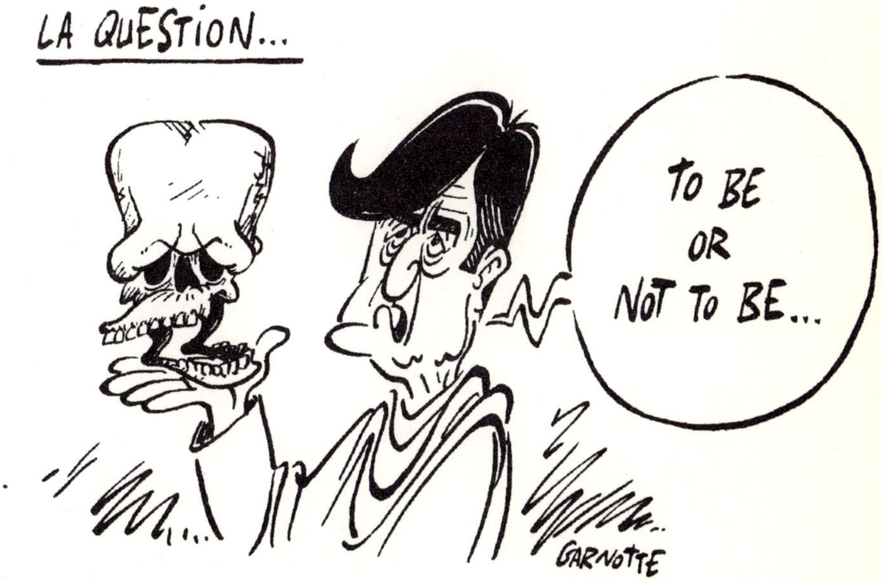
LA QUESTION...
TO BE OR NOT TO BE...
GARNOTTE

GARNOTTE, *Nouvelles CSN*, Montreal

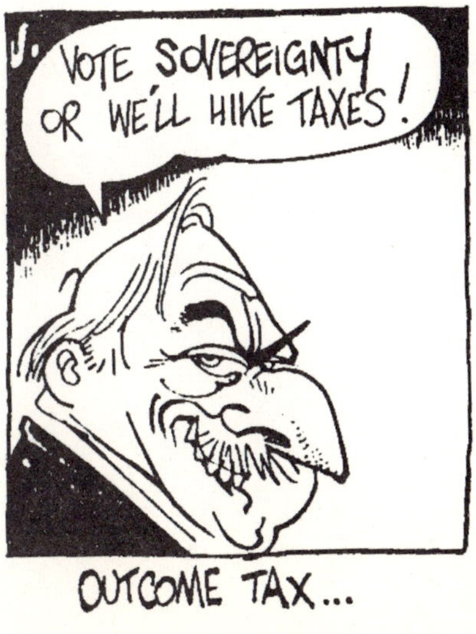
VOTE SOVEREIGNTY OR WE'LL HIKE TAXES!
OUTCOME TAX...

JENKINS, *The Globe & Mail*

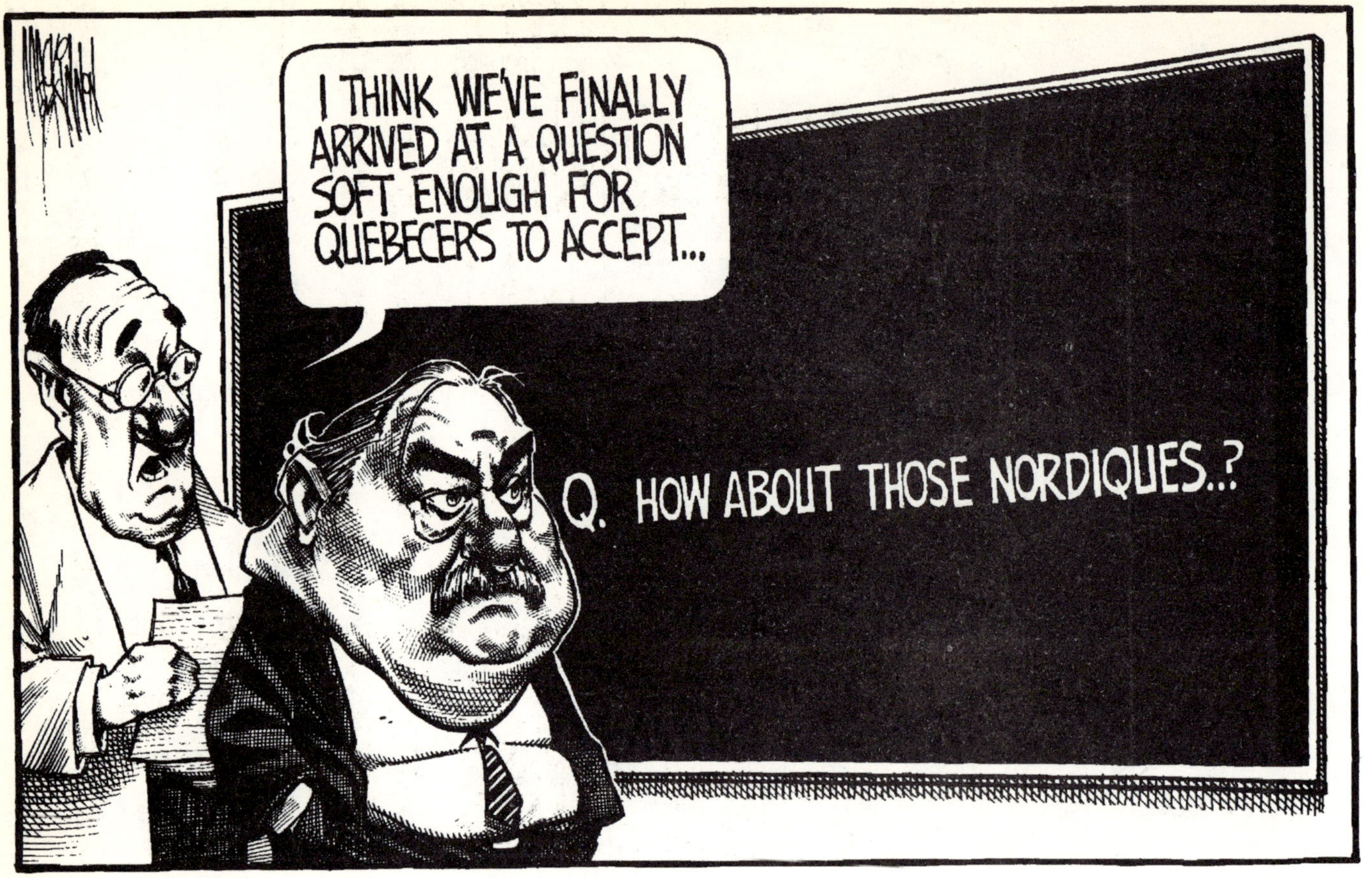
I THINK WE'VE FINALLY ARRIVED AT A QUESTION SOFT ENOUGH FOR QUEBECERS TO ACCEPT...
Q. HOW ABOUT THOSE NORDIQUES..?

MACKINNON, *The Chronicle-Herald*, Halifax

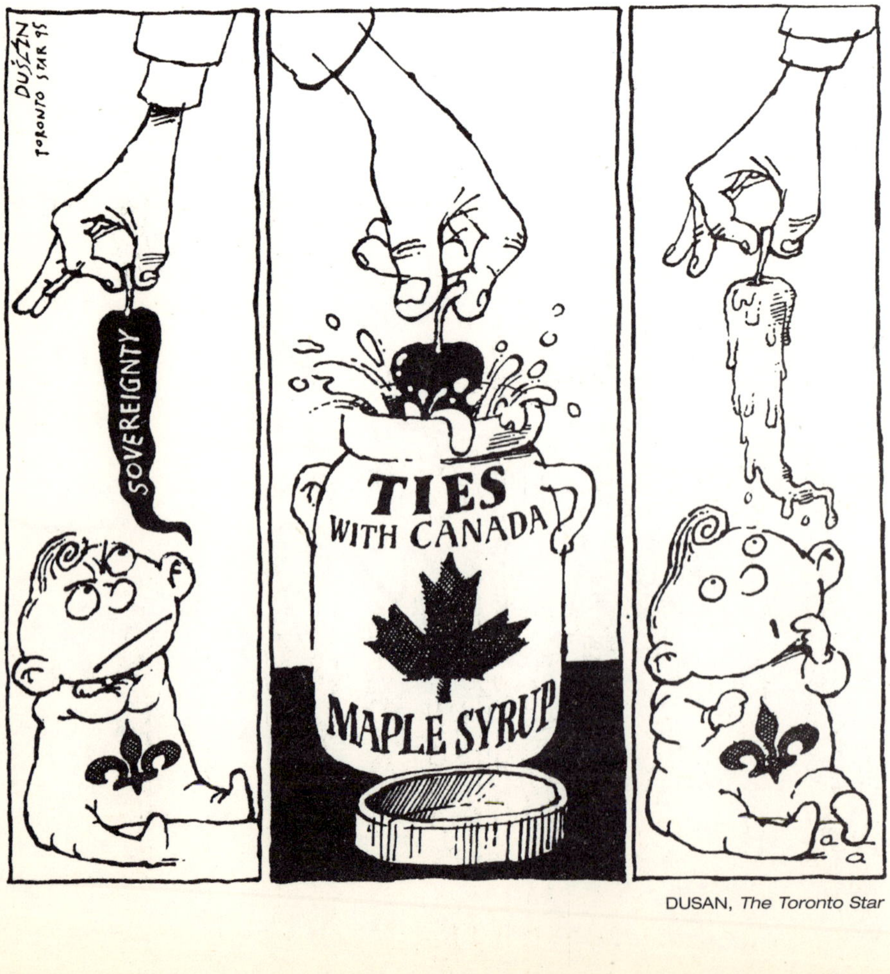
DUSAN TORONTO STAR 95
SOVEREIGNTY
TIES WITH CANADA
MAPLE SYRUP

DUSAN, *The Toronto Star*

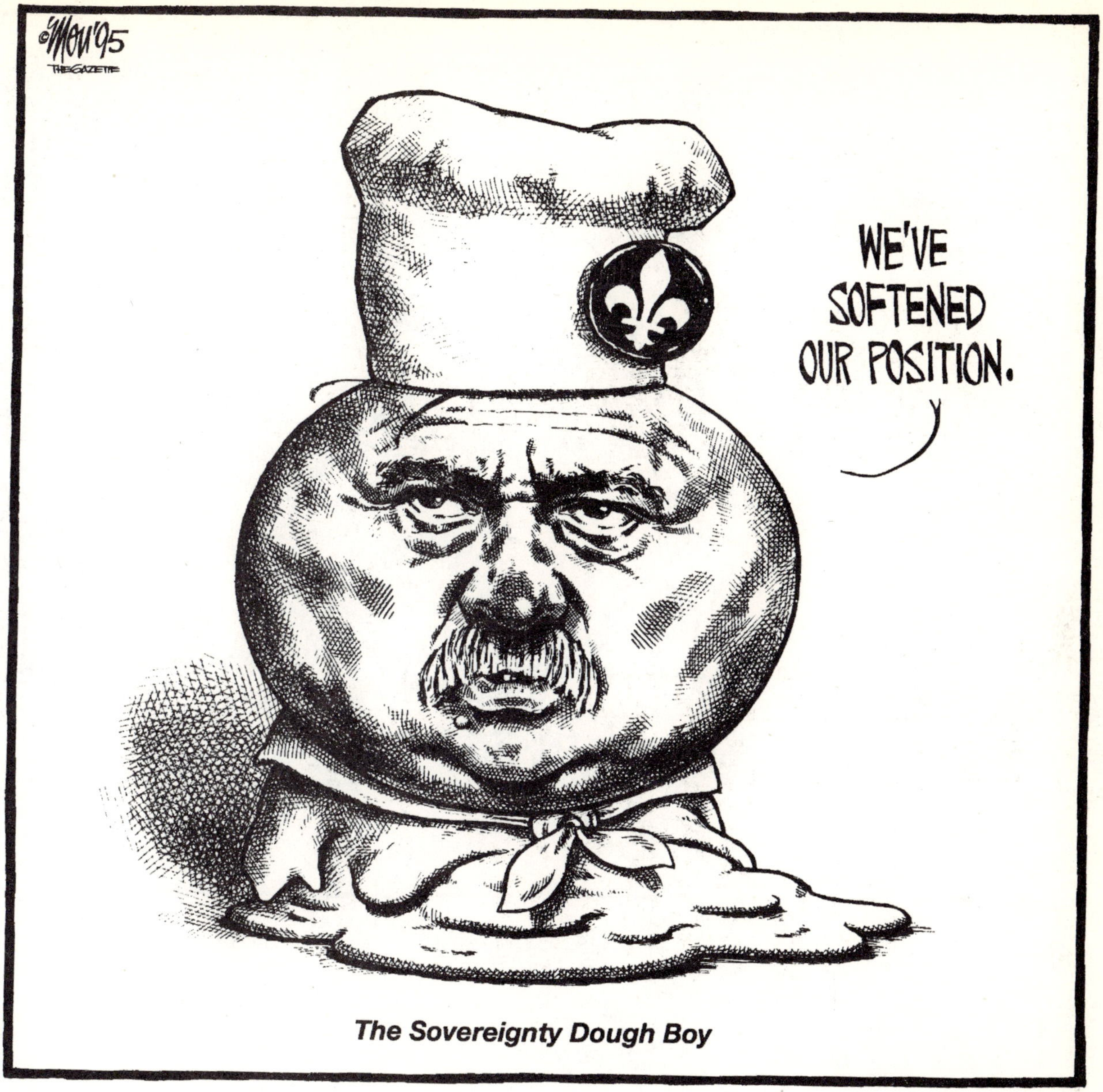
©MOU'95
THE GAZETTE
WE'VE SOFTENED OUR POSITION.
The Sovereignty Dough Boy

MOU, *The Daily News*, Halifax

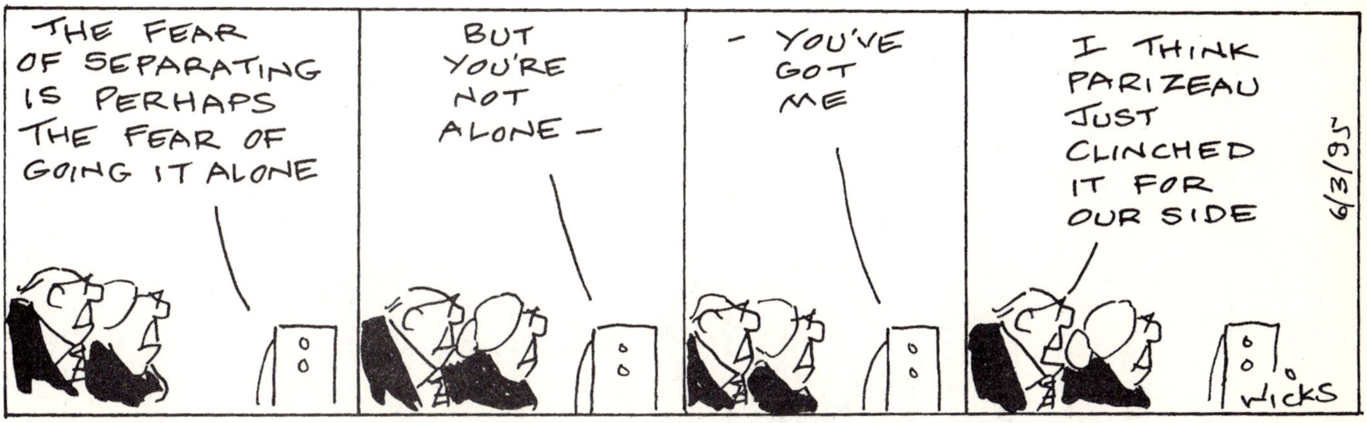
THE FEAR OF SEPARATING IS PERHAPS THE FEAR OF GOING IT ALONE
BUT YOU'RE NOT ALONE –
– YOU'VE GOT ME
I THINK PARIZEAU JUST CLINCHED IT FOR OUR SIDE
6/3/95
WICKS

WICKS

BOUCHARD RETURNS

RICE

ROSEN, *Hour*, Montreal

RAESIDE, *The Times-Colonist*, Victoria

The premier can count on me. I'm behind him!

CHAPLEAU, *Le Devoir*, Montreal

PRITCHARD

GODIN, *Voir*, Montreal

**TOO MANY COOKS...**

NEASE, *The Oakville Beaver*

CUMMINGS, *The Winnipeg Free Press*

ENFIN, APRÈS BIEN DES PÉRIPÉTIES ET DES RÉPÉTITIONS...

Finally, after many fits and starts…

PIER, *Le Journal de Montréal*

AISLIN, *The Gazette*, Montreal

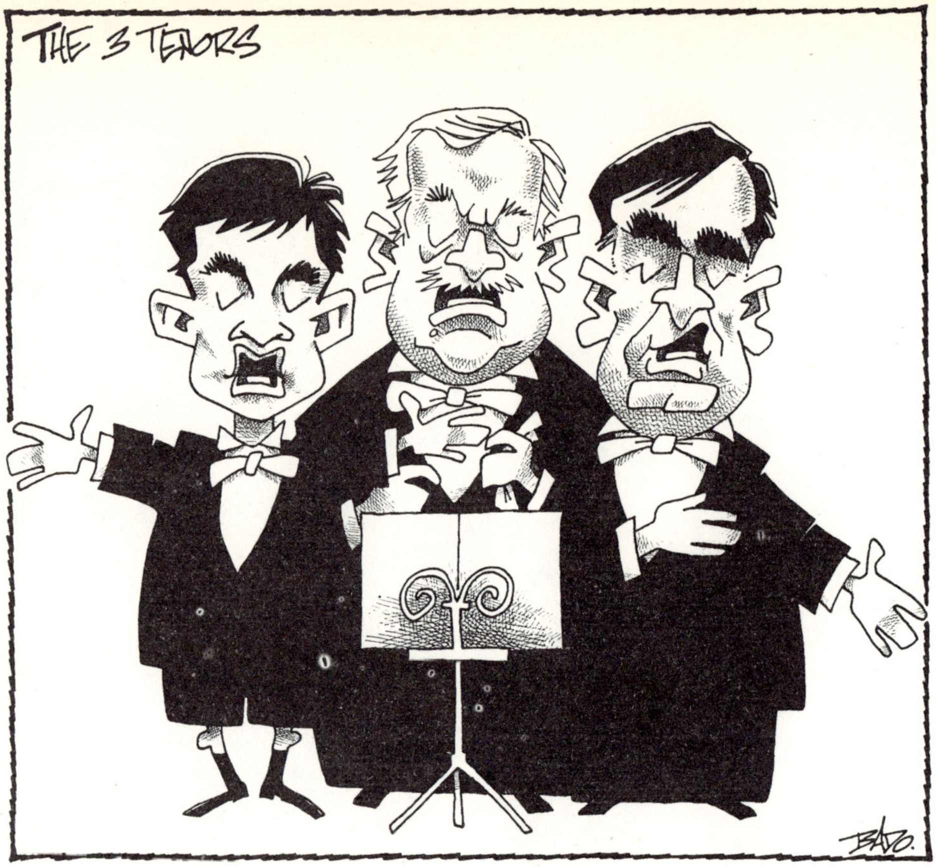
THE 3 TENORS
BADO.

BADO, *Le Droit*, Ottawa

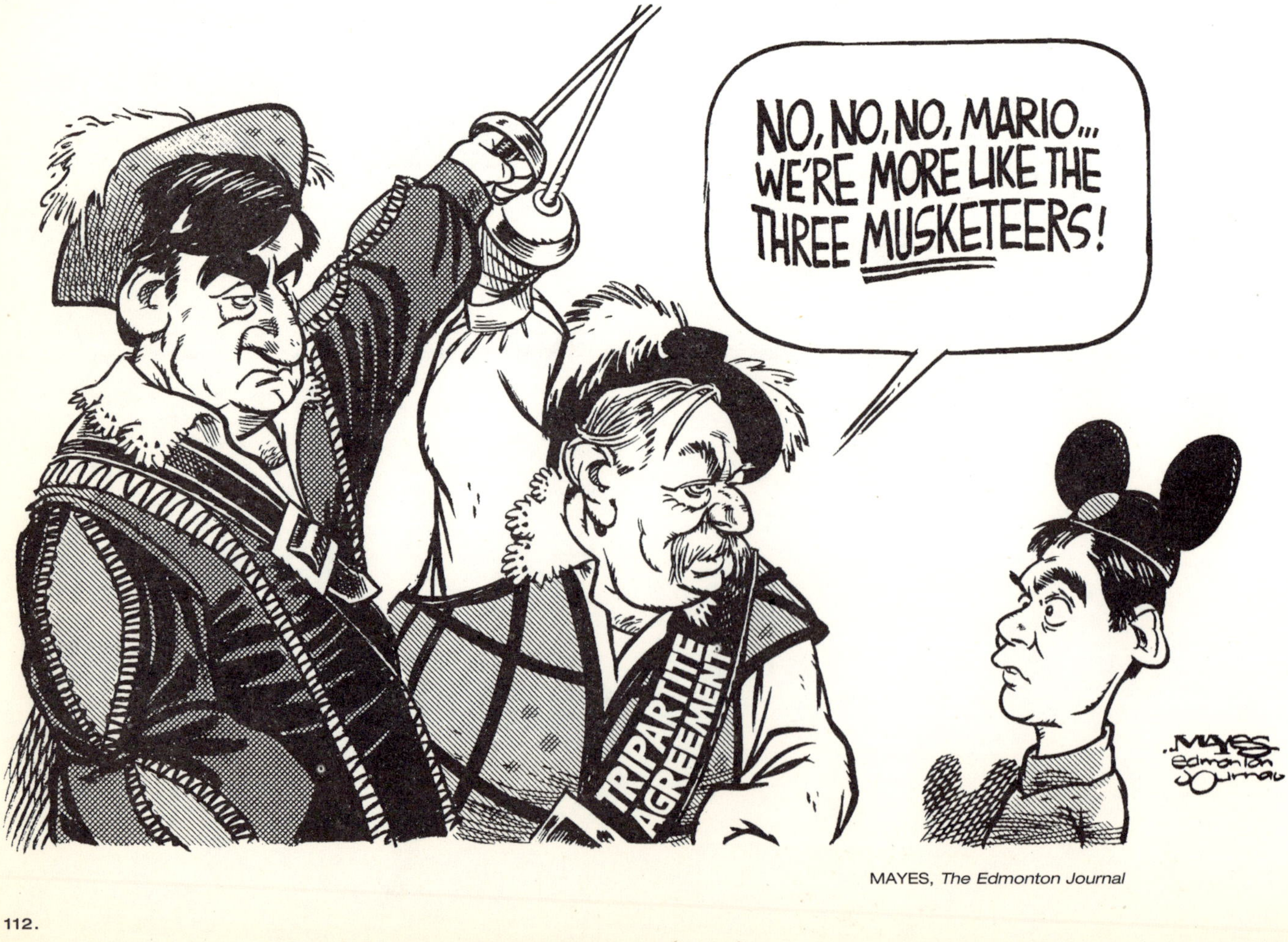
NO, NO, NO, MARIO...
WE'RE MORE LIKE THE
THREE MUSKETEERS!
TRIPARTITE AGREEMENT
MAYES Edmonton Journal

MAYES, *The Edmonton Journal*

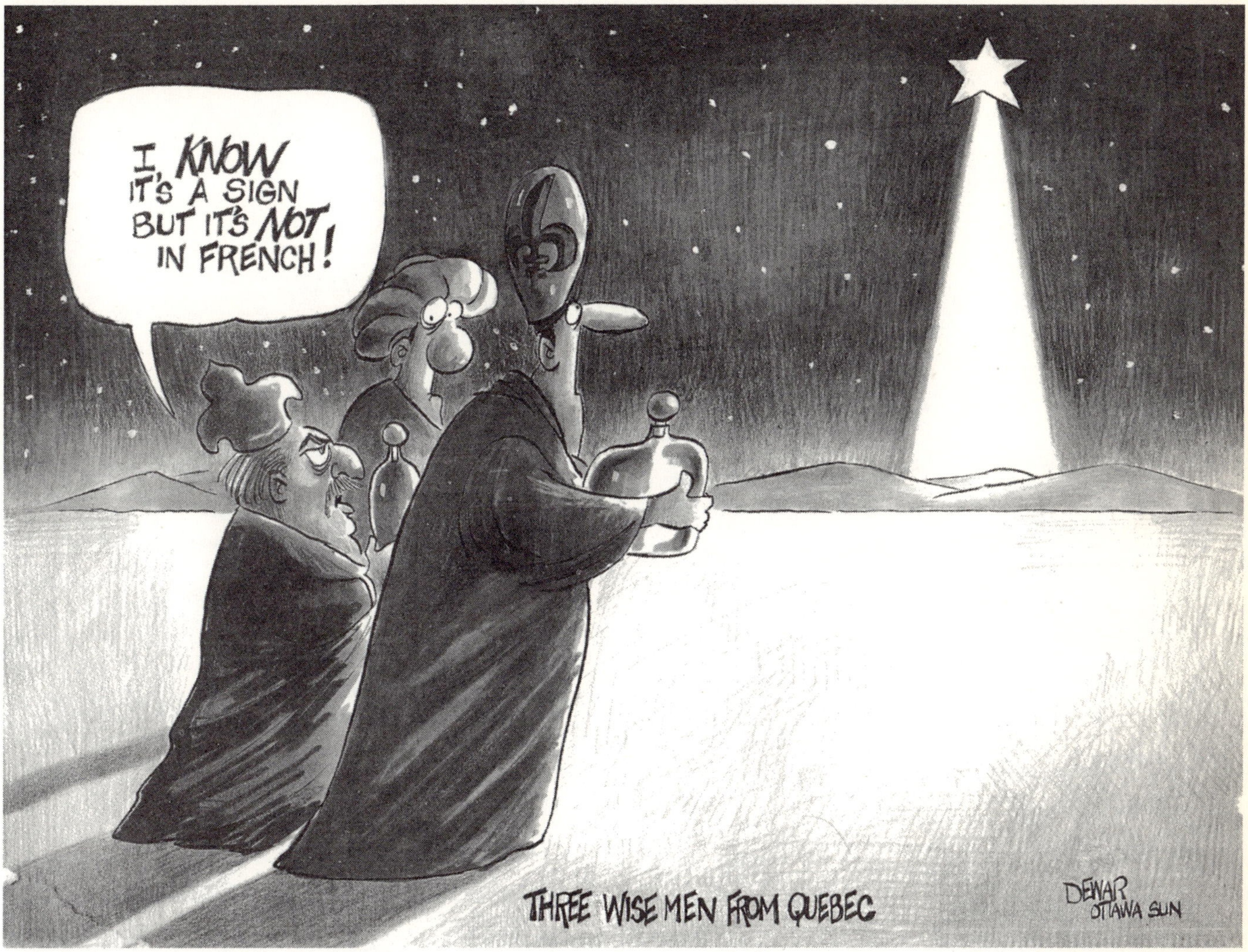
I KNOW IT'S A SIGN BUT IT'S NOT IN FRENCH!
THREE WISE MEN FROM QUEBEC
DEWAR OTTAWA SUN

DEWAR, *The Ottawa Sun*

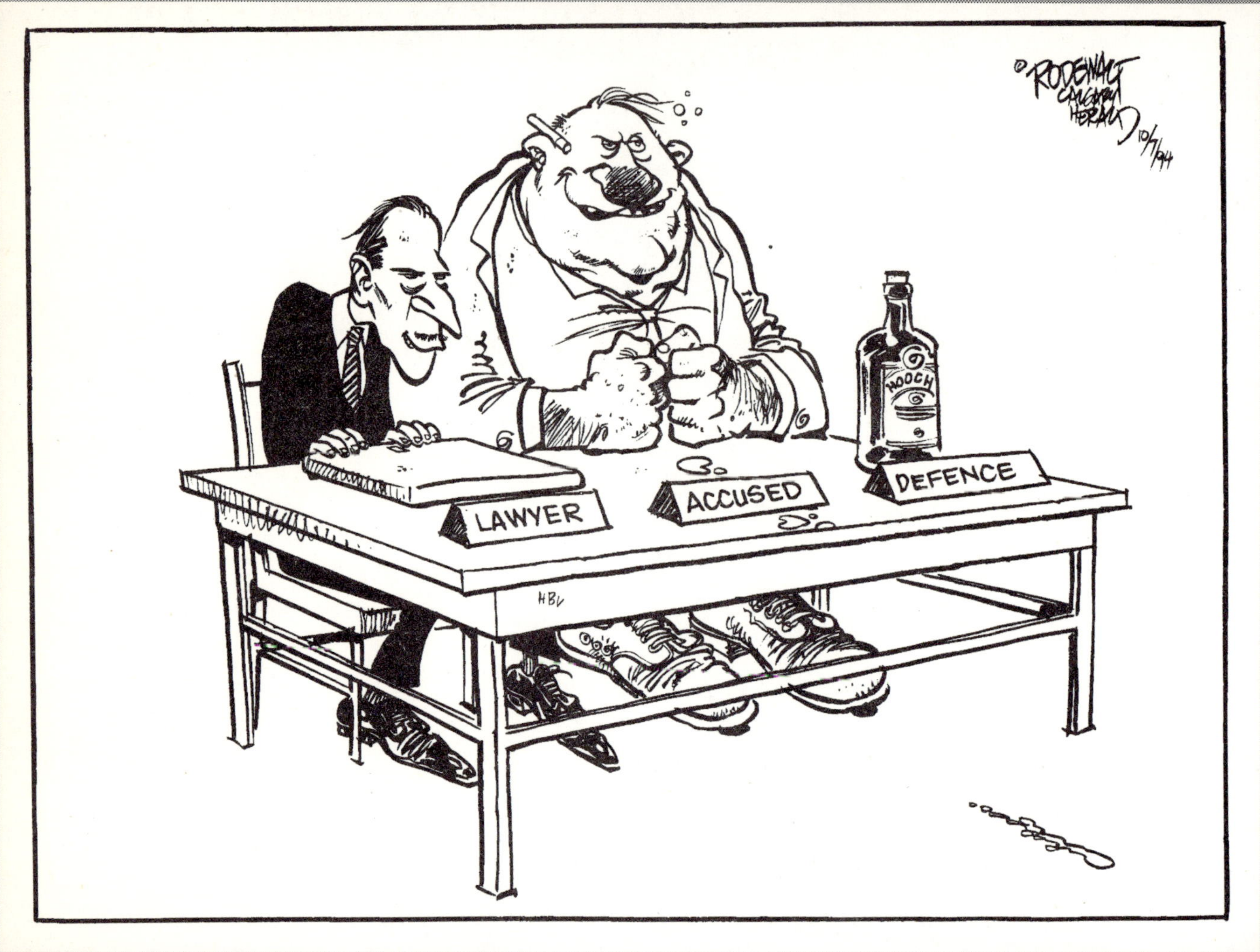
LAWYER
ACCUSED
DEFENCE
HOOCH

Portfoolio 11

# Canadian Life
## This is a negative-option book: keep it or you'll never see "The Rockford Files" again

Everyone has their nomination for the year's greatest nonsense, but you must admit that the "too-drunk defence" ranks right up there. Until new legislation was passed by the kill-joys in the House of Commons and the Senate—your basic chamber of sober (ha!) second thought—the potential for mayhem was limitless. Consider this: "Shorry 'bout that VISA bill, but ash the Shupreme Court shaid, I schouldn't be reshponshible on accounta bein' schnozzled shince Sheptember." Or perhaps we could look forward to: "While it is true that I drove over the entire Shriners Autumn Parade, your Honour, I submit that I was distracted by a plague of rats swarming from my windshield defroster."

Too bad other matters weren't so easily cured, such as the hangover that settled in once the recession was over, and the absolutely relentless push to globalize the economy, which made it ever harder to hold on to our distinctly Canadian icons. Budget cuts slashed the CBC to the point where it had barely 100 vice-presidents to rub together. The railways weren't running…oops, never mind. That was just a strike. And who among us really thought that our mushy determination to keep people from sleeping destitute on the streets would get Canada labelled as a Third World country?

Perhaps no government organization better illustrated the push to a demand economy than the Canadian Security Intelligence Service. Did it sit on its duff because most spies and troublemakers were on long-term layoff? Never. It created a market by hiring its own one-man, neo-Nazi crime wave. Similar spunk was shown by the Unemployment Insurance Commission, which seemed determined to keep its customer base full to overflowing.

The year would not be complete without a word on the news of graphic video-taped evidence that riveted a shocked nation to the murder trial of Paul Bernardo. The word is "yuk."

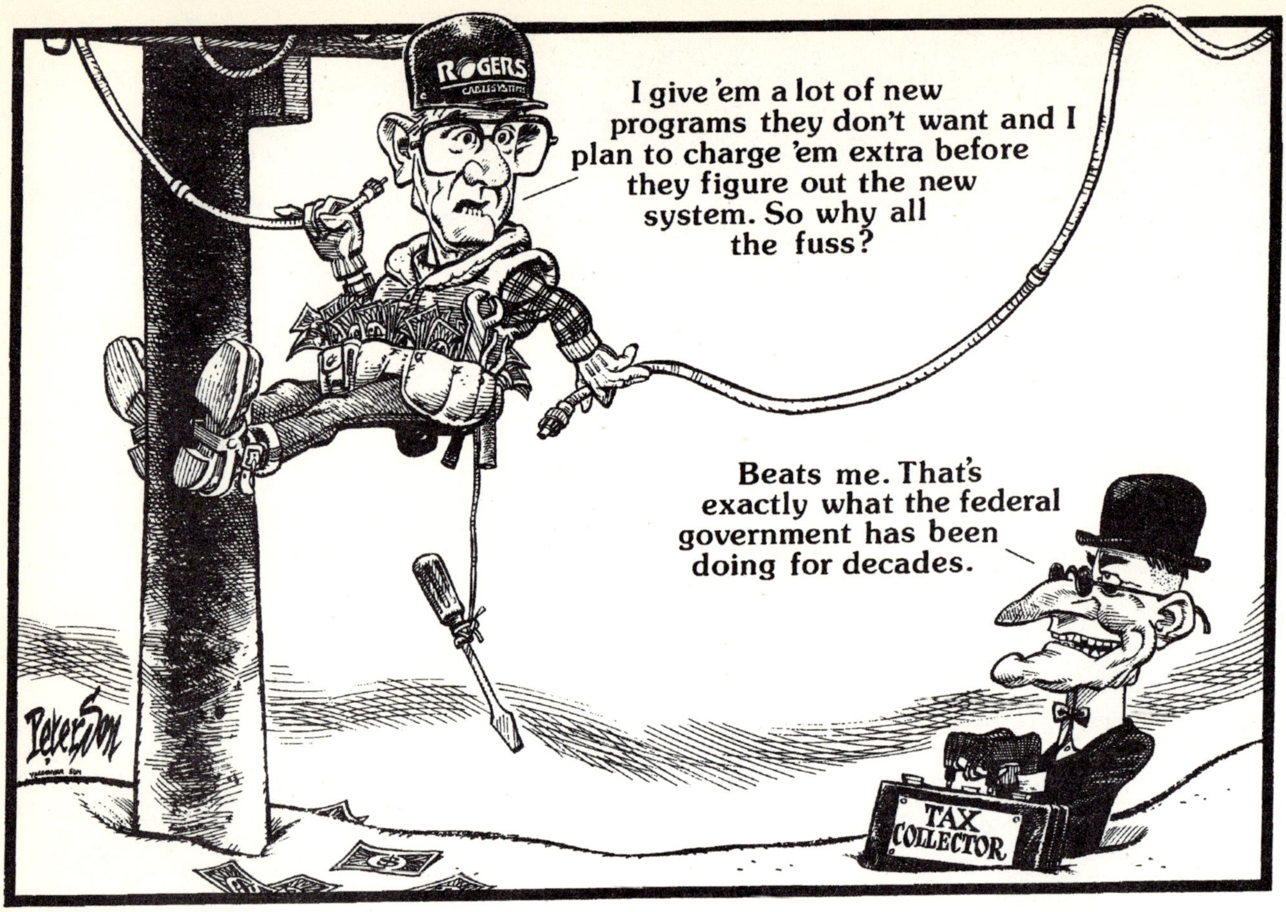
ROGERS
I give 'em a lot of new programs they don't want and I plan to charge 'em extra before they figure out the new system. So why all the fuss?
Beats me. That's exactly what the federal government has been doing for decades.
TAX COLLECTOR

PETERSON, *The Vancouver Sun*

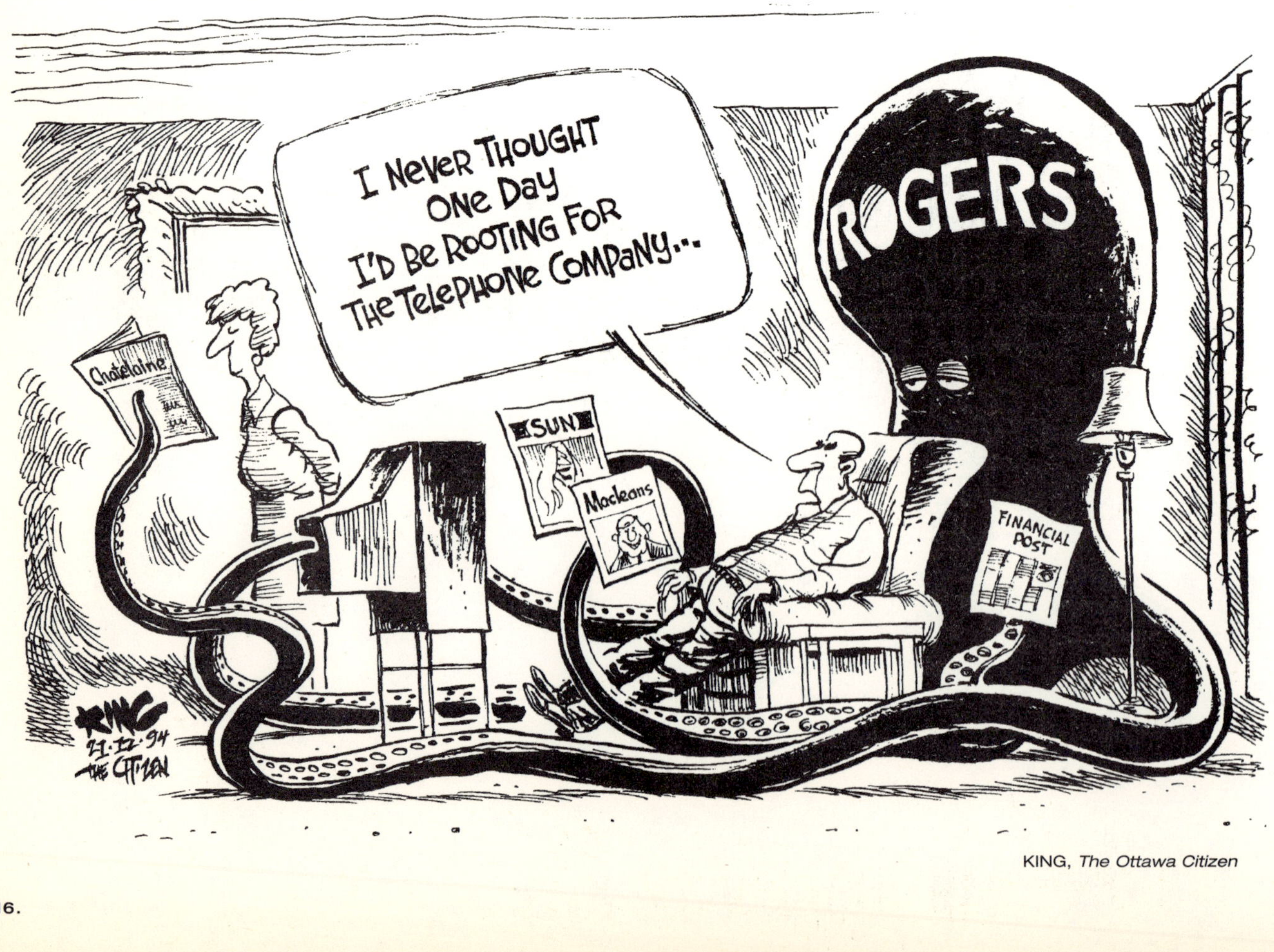
I NEVER THOUGHT ONE DAY I'D BE ROOTING FOR THE TELEPHONE COMPANY...
ROGERS
Chatelaine
SUN
Macleans
FINANCIAL POST

KING, *The Ottawa Citizen*

CORRIGAN, *The Toronto Star*

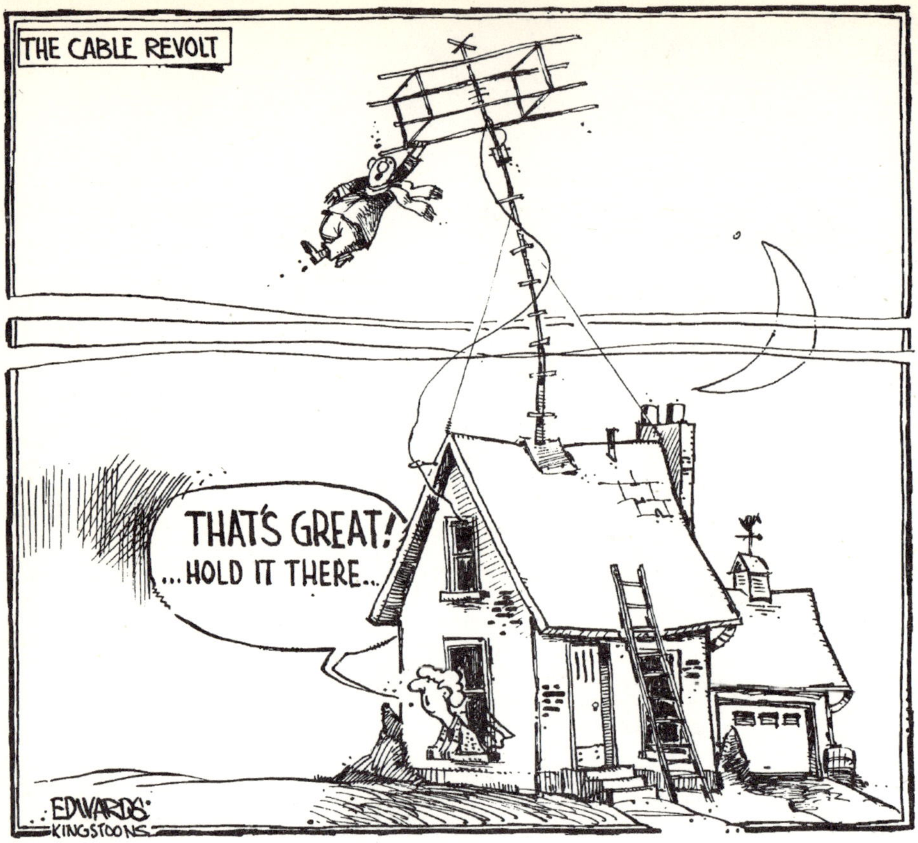
THE CABLE REVOLT
THAT'S GREAT! ...HOLD IT THERE...
EDWARDS KINGSTOONS

EDWARDS

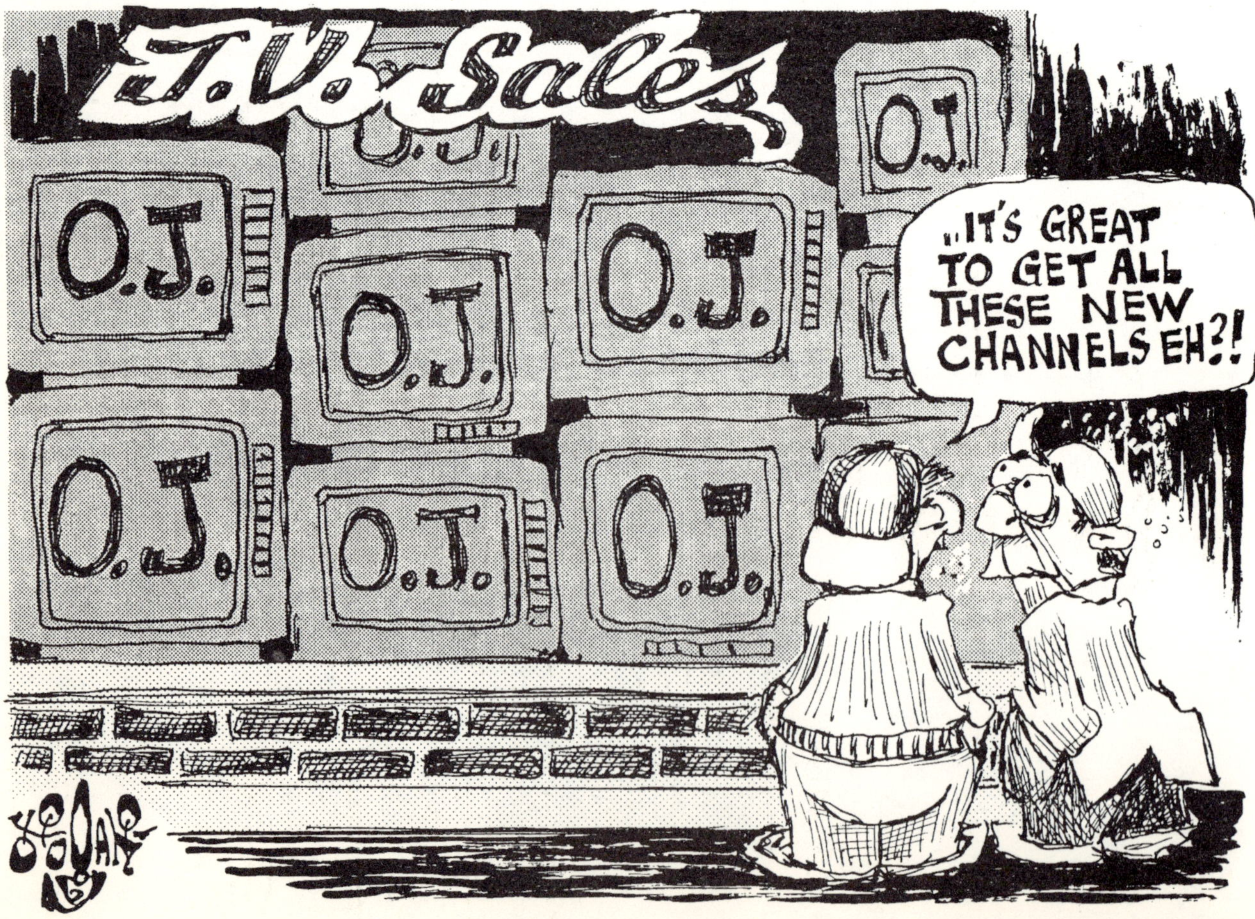
T.V. Sales
O.J.
..IT'S GREAT TO GET ALL THESE NEW CHANNELS EH?!

HOGAN, *The Moncton Times-Transcript*

LACHINE, *The Chatham Daily News*

RICE

MOU, *The Daily News*, Halifax

CORRIGAN, *The Toronto Star*

OLSON, *The Vancouver Courier*

How long job line-ups are used to select the ideal worker.

CONSTABLE, Union Art Services

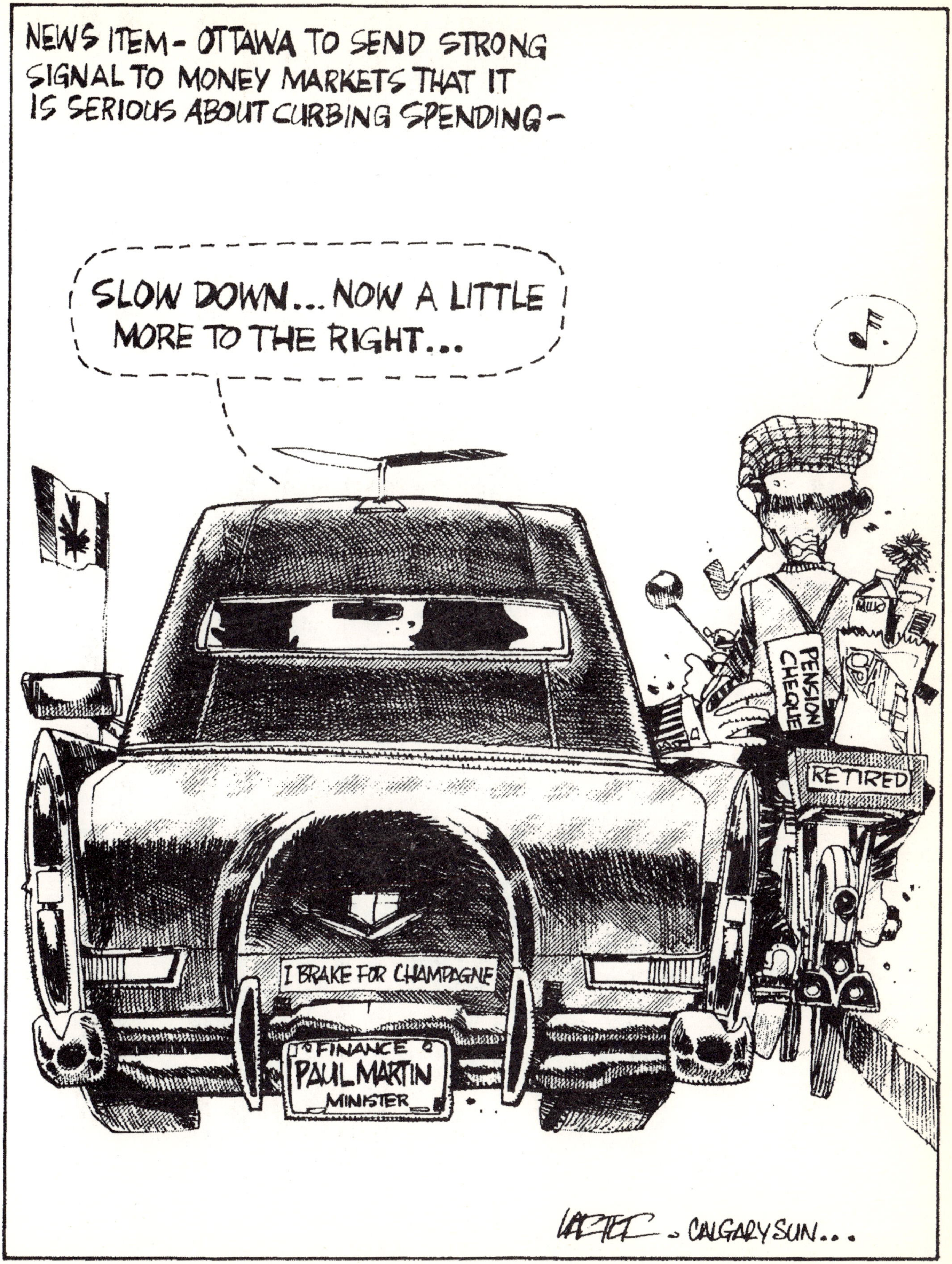
NEWS ITEM - OTTAWA TO SEND STRONG SIGNAL TO MONEY MARKETS THAT IT IS SERIOUS ABOUT CURBING SPENDING -
SLOW DOWN... NOW A LITTLE MORE TO THE RIGHT...
I BRAKE FOR CHAMPAGNE
FINANCE
PAUL MARTIN
MINISTER
PENSION CHEQUE
MILK
RETIRED
LARTER - CALGARY SUN...

LARTER, *The Calgary Sun*

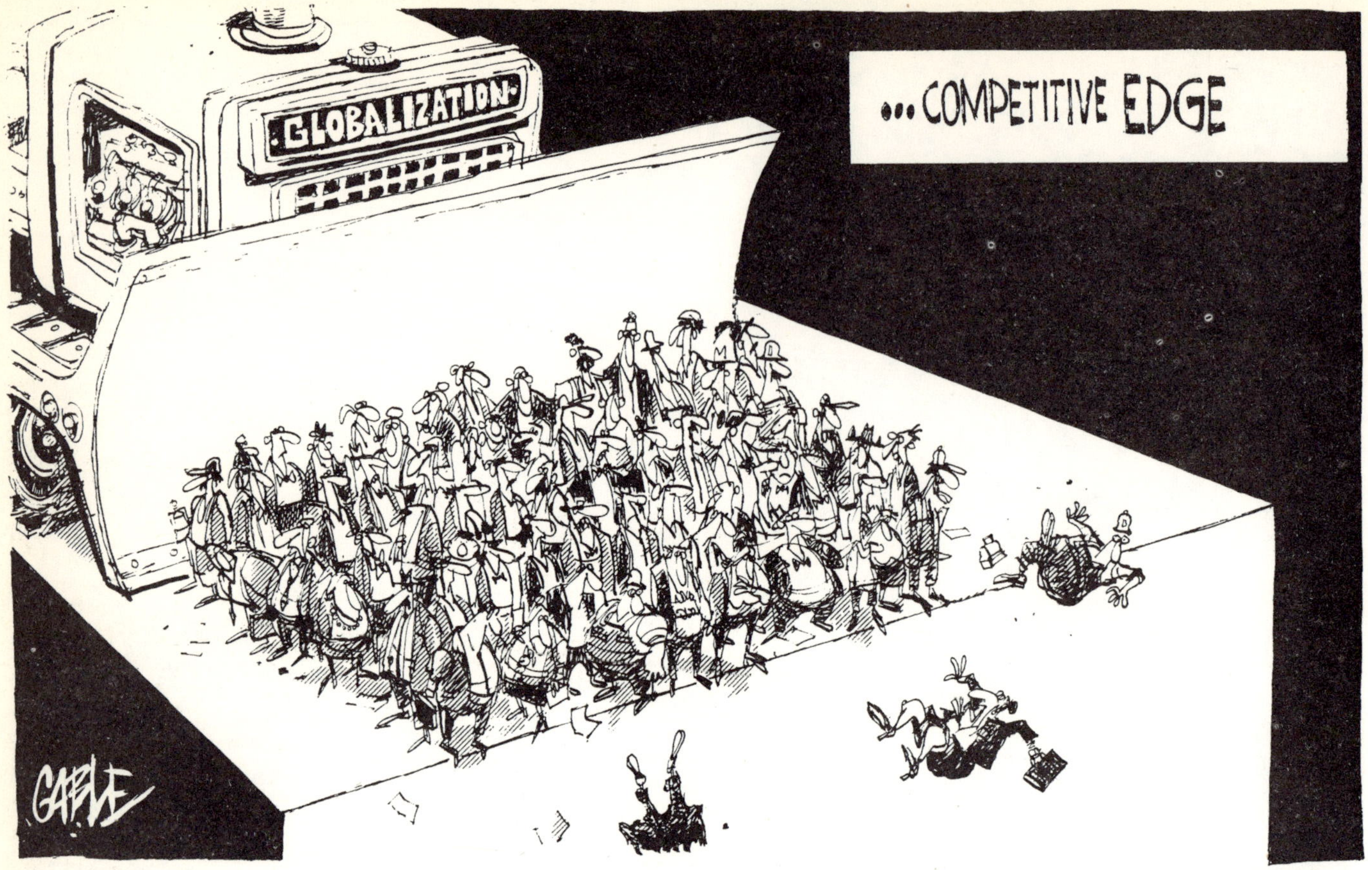
GLOBALIZATION
...COMPETITIVE EDGE
GABLE

GABLE, *The Globe & Mail*

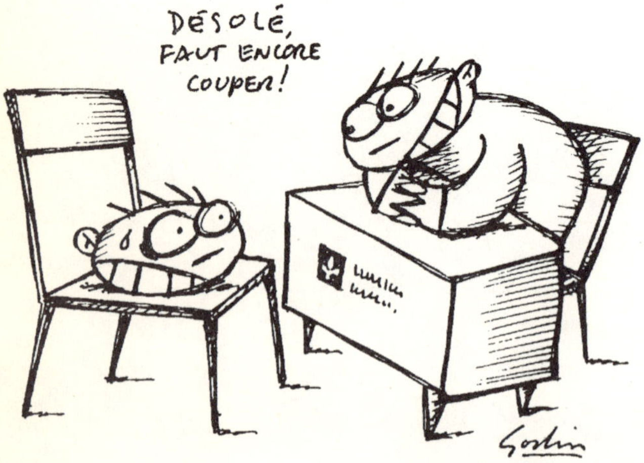
DÉSOLÉ, FAUT ENCORE COUPER!

Sorry, we have to cut!

GODIN, *Voir*, Montreal

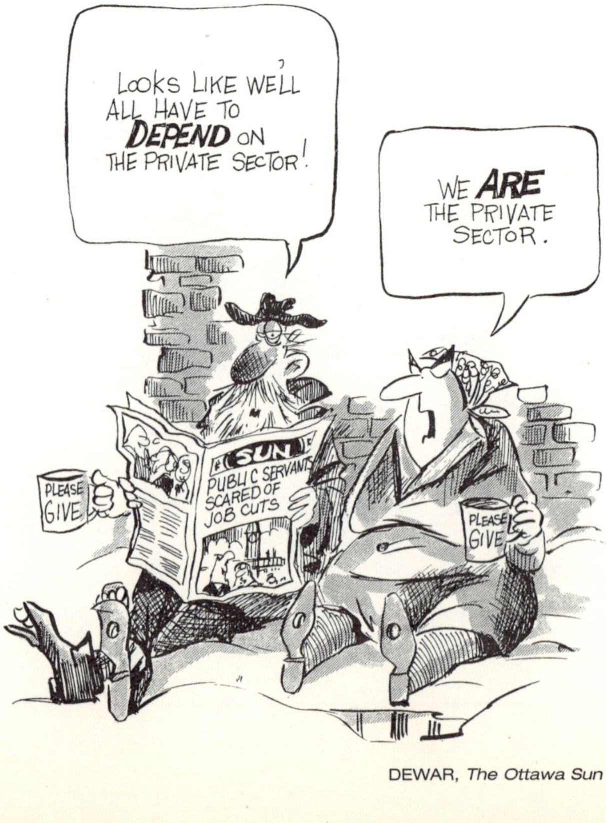
LOOKS LIKE WE'LL ALL HAVE TO **DEPEND** ON THE PRIVATE SECTOR!
WE **ARE** THE PRIVATE SECTOR.
SUN
PUBLIC SERVANTS SCARED OF JOB CUTS
PLEASE GIVE
PLEASE GIVE

DEWAR, *The Ottawa Sun*

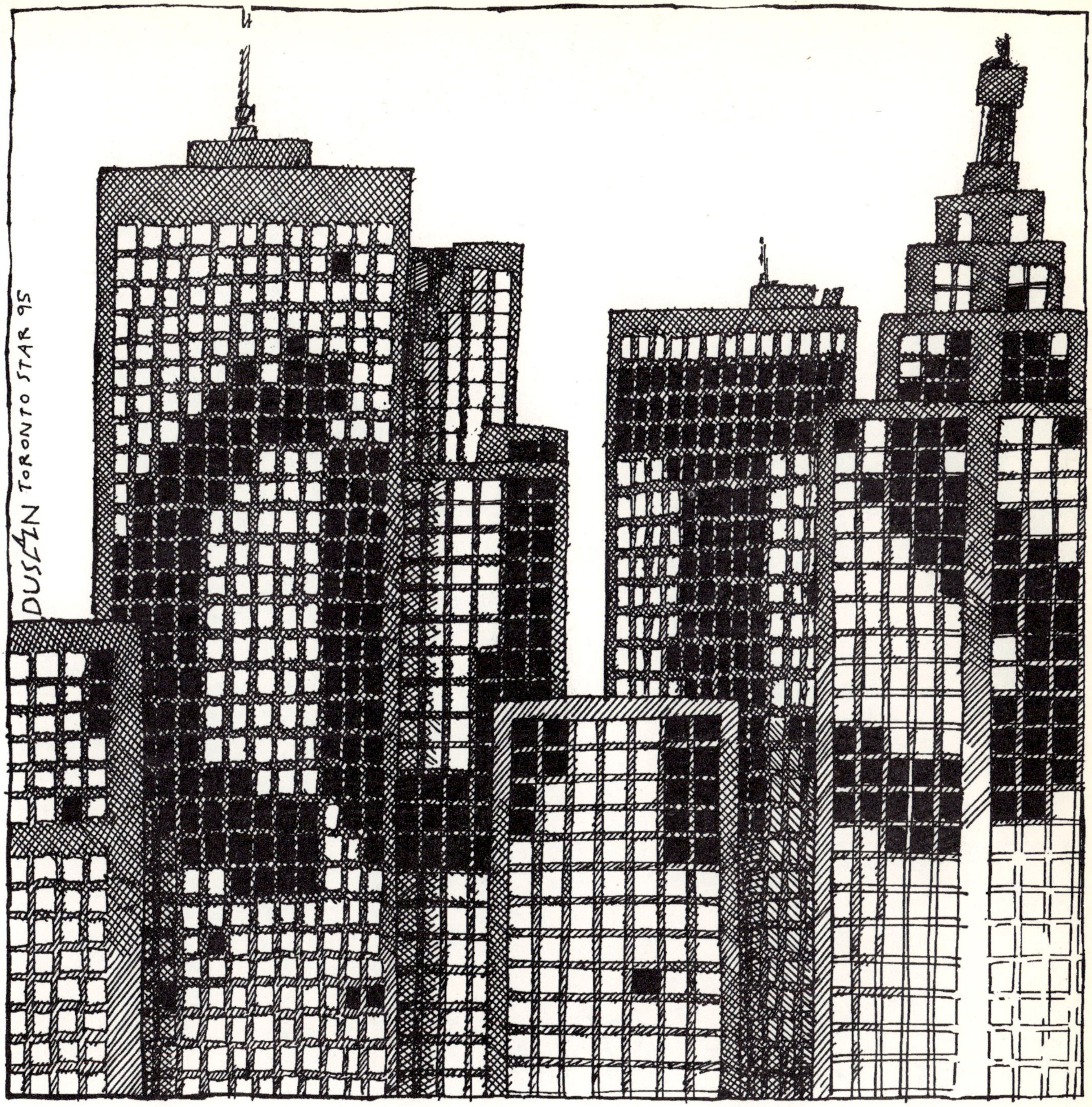
DUSAN TORONTO STAR 95

DUSAN, *The Toronto Star*

MACKINNON, *The Chronicle-Herald*, Halifax

Everything we receive during this consultation will be passed on to needy families!

GARNOTTE, *Nouvelles CSN*, Montreal

PRITCHARD

DEWAR, *The Ottawa Sun*

PRITCHARD

KING, *The Ottawa Citizen*

NEASE, *The Oakville Beaver*

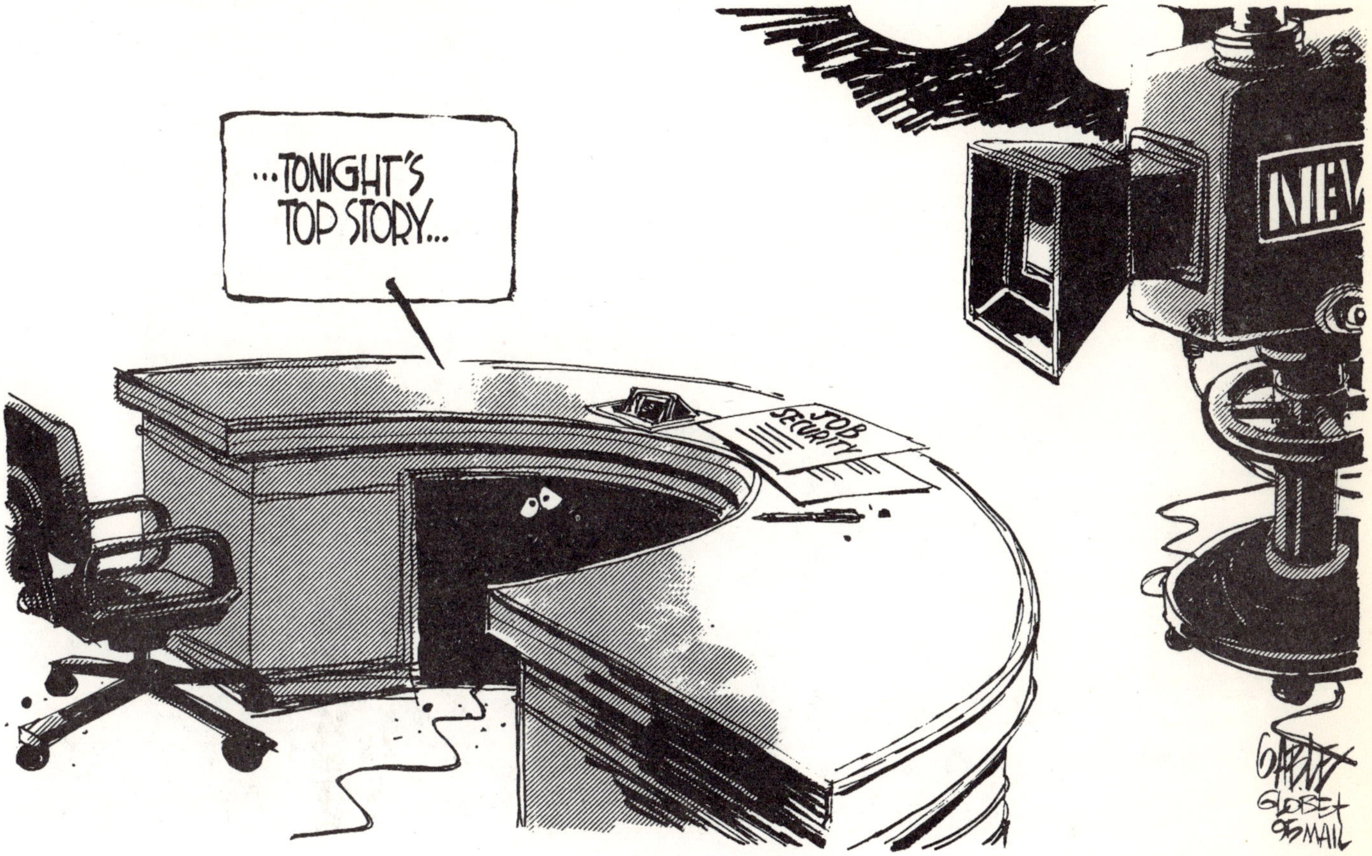
...TONIGHT'S TOP STORY...
JOB SECURITY
NEW
GABLE GLOBE & MAIL 95

GABLE, *The Globe & Mail*

CORRIGAN, *The Toronto Star*

PRITCHARD

HARROP, *The Globe and Mail*

MAYES, *The Edmonton Journal*

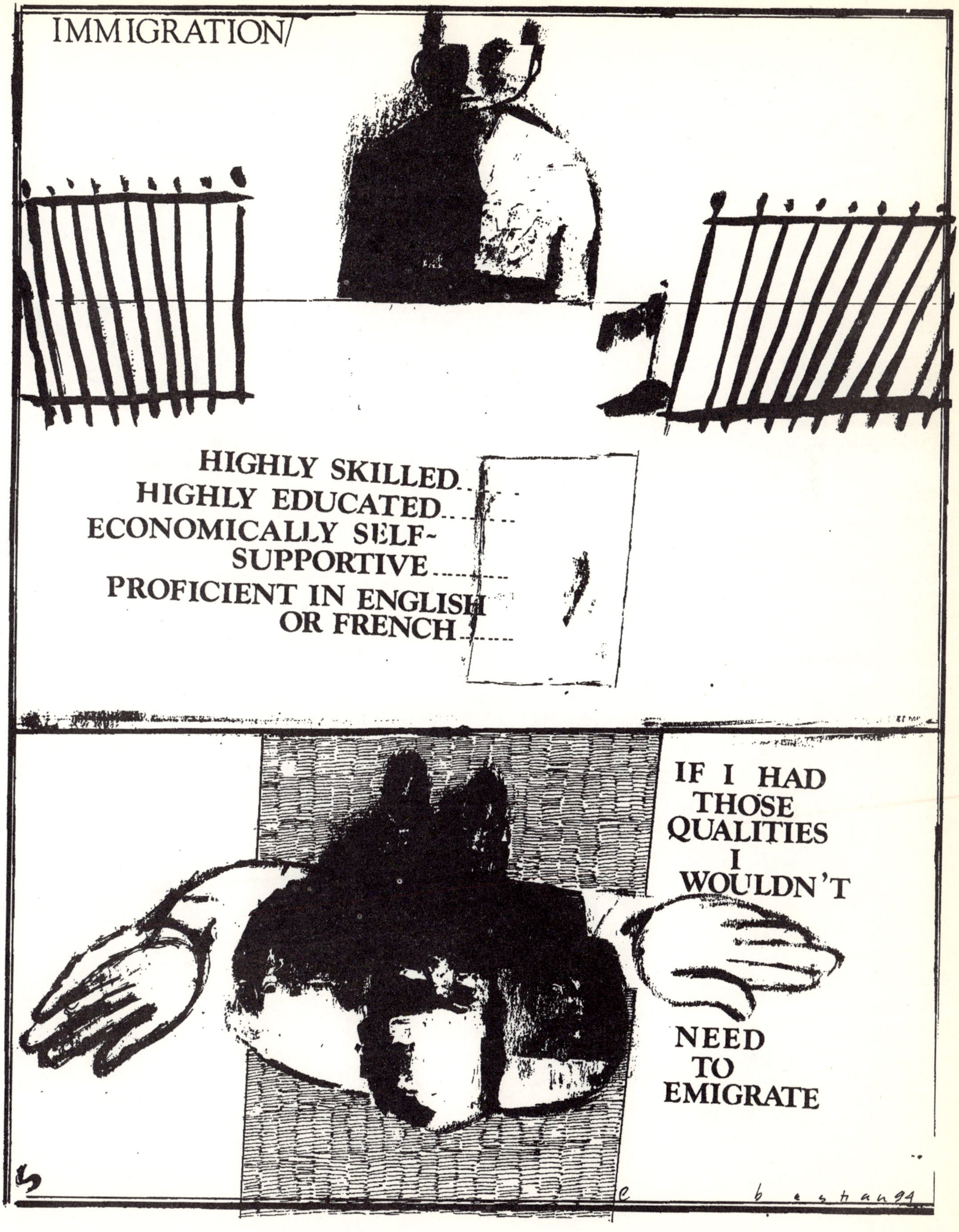
IMMIGRATION/
HIGHLY SKILLED
HIGHLY EDUCATED
ECONOMICALLY SELF-SUPPORTIVE
PROFICIENT IN ENGLISH OR FRENCH
IF I HAD THOSE QUALITIES I WOULDN'T NEED TO EMIGRATE

SEBASTIAN

**SIRC + CSIS = CIRCUS**

CUMMINGS, *The Winnipeg Free Press*

THE COLD WAR ENDS, A GOVERNMENT SECURITY SERVICE LOSES ITS RAISON D'ÊTRE...

SO WHAT DOES IT DO? IT HIRES SOMEONE TO FOUND A NEO-NAZI ORGANIZATION...

POOF! INSTANT NATIONAL SECURITY THREAT AND A NEW RAISON D'ÊTRE...

GOD, I LOVE THIS COUNTRY!

ROSEN, *Hour*, Montreal

OLSON, *The Vancouver Courier*

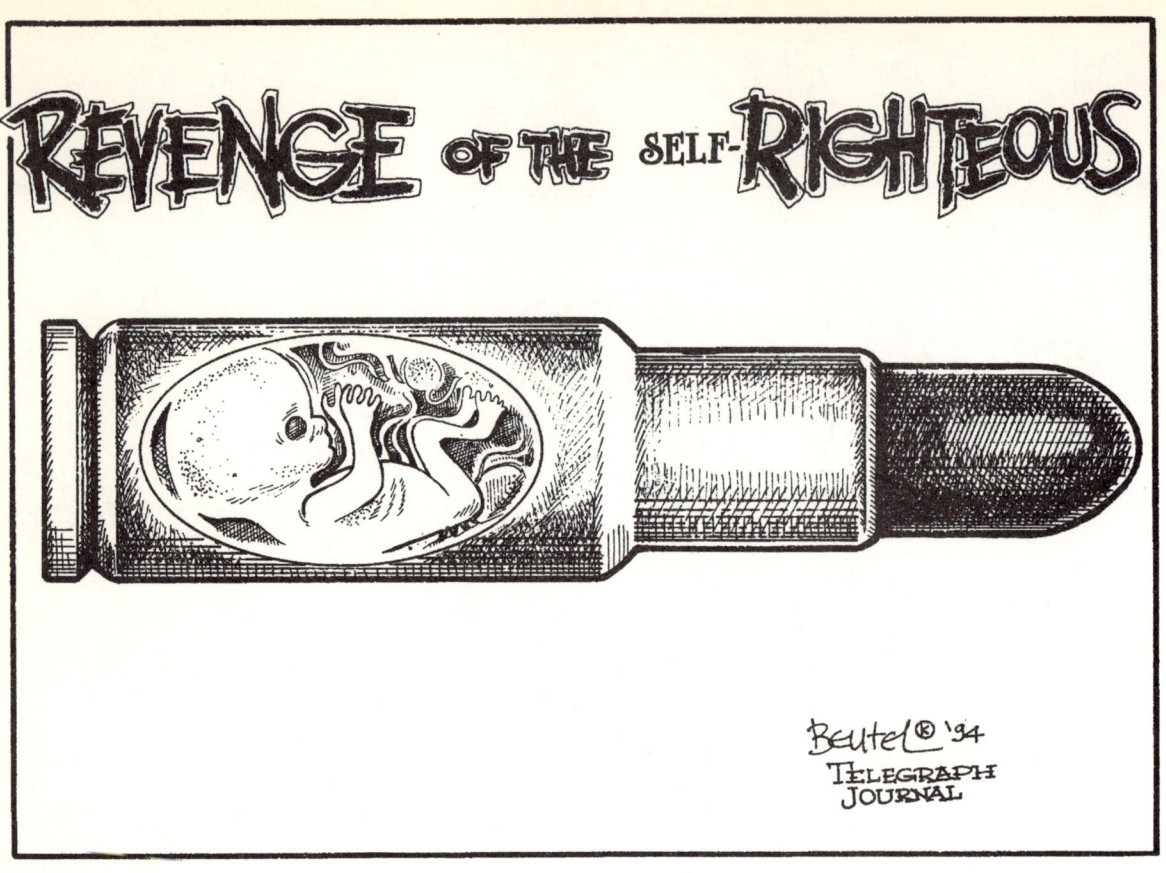

BEUTEL, the *Telegraph-Journal*, Saint John

KEMPKES, Union Art Services

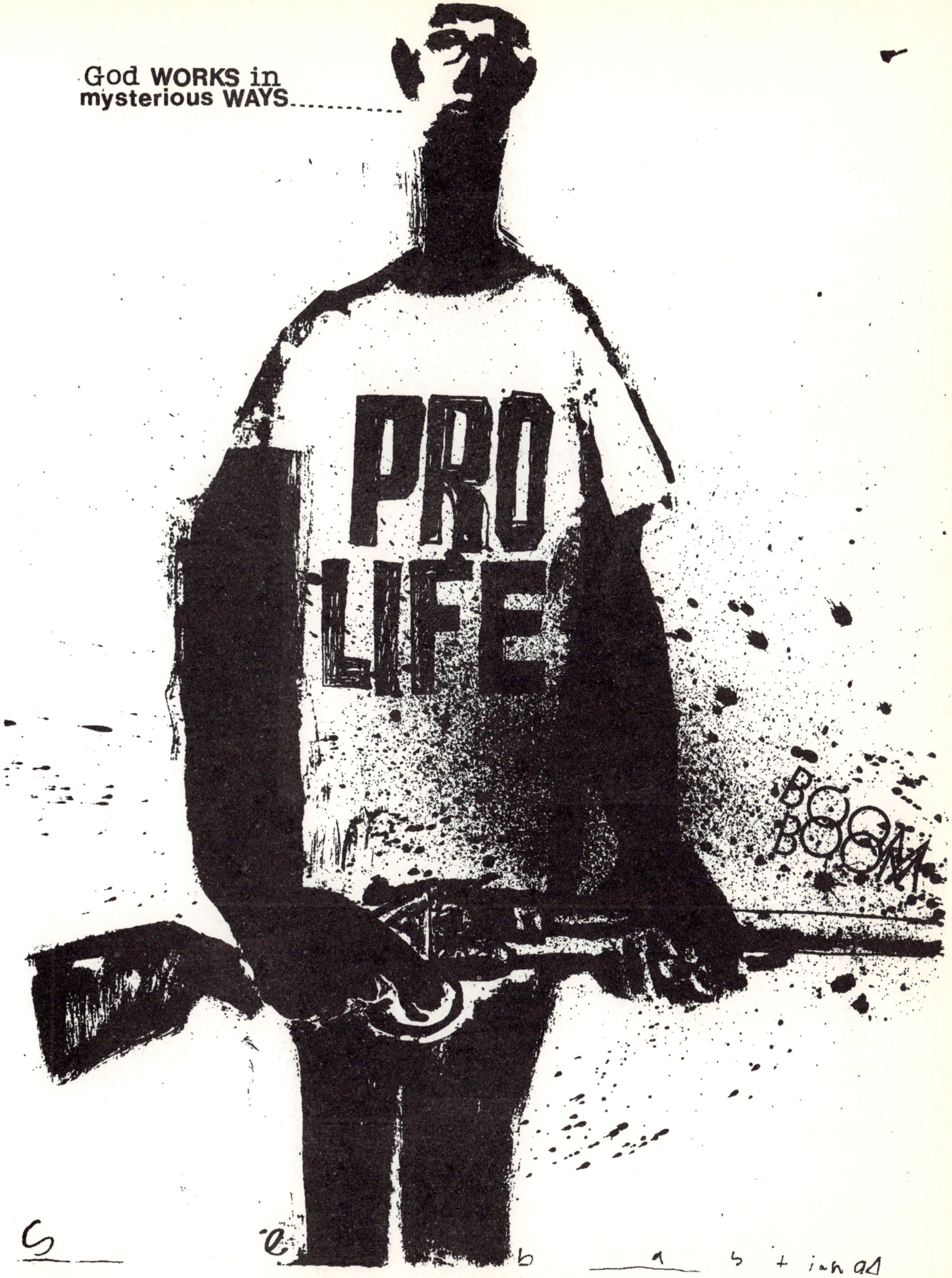
God WORKS in
mysterious WAYS
PRO
LIFE
BOOM
BOOM

SEBASTIAN

CUMMINGS, *The Winnipeg Free Press*

Isn't this fun?   WICKS

JENKINS, *The Globe & Mail*

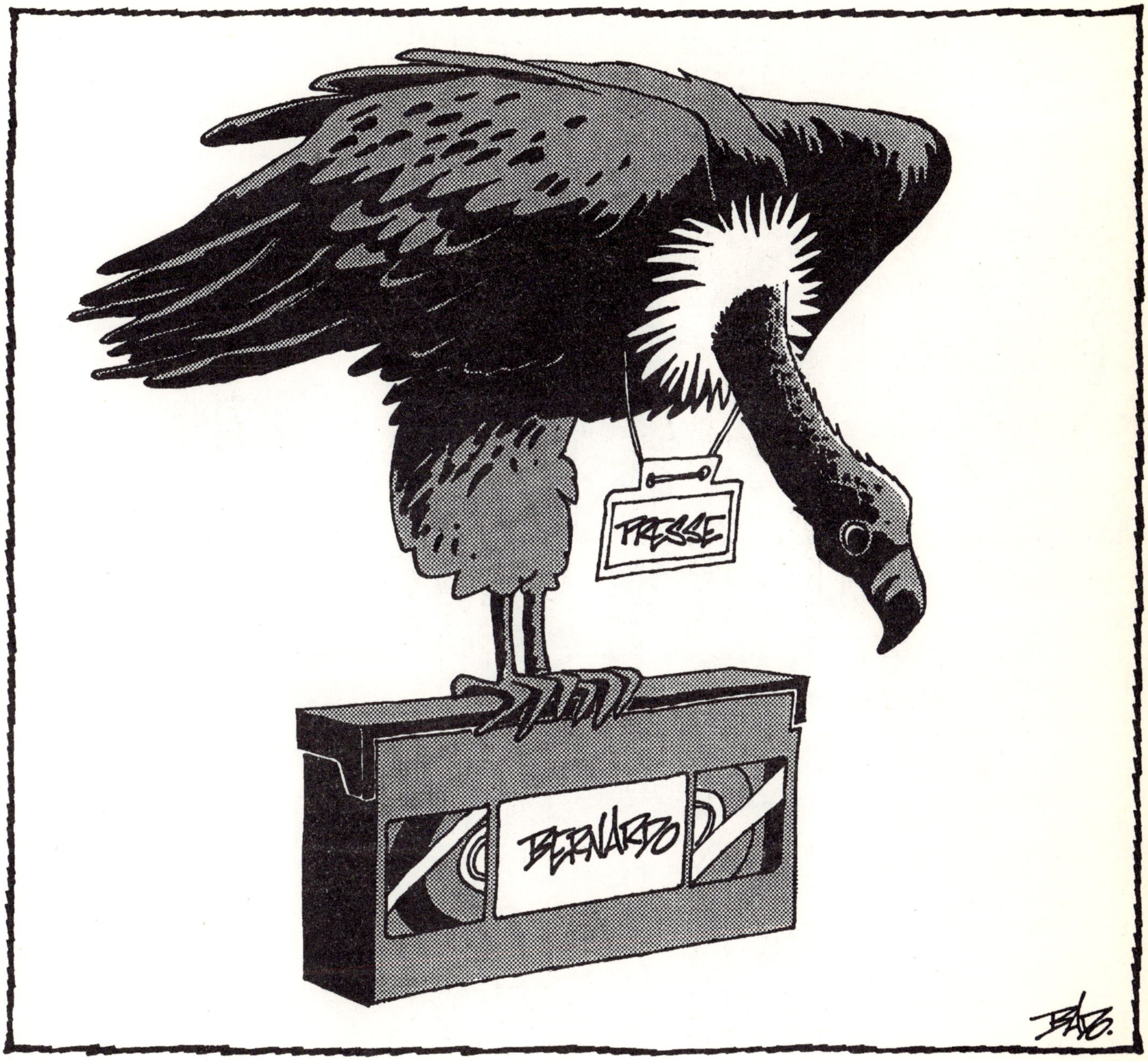
PRESSE
BERNARDO
BADO

BADO, *Le Droit*, Ottawa

Q: what film grossed the most in Toronto....?

A: the Bernardo videos.

SEBASTIAN

# BIOGRAPHIES

 **AISLIN** (Terry Mosher) is the editorial page cartoonist for *The Gazette* in Montreal. Self syndicated, he has freelanced in the U.S. and abroad for such publications as *The New York Times, Time, National Lampoon, Harper's, The Atlantic Monthly* and *Punch.* Born in Ottawa in 1941, he is a graduate of Quebec City's École des Beaux-Arts. Aislin has won a number of citations, including Canadian National Newspaper Awards (1977 and 1978), the prestigious Quill Award and five individual prizes from the International Salon of Caricature. In May of 1985, Aislin was inducted into the Canadian News Hall of Fame.

 Born in 1952 in South Africa, David Anderson, **ANDY** or ERIC, worked for several newspapers in that country. He was the cartoonist for *The Rand Daily Mail* until its closure in 1985 and then for *The Johannesburg Star*. Freelancing in Toronto since 1990, he still faxes two editorial cartoons a week back to the *Star*.

 **BADO** is Guy Badeaux's last name pronounced phonetically. Born in Montreal in 1949, he worked there for ten years before moving to Ottawa in 1981 to become the editorial page cartoonist for *Le Droit*. He won the 1991 National Newspaper Award for political cartooning.

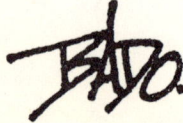

 Born in the winter of 1946 in Winnipeg, **ERIC BARDAL** moved to Thunder Bay, Ontario in 1971 to work in television graphics. Two years later, he was in Vancouver drawing 70 cartoons a week for the network game show "What's the Good Word." In 1976, Bardal became a freelance designer, illustrator and cartoonist and enjoyed working for 13 years as a courtroom sketch artist for television news. In 1989, he began producing editorial cartoons and now syndicates across Canada.

 **JOSH BEUTEL** was born in Montreal in 1945. He presently cartoons for *The Telegraph Journal* in New Brunswick as well as for syndication.

 **BLAINE** was born in Glace Bay, Nova Scotia. He has been the editorial page cartoonist of *The Spectator* in Hamilton since 1961. Winner of the National Newspaper Award in 1974 and again in 1982, he was the first Canadian cartoonist to win the coveted Reuben Award in New York (1970). First winner of the Grand Prize at Montreal's International Salon of Caricature in 1965, Blaine has also freelanced for *The New York Times, Time* and *Playboy*. A black belt instructor in karate, he also writes music and sings.

 Born in Ottawa in 1960, Cameron Cardow (**CAM**) began his career in newspapers at *The Ottawa Citizen* in 1984. In November 1987 he accepted the position of editorial cartoonist at *The Regina Leader-Post*, where he currently draws five cartoons a week. His work appears frequently in other newspapers across Canada.

 Born in Montreal in 1945 and having studied painting and graphic arts at l'École des Beaux-Arts, **SERGE CHAPLEAU** became an instant celebrity in Quebec in 1972 with a weekly full colour caricature for *Perspectives*. He joined *Montreal Matin* two years later where he did editorial cartoons until the paper folded following a long strike. He regained stardom (or at least his voice did) when a puppet character of his, Gérard D. Laflaque, became a supper-time regular on public TV. Serge resurfaced at the very sedate *Le Devoir* in the mid eighties, left for a two-month stint at *Le Matin*, and has been back at *Le Devoir* since June 1992.

 **MIKE CONSTABLE** was born in Woodstock, Ontario, in 1943. After studying sculpture at the Ontario College of Art, he moved on to Carleton University in Ottawa, where he studied sociology. He was a co-founder of *Guerilla*, a Toronto underground newspaper from 1969 through 1974. In 1977 he was one of the founders of Union Art Services, a co-operative mailing service of graphics and cartoons. Besides freelancing for *Canadian Tribune*, he is the editor of *Piranha* (Toronto's National Humour Magazine).

 Born in Toronto in 1951, **PATRICK CORRIGAN** studied fine arts at the Ontario College of Art, which led to a career of night-shift taxi driving. He forsook his extensive art training and freelanced for *The Financial Post*, *Maclean's* and *The Toronto Star*. He joined the *Star* in 1983 as a full-time illustrator, while filling in for Duncan Macpherson whenever possible. Twice nominated for a National Newspaper Award and winner of several awards in illustration and graphics (Society of Newspaper Design, New York Art Directors Club, Advertising Design Club of Canada, Toronto Art Directors Club). He was named the editorial page cartoonist in 1995 at *The Toronto Star* and can still quote you a return fare from the airport.

 Born in 1948 in St. Thomas, Ontario, **DALE CUMMINGS** studied animation and illustration at Sheridan College in Oakville. During a brief stay in New York he did some cartoons for *The New York Times*. He returned to Toronto in 1976, where he freelanced for *Last Post*, *Canadian Forum*, *Maclean's*, *The Toronto Star*, *Canadian Magazine* and *This Magazine*. Full-time editorial cartoonist with *The Winnipeg Free Press* since 1981, he won the National Newspaper Award in 1983.

 Born December 29th, 1958, **FRED CURATOLO** published his first cartoon in *The Toronto Sun* in 1982. Syndicating his work in various dailies, he was staff cartoonist for *The Brampton Guardian* and Metroland newspapers before moving to *The Edmonton Sun* in 1989.

 Born in Montreal in 1949, **SUSAN DEWAR** attended high school in Toronto, went to the University of Western Ontario in London, and graduated from Toronto Teachers' College. After working in commercial art in Toronto, she freelanced for *Canadian Forum, Teen Generation Current* and *The Toronto Sun*. She joined *The Calgary Sun* as full-time editorial cartoonist in 1984 and won the 1987 National Business Writing Award for political cartooning. In October 1988 she moved to Ottawa to become the editorial cartoonist with *The Ottawa Sun*. She is the mother of James Geoffrey.

DEWAR

 **ANDY DONATO** was born in Scarborough in 1937. He graduated from Danforth Technical School in 1955 and worked at Eaton's as a layout artist. He joined the Toronto *Telegram* in 1961 as a graphic artist working in the promotion department. In 1968 he was appointed art director and began cartooning on a part-time basis. After the demise of the *Telegram*, he joined *The Toronto Sun* and in 1974, started cartooning on a full-time basis. In 1985-86 he served as president of the Association of American Editorial Cartoonists.

Donato

 **DUŠAN PETRIČIĆ** was born in Belgrade, Yugoslavia, in 1946. He graduated from Belgrade's Academy for Applied Arts where he has also taught illustration. Editorial cartoonist for the daily *Večernje Novosti* (Evening News) and the weekly magazine *Nin,* Petricic is the author of numerous children's books and has directed many animated films. He has won several awards: Grand Prix in Tokyo, Silver medal in Istanbul, Grand Prix in Skopje and Golden Pen in Amsterdam. In Canada since September 1993, he has had cartoons published regularly in *The Toronto Star* and the book review section of *The New York Times*.

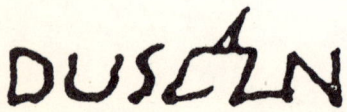

**FRANK A. EDWARDS** was born in Belleville, Ontario, in 1940. After graduating from the Ontario College of Art, he worked as a commercial artist for several printing companies. In 1965, Frank accepted a position with Queen's University where he worked for 13 years as a medical illustrator. In 1978 he joined *The Whig Standard* in Kingston as its first full-time cartoonist but was "downsized" in 1994. His work is syndicated in Canada and the United States.

Born in 1949 in Saskatoon, **BRIAN GABLE** studied fine arts at the University of Saskatchewan. Graduating with a B.Ed. from the University of Toronto in 1971, he taught art in Brockville and began freelancing for the Brockville *Recorder and Times* in 1977. In 1980 he started full-time with the Regina *Leader-Post* and won the National Newspaper Award in 1986. He is presently the editorial cartoonist for *The Globe and Mail*.

Born in Montreal in 1951, and after studies having nothing to do with drawing, Michel Garneau (**GARNOTTE**) has contributed to many newspapers and magazines in Montreal, including *CROC, TV Hebdo, Protégez-vous (Protect Yourself), Titanic* (of which he was editor-in-chief), *Les Expos, Les débrouillards, La Terre de chez nous* and *Nouvelles CSN*, which has carried his cartoons since 1986.

Illustrator, graphic artist and painter, **ÉRIC GODIN** was born in Montreal in 1964. Drawing for the weekly *Voir* since 1988, he is also known for his theatre posters and his advertising work. He has, since 1983, exhibited in group shows or solo both in Canada and Europe.

Born and raised in Edmonton, **JAMES GRASDAL** began freelancing at *The Edmonton Journal* in 1992, drawing 1-2 editorial cartoons and 2-3 illustrations per week. He is currently the regular cartoonist for *SEE* magazine in Edmonton.

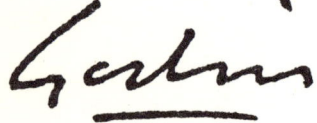

Born in Liverpool, England, **GRAHAM HARROP**'s first cartoons appeared in *The Powell River News*. His former jobs include being a copy boy for *The Vancouver Sun*, mill-worker and taxi driver. He has done freelance cartoons for the Vancouver *Province*, a cartoon strip for the Victoria *Times-Colonist* and he is the author of "Back Bench" in *The Globe and Mail*.

 **W.A. (Bill) HOGAN** was born in Montreal, but spent most of his life in Chatham, New Brunswick. He is presently the editorial cartoonist for the Moncton *Times-Transcript* and he does cartoons for several New Brunswick weeklies. He is the author of the strip *The River Rats* and he has also traveled across the province doing courtroom drawing for CBC TV. Winner of numerous Atlantic Community Newspaper Association Awards and the 1994 Atlantic Journalism Award for editorial cartooning, he has published two collections of his cartoons.

 **CHARLES JAFFE (JÉ)** was born in 1952 and 1963. He was raised in southern Ontario, but tripped and fell down in western Manitoba. He started doing cartoons for *The Varsity* at the University of Toronto. Then the commies got him and his drawings appeared in *Canadian Forum*, *This Magazine* and *Last Post*. Later he drew regularly for *Maclean's*, *The Financial Post*, *Toronto Life* and many other capitalist consumer running dogs. He was a founding contributor to *The Idler*. Now, however, this once glorious talent is reduced to scribbling for the notorious *Frank* magazine, available in disreputable variety stores everywhere.

"Ah Hoskins! Do come in! Have a seat."

 **ANTHONY JENKINS** was born in Toronto in 1951 and stayed there after graduating from the University of Waterloo and taking three trips around the world. His work has appeared in *The Globe and Mail* since 1974; kids Adriana and Zoe have appeared more recently.

 **JIM KEMPKES** was born in Buffalo, New York, in 1947 and came to Canada in 1969. He studied fine arts at York University in Toronto where he was especially influenced by the drawing and sculpture of Honoré Daumier. Since then he has worked freelance, specializing in sculptural caricature in addition to contributing drawings to Union Art Services and other publications.

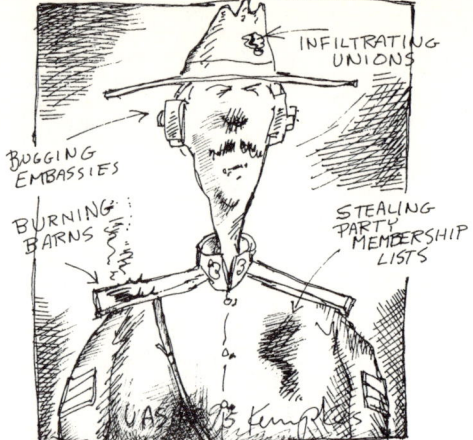

---

 Born in Belfast, Northern Ireland, in 1947, **ALAN KING** came to Canada with his family at the age of two. After graduating in English Literature from the University of Western Ontario, he taught high-school English, and worked as a piano salesman, taxi driver, engineering technician, illustrator and ad agency art director. Father of Christopher and Chloe, he has been with *The Ottawa Citizen* since 1979.

---

 Born in 1965, **PAUL LACHINE** lives in Chatham, Ontario, with his wife Deborah and their children Katie and Michael. His freelance editorial cartoons and illustrations appear regularly in *The Chatham Daily News*, Kingston's *Whig Standard*, and various southern Ontario weeklies. Paul's work also appears occasionally in *The Toronto Star* and *The London Free Press*.

 Born in Swift Current, Saskatchewan, in 1950, **JOHN LARTER** started at *The Lethbridge Herald* in 1974 and went to *The Edmonton Sun* in 1978. He was *The Toronto Star's* editorial cartoonist from 1980 until he returned west in 1989 to take the same position at *The Calgary Sun*.

 Born in Kitchener, Ontario, in 1964, **JACK LEFCOURT** graduated with a B.A. in fine arts from the University of Waterloo. He started cartooning for the university student paper syndicate in 1985 and has been drawing professionally since 1988. His work is published in about 15 dailies and weeklies across Canada and he is currently the regular editorial cartoonist for *NOW* in Toronto.

 **BRUCE MACKINNON** grew up in Antigonish, N.S., studied fine arts at Mount Allison University, and was a member of the Graphic Design program at the Nova Scotia College of Art and Design. He started doing a weekly editorial cartoon with *The Halifax Herald* in 1985, working at home while raising his newborn daughter, Robyn. Through the miracle of day-care, he was able to join the *Herald* on a full-time basis in August of 1986. He has won several Atlantic Journalism Awards for editorial cartooning, was named "journalist of the year" in 1991, and was the National Newspaper Award winner for both 1992 and 1993.

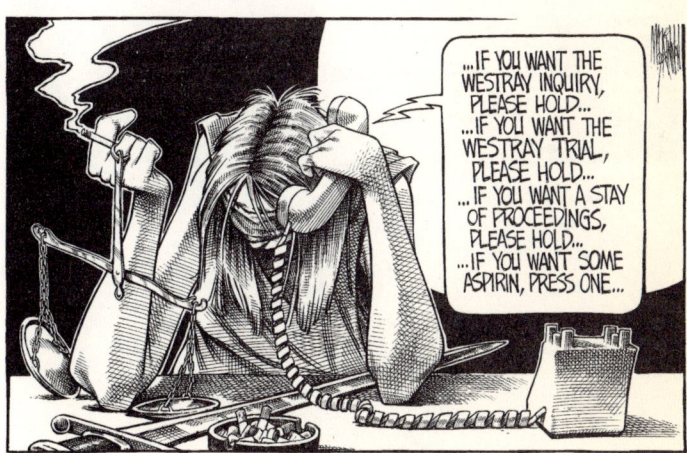

**DAVID MACLEAN** was born in Oshawa in 1952. He has worked as an editorial artist at *The Vancouver Sun* for the past 12 years and has won the B.C. Newspaper Award for best cartoon twice. His cartoons are syndicated throughout B.C., and have appeared in various papers and magazines across Canada and in the States. MacLean is also a published poet and playwright despite the fact he can't spell to save his life.

**MALCOLM MAYES** was born in Edmonton in 1962. Editorial cartoonist for *The Edmonton Journal* since June 1986, his work has appeared in most major Canadian newspapers and many major American newspapers, as well as numerous books and magazines including *Best Editorial Cartoons of The Year* (USA), *Reader's Digest*, and *The Great Big Book of Canadian Humour*. In addition, his cartoons have been featured on CBC, CNN, and at Montreal's International Museum of Humour.

Theo Moudakis (**MOU**) was born in Montreal in 1965. He was first hired by *The Chronicle*, a Montreal weekly, in 1983, and since then his work has appeared in most major Canadian dailies as well as *The New York Times* and *MAD* magazine. In January 1991, he left Montreal to become the full-time cartoonist for the Halifax *Daily News*. He is also the Sunday editorial cartoonist for *The Gazette* in Montreal.

 **DAN MURPHY** was born in Missouri. He moved to Canada in the early seventies, drawing for various underground newspapers and aboveground magazines. He currently cartoons for *The Vancouver Province* and the Rothco syndicate.

 Born in Woodbridge, Ontario, in 1955, **STEVE NEASE** is currently art director of *The Oakville Beaver*, producing both editorial cartoons and his *Pud* comic strip, which are syndicated by Southam. He is a four-time recipient of the (Canadian Community News Association) Jasper Awards for cartooning. Nease and his wife Dian have three sons: Robert, Benjamin and Sam.

 **GEOFF OLSON** is editorial cartoonist and columnist for *The Vancouver Courier*. His artwork and articles have also appeared in *The Vancouver Sun* and numerous Canadian and American magazines.

Born in Winnipeg in 1936, **ROY PETERSON** works for *The Vancouver Sun* and *Maclean's*. His work has appeared in all major Canadian and most major American newspapers and magazines. He worked with Stanley Burke on the best-selling *Frog Fables & Beaver Tales* series and has illustrated many book covers and produced his own children's book, *The Canadian ABC Book*, as well as two collections of his cartoons: *The World According to Roy Peterson*, and *Drawn & Quartered*. Married with five children, he was, in 1982-83, the first Canadian-born president of the Association of American Editorial Cartoonists. He won the Grand Prize at the International Salon of Caricature in Montreal in 1973 and is a five-time winner of the National Newspaper Award.

---

**ROLAND PIER** was born in France in 1936. He came to Canada in 1960, traveled extensively, and had various jobs, including construction and working in a gold mine. Arriving in Montreal in 1962, he began freelancing and was eventually hired by *Le Journal de Montréal*. *Le Journal* has since become the largest French-language newspaper in North America. As Pier's cartoons also appear in a sister publication, *Le Journal de Québec*, he is undoubtedly the most widely read cartoonist in Quebec today.

---

Born in 1935 in Hamilton, Ontario, **DENNY PRITCHARD** worked in auto plants in Ontario and began cartooning as a freelancer in 1975. He was employed as staff cartoonist with *The Saskatoon Star Phoenix* until July 1988 and is now based in Perth, Ontario, where he has resumed freelance work.

Born July 1st, 1957, in Dunedin, New Zealand, **ADRIAN RAESIDE** got his start in cartooning drawing on the back of bus seats on his way home from school. Moving to Canada in 1972 after a brief period in England, he worked at various jobs, before realizing he wasn't much good at any of them. Getting his first break in 1976, illustrating five children's books that his mother, Joan, had written, he became editorial cartoonist of the Victoria *Times-Colonist* in 1980 and is widely syndicated in Canada. He has never won an award, and is not president of anything.

---

**INGRID RICE** is a self-syndicated cartoonist published in over 50 markets across Canada and throughout B.C. Although she has not won any contests, she has appeared before the B.C. Press Council and been found to be reprehensible. Her free time is spent caring for assorted guinea pigs and a cat.

---

Born in Edmonton in 1946, **VANCE RODEWALT** did advertising cartoons at *The Roughneck* after completing high school. Working for Marvel Comics for five years, he traveled to Europe and, upon his return, began doing political cartoons for the Calgary *Albertan*. When the *Albertan* was bought by *The Calgary Sun*, he remained there for 3 1/2 years before moving on to *The Calgary Herald* where he shared editorial page cartooning duties with Tom Innes. He has assumed full duties since 1987 and won the 1988 National Newspaper Award for Cartooning. He is also the author of the *Chubb & Chauncey* comic strip.

 **DAVE ROSEN** was born in Montreal in 1955. At 16, he started cartooning for the underground newspaper, *Logos*. Since then his cartoons have appeared in *Briarpatch*, *This Magazine*, *Canadian Forum*, the *Globe and Mail* and the Sherbrooke *Record*, as well as a host of other publications. In 1984 he edited a book, *Megatoons*, a collection of antiwar cartoons by artists from across Canada. In 1988 he quit cartooning for a career in radio and, ultimately, stand-up comedy. While continuing his broadcasting and stand-up activities, he returned to the drawing board in 1993 and currently draws for the alternative Montreal weekly, *Hour*.

R O S E N

 Editorial cartoonist for the *Ottawa Business News*, **FRED SEBASTIAN** was born (in 1964) and bred in Ottawa. A graduate of Algonquin College's Commercial Art/Graphic Design program, his work appears in *Legion*, *The Ottawa Citizen*, *The Province* (Vancouver), *The Toronto Star* and *Law Times*. He won, in 1994, a *Studio* magazine merit award for illustration and is currently syndicated by Cartoonists and Writers.

 Born in Hamburg, **TAB** (Thomas Boldt) came to Canada seeking more than the 3m² allocated to be his personal space in Germany. Since he flunked art and English in high school, he naturally aspired to become an editorial cartoonist. First though he was forced into being a car mechanic, gold miner, newspaper publisher (he's still paying for the legal bills and his soul is spoken for...), brakeman, engineer on a sail ship and, while waiting for a permanent position with a big daily newspaper (Hint: TAB's phone number can be obtained through the editor of this book), he continues to freelance for his esteemed clients. The only fan mail he's ever received prompted an investigation by the local R.C.M.P.

 **TING** is the pen name of Merle Tingley. Born and raised in Montreal, he studied art for one year and then worked briefly as a draftsman until joining the army at the beginning of the Second World War. He began drawing cartoons on a full-time basis for *The London Free Press* in 1947 and received the National Newspaper Award in 1955. He has now retired, but still draws on a freelance basis.

 **JIM TODD** is a nationally syndicated cartoonist and illustrator with Southam Syndicate and lives in Nova Scotia. He is the winner of the 1990 Atlantic Journalism Award for editorial cartooning.

 Since his debut at *The Edmonton Journal* in 1968, **EDD ULUSCHAK**'s acclaim and popularity have been indisputable. Twice the recipient of the National Newspaper Award for cartooning, he has also won many international awards and prizes. Edd, his wife Susan, and their two children and his pet raccoon now make their home on five acres of paradise on Gabriola Island, BC

 Born in London, England, in 1926, **BEN WICKS** claims to have held the Nazis at bay during the war as a swimming pool attendant at a Canterbury army camp. Having learned to play the saxophone in the army, he toured Europe with a band and was later to play in the orchestra on the liner *Queen Elizabeth*. Wicks moved to Canada in 1957, working as a milkman in Calgary. He sold several gag cartoons to *The Saturday Evening Post* and has never looked back. Moving to Toronto in 1960, he produces a daily syndicated cartoon ("Wicks") and was named to the Order of Canada in 1986.

"There must be some mistake. I'm wealthy."

 Michael **ZAHARUK** was born in Toronto in 1965. After graduating from the Ontario College of Art in 1991, he began freelancing as an illustrator and political cartoonist. His work has appeared in such publications as *The Toronto Star*, *The Globe and Mail*, *NOW* magazine and the Guelph *Mercury*, as well as many Canadian and, more recently, American magazines. Since 1994 he has been a regular contributor to Union Art Services, a co-operative mailing service distributing political cartoons and graphics.

 Born in Ottawa in 1961, **PETER ZAZULAK** lives in Gloucester, Ontario. He is editorial cartoonist for *The Hill Times* (Ottawa). Freelancing since 1990, his work appears in *The Ottawa Citizen*, *The London Free Press*, *The Toronto Star* and 12 dailies across Canada.

**IN ADDITION TO *PORTFOOLIO*, HERE IS A LIST OF RECENT EDITORIAL CARTOON COLLECTIONS:**

CHAPLEAU, *L'Année Chapleau 1995,* Boréal, Montreal
MACKINNON, *Inklings 2*, Nimbus, Halifax
MOU, *No Friends in High Places*, Pottersfield Press, Halifax

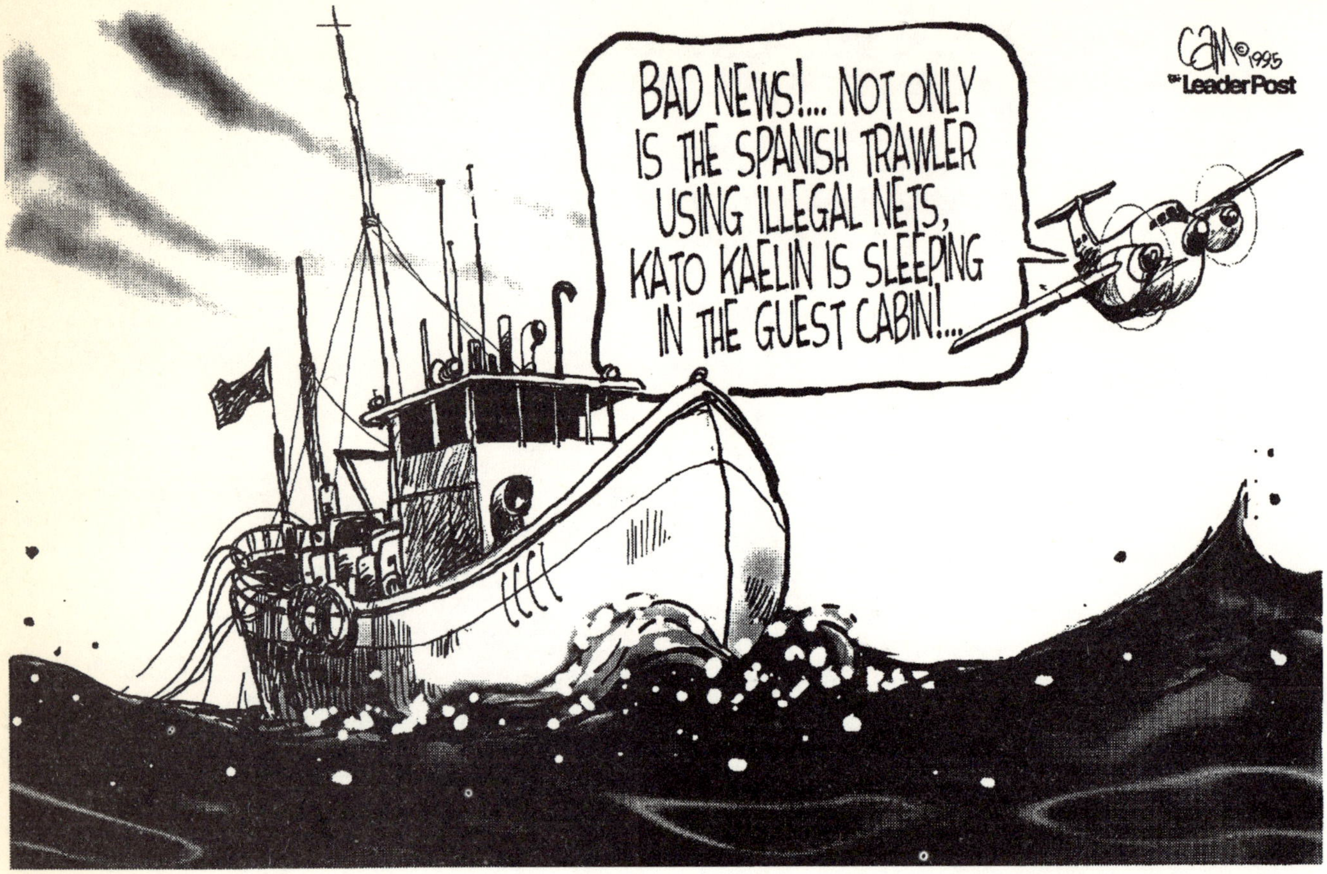
BAD NEWS!... NOT ONLY IS THE SPANISH TRAWLER USING ILLEGAL NETS, KATO KAELIN IS SLEEPING IN THE GUEST CABIN!...
CAM ©1995
Leader Post